OCCASIONAL PAPER 218

Fiscal Vulnerability and Financial Crises in Emerging Market Economies

Richard Hemming, Michael Kell, and
Axel Schimmelpfennig

INTERNATIONAL MONETARY FUND
Washington DC
2003

© 2003 International Monetary Fund

Production: IMF Multimedia Services Division
Typesetting: Alicia Etchebarne-Bourdin
Figures: Theodore F. Peters, Jr.

Cataloging-in-Publication Data

Hemming, Richard

Fiscal vulnerability and financial crises in emerging market economies / Richard Hemming, Michael Kell, and Axel Schimmelpfennig — Washington, D.C.: International Monetary Fund, 2003

  p. cm. — (Occasional paper, ISSN 0251-6365; 218)
 Includes bibliographical references.
 ISBN 1-58906-196-9

  1. Fiscal policy. 2. Financial crises. 3. Currency question. I. Kell, Michael. II. Schimmelpfennig, Axel. III. International Monetary Fund. IV. Occasional paper (International Monetary Fund); no. 218
HJ192.5.H35 2003

Price: US$25.00
(US$17.50 to full-time faculty members and
students at universities and colleges)

Please send orders to:
International Monetary Fund, Publication Services
700 19th Street, N.W., Washington, D.C. 20431, U.S.A.
Tel.: (202) 623-7430 Telefax: (202) 623-7201
E-mail: publications@imf.org
Internet: http://www.imf.org

recycled paper

Contents

Preface		vii
I	**Overview**	1
II	**Background**	3
	Definitions	3
	Assessing Fiscal Vulnerability	4
	Conclusions from the Literature	5
III	**Data and Event Studies**	7
	Data	7
	Event Studies	9
	Summary of Findings	14
IV	**EWS Models and the Severity of Currency Crises**	15
	Using Fiscal Variables to Predict Crises	15
	Fiscal Variables and the Severity of Currency Crises	19
	Summary of Findings	20
V	**Case Studies**	22
	Fiscal Causes of Crises	22
	Fiscal Indicators	25
	Fiscal Consequences of Crises	25
VI	**Conclusions**	29
	What Are the Fiscal Causes of Crises?	29
	Which Fiscal Vulnerability Indicators Help to Predict Crises?	29
	Can Fiscal Variables Explain the Severity of Currency Crises?	30
	What Are the Fiscal Consequences of Crises?	30
Appendixes		
I	**Literature Review**	32
II	**Country and Area Coverage and Data Availability**	47
III	**Event Studies**	54
IV	**EWS Models and the Severity of Currency Crises**	63
V	**Case Studies**	87
References		119

Boxes

2.1.	Currency, Debt, and Banking Crises	4
3.1.	Fiscal Variables	9

Text Tables

4.1.	Summary Results from the Signals Approach	17
4.2.	Summary of Probit EWS Results	18
4.3.	Explaining the Severity of Currency Crises (STV Approach)	20
4.4.	Explaining Changes in the FMP Index (Panel Approach, Fixed Effects)	21
5.1.	Causes of Crises	23
5.2.	Fiscal Consequences of Crises	26

Appendix Tables

A1.1.	Literature Review: Empirical Studies of Financial Crises	35
A2.1.	Countries and Areas Included in EWS and Event Studies	47
A2.2.	Dates of Crisis Episodes	49
A2.3.	Description and Sources of Fiscal Variables	50
A2.4.	Data Availability	51
A4.1.	Performance of Indicators of Currency Crises Using the Signals Approach	65
A4.2.	Performance of Indicators of Debt Crises Using the Signals Approach	66
A4.3.	Performance of Indicators of Banking Crises Using the Signals Approach	67
A4.4.	Country-Specific Thresholds for Currency Crises	69
A4.5.	Country-Specific Thresholds for Debt Crises	70
A4.6.	Country-Specific Thresholds for Banking Crises	72
A4.7.	Regression Results for the DCSD Specification (Maximum Sample)	74
A4.8.	Regression Results for Deficit and Financing Variables (Joint Sample)	75
A4.9.	Regression Results for Reduced Set of Deficit and Financing Variables (Maximum Sample)	76
A4.10.	Regression Results for Selected Fiscal Variables	78
A4.11.	Explaining Crisis Depth (Benchmark Specification)	79
A4.12.	Best Performers Among Fiscal Variables	80
A4.13.	Benchmark Specification for Panel Approach (Fixed Effects)	82
A4.14.	Including Deficit and Financing Variables in the Benchmark Specification (Panel Approach, Fixed Effects)	83
A4.15.	Including Public Debt Variables Individually in the Benchmark Specification (Panel Approach, Fixed Effects)	84
A4.16.	Including Government Expenditure Variables in the Benchmark Specification (Panel Approach, Fixed Effects)	85
A4.17.	Best Performers Among Fiscal Variables (Panel Approach, Fixed Effects)	86
A5.1.	Mexico: Selected Fiscal Vulnerability Indicators (Annual)	89
A5.2.	Mexico: Selected Fiscal Vulnerability Indicators (Quarterly)	90
A5.3.	Argentina: Selected Fiscal Vulnerability Indicators (Annual)	93
A5.4.	Argentina: Selected Fiscal Vulnerability Indicators (Quarterly)	93
A5.5.	Bulgaria: Selected Fiscal Vulnerability Indicators	96
A5.6.	Czech Republic: Selected Fiscal Vulnerability Indicators	99
A5.7.	Thailand: Selected Fiscal Vulnerability Indicators (Annual)	100
A5.8.	Thailand: Selected Fiscal Vulnerability Indicators (Quarterly)	101

A5.9.	Korea: Selected Fiscal Vulnerability Indicators (Annual)	103
A5.10.	Korea: Selected Fiscal Vulnerability Indicators (Quarterly)	104
A5.11.	Pakistan: Selected Fiscal Vulnerability Indicators	107
A5.12.	Russia: Selected Fiscal Vulnerability Indicators (Annual)	109
A5.13.	Russia: Selected Fiscal Vulnerability Indicators (Quarterly)	110
A5.14.	Ukraine: Selected Fiscal Vulnerability Indicators	112
A5.15.	Brazil: Selected Fiscal Vulnerability Indicators	115
A5.16.	Ecuador: Selected Fiscal Vulnerability Indicators	118

Figures

3.1.	Number of Crises in the Sample	8
3.2.	Overall Balance	11
3.3.	Public External Debt	12
3.4.	Short-Term Debt	13

Appendix Figures

A3.1.	Actuarial Deficit	55
A3.2.	Total Financing	56
A3.3.	Change in Net Claims on Government	57
A3.4.	Foreign Debt	58
A3.5.	Total Expenditure	59
A3.6.	Interest Expenditure	60
A3.7.	Social Expenditure	61
A3.8.	International Trade Taxes	62

The following symbols have been used throughout this paper:

... to indicate that data are not available;

— to indicate that the figure is zero or less than half the final digit shown, or that the item does not exist;

– between years or months (e.g., 2001–02 or January–June) to indicate the years or months covered, including the beginning and ending years or months;

/ between years (e.g., 2001/02) to indicate a fiscal (financial) year.

"n.a." means not applicable.

"Billion" means a thousand million.

Minor discrepancies between constituent figures and totals are due to rounding.

The term "country," as used in this paper, does not in all cases refer to a territorial entity that is a state as understood by international law and practice; the term also covers some territorial entities that are not states, but for which statistical data are maintained and provided internationally on a separate and independent basis.

Preface

This Occasional Paper focuses on the fiscal aspects of financial crises in emerging market economies, and as such fills a gap in the crisis literature. The discussion in the paper is based on statistical analysis of a large dataset of fiscal variables and case studies of eleven emerging market crises during the 1990s. The paper concludes that there are several important fiscal causes of crises, related to the size of deficits and their financing, the level and composition of public debt, and structural fiscal factors. Some fiscal indicators are useful for predicting crises, including banking crises. That said, fiscal indicators add little to existing early warning system models in terms of calling crises, but may be useful in improving the ability of such models to predict tranquil periods. It is found that crises tend to put upward pressure on deficits and add to debt as output falls, the exchange rate depreciates, and the government has to cover the costs of bank restructuring. However, the fiscal adjustment usually required in response to a crisis more than offsets the underlying increase in deficits. Crises have also proved to be a catalyst for difficult structural fiscal reforms.

The authors are especially indebted to Teresa Ter-Minassian for her overall guidance and support, to Nigel Chalk and Tony Annett for their contributions to the case studies, and to Estella Macke for excellent research assistance. They would also like to thank Andy Berg, Marco Cangiano, Luis Cubeddu, James Daniel, Liam Ebrill, Hali Edison, Anne-Marie Gulde, Paolo Manasse, Luiz de Mello, Eric Mottu, Saleh Nsouli, Carmen Reinhart, Nouriel Roubini, Gerd Schwartz, and Hung Tran for their helpful comments on earlier drafts, and colleagues in area departments and the offices of Executive Directors who commented on the case studies. Administrative assistance was provided by Constanza Bryant, Veronique Catany, and Mileva Radisavljeviç. Esha Ray of the External Relations Department edited the paper and coordinated its publication.

The opinions expressed in the paper are those of the authors and do not necessarily reflect the views of national authorities, the IMF, or IMF Executive Directors.

I Overview

Fiscal problems have long been considered a central feature of financial (i.e., currency, debt, and banking) crises. However, fiscal problems received less attention at the time of the Asian crisis, because financial and corporate sector vulnerabilities were seen to be more important than fiscal vulnerability.[1] But the recent crises in Argentina and Turkey illustrate the continuing importance of fiscal problems in precipitating crises. Moreover, whatever their cause, financial crises always have important fiscal dimensions.

This paper focuses on the fiscal aspects of financial crises in emerging market economies. As such, it is intended to complement other IMF work in progress on vulnerability and crises.[2] In particular, the paper seeks to provide answers to the following four questions:

- What are the fiscal causes of crises?
- Which fiscal vulnerability indicators help to predict crises?
- Can fiscal variables explain the severity of crises?
- What are the fiscal consequences of crises?

Two empirical approaches are followed. First, a large set of fiscal variables for 29 emerging market economies over the period 1970–2000 is used to examine whether: there are systematic patterns in fiscal variables in the periods before and after crises; fiscal variables can improve the performance of existing early warning system (EWS) models in predicting crises; and fiscal variables help to explain the severity of currency crises. Second, detailed case studies of 11 recent crises in emerging market economies focus on some of the structural and institutional dimensions of fiscal vulnerability.

The main conclusions of the paper are the following:

- Fiscal policy has contributed significantly to past crises. While previous cross-country empirical studies have not found a significant role for fiscal variables in explaining currency crises, this paper concludes that fiscal variables are correlated with crises. The change in net claims of the banking sector on government, together with public debt level and composition variables, are consistently important. Some structural variables, reflecting expenditure and revenue rigidities, also matter. Country case studies reveal the importance of fiscal variables even more clearly, with fiscal problems being the direct cause of crises in a number of countries, and a contributing factor elsewhere. But in a few countries, fiscal problems did not play a catalytic role.

- Fiscal variables add relatively little to the predictive capabilities of existing EWS models. The main contribution of fiscal variables to such models is that their inclusion reduces the chances of sending false alarms. However, closer analysis of crisis events suggests that fiscal deficits are higher than normal in the run-up to crises. This is not the case for debt as whole, but short-term debt turns out to be one of the best predictors of currency, debt, and banking crises. Fiscal variables are also found to contribute to pressure on the foreign exchange market in both crisis and noncrisis periods, although their impact is dominated by other variables.

- Crises have significant fiscal consequences. Fiscal deficits tend to decline following crises, the adverse impact of slower growth on revenue and expenditure being more than offset by the discretionary fiscal adjustment normally called for in response to a crisis. Debt tends to increase, driving forces being the recognition and securitization of contingent liabilities associated with bank restructuring and often sizable exchange rate effects. But the share of short-term debt in the total is reduced. Expenditure and revenue changes are not particularly marked.

---

[1]For example, in several recent overviews of the emerging market crises of the 1990s—Beim and Calomiris (2001); Glick, Moreno, and Spiegel (2001); and Feldstein (2002)—the coverage of fiscal issues is marginal at best.

[2]As reported in IMF (2002a); Allen and others (2002); and Berg, Borensztein, and Pattillo (2003).

I OVERVIEW

The paper is structured as follows. Section II provides background: it defines financial crises and fiscal vulnerability; discusses the different ways in which fiscal vulnerability can be assessed; and reports the main conclusions from the theoretical and empirical literature on financial crises. This literature is more extensively reviewed in Appendix I. Section III describes the dataset constructed for this study, and presents an event study analysis that summarizes the univariate correlations between crises and fiscal variables. More details about the dataset and the event studies are provided in Appendixes II and III. Section IV reports the main results of econometric analysis that uses fiscal variables to predict the timing of financial crises and investigates the role of fiscal variables in explaining the severity of currency crises. Further details of the methodology and results are contained in Appendix IV. Section V presents the results from 11 case studies of emerging market crises in the 1990s; the case studies themselves are in Appendix V. Section VI concludes by providing answers to the four questions listed above.

II Background

Financial crises in emerging market economies have been the subject of considerable analysis. This section draws on work to date to provide essential background for the subsequent sections.

Definitions

Financial Crises

Most studies of financial crises distinguish between currency, debt, and banking crises.[3] These three types of crisis are discussed in Box 2.1. Empirical studies—including this one—typically make such a distinction because it is helpful to use specific, and therefore relatively narrow, crisis definitions.[4] But many of the recent financial crises in emerging market economies, such as the Mexican crisis of 1994–95 and the Asian crisis of 1997–98, have been characterized by currency, debt, and banking crises occurring at the same time or in rapid succession. Indeed, as international capital and domestic financial markets have become increasingly integrated, the distinction between different types of financial crisis has become blurred.

For this reason, recent analyses of emerging market crises have focused on the linkages between the corporate, banking, and public sectors during times of external financing pressure. In particular, attention is paid to crisis dynamics and spillover effects propagated through sectoral and aggregate balance sheets, as opposed to through more traditional flow variables such as the current account and fiscal deficits.[5] From this perspective, financial crises occur when there is a plunge in demand for financial assets of one or more sectors (Allen and others, 2002). Thus creditors may lose confidence in the government's ability to service its debt, in the banking system's ability to finance deposit outflows, or in the corporate sector's ability to service its loans. Problems in one sector are then liable to spread to other sectors: for example, concerns about the government's balance sheet could undermine confidence in banks holding government debt, and could spark a run on deposits; or banking sector problems could expose large contingent liabilities that could lead to difficulties for the government in servicing its debt, and could even give rise to solvency concerns that could cause a run on the currency.[6]

Fiscal Vulnerability

Fiscal vulnerability is related to vulnerability to crises more generally.[7] Furman and Stiglitz (1998, p. 6) equate vulnerability with the causes of crises in a stochastic sense:[8] "an increase in vulnerability means an increase in the probability that . . . shocks, rather than being absorbed by the economy, will be translated into a . . . currency or financial crisis." IMF (1998) argues that vulnerability depends on: the magnitude of economic imbalances, in terms of stocks and flows; misalignments of asset prices, including the exchange rate; the extent of financial sector distortions and structural rigidities; and the credibility of policies. Fiscal vulnerability can then be seen as a component of overall vulnerability that derives from the design and implementation of fiscal policy. Allen and others (2002) adopt a more precise definition, namely the risk that liquidity or solvency conditions are violated and a crisis results.

Fiscal vulnerability can also be defined in its own right. At a fairly general level, Hemming and Petrie (2002, p. 161) see fiscal vulnerability as reflecting a situation in which a government is exposed to the possibility of failing to achieve its aggregate fiscal policy

---

[3]See, for example, IMF (1998); Eichengreen and Rose (1998); and Aziz, Caramazza, and Salgado (2000).

[4]The quantitative crisis definitions used in the empirical work in this study are discussed in Section IV.

[5]See, for example, Krugman (1999), Dornbusch (2001), and IMF (2002b).

[6]The case studies in Appendix V explain how these linkages and spillover effects played out in different crises.

[7]A typical dictionary definition is "being open to attack or damage."

[8]As opposed to the traditional sense of causality—a factor that inevitably leads to a given consequence—because many factors interact in causing crises.

> **Box 2.1. Currency, Debt, and Banking Crises**[1]
>
> A currency crisis occurs when a speculative attack on the exchange rate results in a devaluation or sharp depreciation, or forces country authorities to defend the currency by expending large volumes of reserves or by significantly raising interest rates. Dornbusch (2001) distinguishes between "old style" or "slow motion" currency crises—where a cycle of overspending and real appreciation weakens the current account, often in a context of extensive capital controls, and ends in devaluation—and "new style" crises—where investor concerns about the creditworthiness of the balance sheet of a significant part of the economy (public or private) lead to a rapid buildup of pressure on the exchange rate in an environment of more liberal and integrated capital and financial markets.
>
> A debt crisis occurs either when the borrower defaults or lenders perceive this as a significant risk and therefore withhold new loans and try to liquidate existing loans. Debt crises can apply to commercial (private) and/or sovereign (public) debt. If there is a perceived risk that the public sector will cease to honor its repayment obligations, this is likely to lead to a sharp curtailment of private capital inflows, in part because it casts doubt on the government's commitment to allowing private sector debt repayment. By contrast, if (part of) the private sector is unable to discharge its external obligations, this need not lead to a wider crisis; but, in practice, if private sector default is on a significant scale, commercial debt often becomes sovereign debt, through guarantees, bank bailouts, and so on. In an emerging market context, sovereign debt crises will primarily concern debt held by nonresidents and/or denominated in foreign currency. The term debt crisis clearly applies to cases of outright default (such as Russia in 1998), but may also include situations where there is a negotiated "voluntary" restructuring against the background of a real prospect of default (such as Ukraine in 2000), and/or cases where default is only avoided as a result of large and exceptional financing from official donors (such as Mexico in 1994–95).
>
> A banking crisis occurs when actual or potential bank runs or failures induce banks to suspend the internal convertibility of their liabilities or compel the government to intervene to prevent this by extending assistance on a large scale. Banking crises tend to be protracted, and have severe effects on economic activity, through their impact on financial intermediation, confidence, capital flight, currency substitution, and public finances. Banking crises were relatively rare during the Bretton Woods era, due to capital and financial controls, but have become increasingly common since the 1970s, often in tandem with currency crises (Kaminsky and Reinhart, 1999).
>
> ---
> [1]These definitions are taken from IMF (1998).

(or macrofiscal) objectives. The latter are characterized as: avoiding excessive deficits and debt; ensuring that fiscal policy contributes to effective demand management; and raising revenue in a manner consistent with maintaining reasonable and stable tax rates (and a stable tax system more generally). Brixi and Schick (2002) define a closely related concept—fiscal risk—which is "a source of financial stress that could face a government in the future," and focus, in particular, on contingent liabilities and off-budget fiscal activities. This paper is concerned very much with public sector liquidity and solvency risks, although there is increasing recognition of the difficulties involved in distinguishing between the two in emerging market economies.[9] However, the paper also pays attention to sources of fiscal vulnerability more broadly defined.

Assessing Fiscal Vulnerability

In principle, fiscal vulnerability can be assessed using financial market indicators. For example, spreads on foreign currency long-term government debt should reflect all information relevant to the risk of a sharp depreciation or debt default, including information about fiscal vulnerability. However, the evidence suggests that financial market indicators have often failed to signal impending crises in a timely fashion.[10] Moreover, to the extent that financial market indicators do contain useful information for predicting and explaining crises, there is the separate issue concerning how to identify the specific contribution of fiscal factors.

A second approach would be to apply the "Value at Risk" (VaR) methodology to the public sector. The VaR methodology, which was developed as a means for assessing risks in private sector financial institutions, provides a single measure of the multiple risks applying to a portfolio or balance sheet.[11] The growing emphasis on balance sheet problems as a major

---
[9]As Krugman (1985, p. 79) puts it: "it is difficult to explain a liquidity crisis unless there is a real possibility that the debtor is truly insolvent."

[10]See Goldstein, Kaminsky, and Reinhart (2000) and the references therein.

[11]More specifically, the VaR of a portfolio is the expected maximum loss over a specific time horizon within a given confidence interval, based on explicit assumptions about the distribution and covariance of shocks or risks, usually based on past information on prices.

cause of financial crises led Dornbusch (2001, p. 5) to suggest that "vulnerability can, at least conceptually, be determined through a value at risk exercise: What are the relevant shocks? What are the exposure areas? How large a deterioration of the balance sheet would result?" In principle, this could be applied to the public sector balance sheet, to derive a measure of solvency—and hence vulnerability—explicitly accounting for the expected volatility of the macroeconomic and financial environment.[12]

There are, however, significant conceptual and practical problems with implementing the VaR methodology. An obvious problem is the lack of comprehensive data on public sector balance sheets for even the most advanced economies. Variances and covariances drawn from past periods of relative calm have also been shown to be unreliable in periods of market turbulence; the same drawback might well apply in the context of the macroeconomy and public finances. Furthermore, whereas the asset prices that are typically used in VaR models tend to follow a random walk with movements dominated by a probability distribution, this is less likely to be true for macroeconomic and public finance aggregates, which depend on behavioral relationships, including policy responses.

A more comprehensive approach to assessing country-specific fiscal vulnerability has recently been proposed. Hemming and Petrie (2002) outline a framework based on assessments of four sources of fiscal vulnerability: the initial fiscal position (i.e, deficit and debt levels), which should relate to the full range of government operations, including quasi-fiscal activities and contingent liabilities; short-term fiscal risks, including the sensitivity of fiscal outcomes two or three years ahead to variations in key underlying assumptions about the economic environment, the calling of contingent liabilities, and unanticipated spending needs; longer-term fiscal sustainability, based on the standard analysis of debt dynamics, supplemented by alternative scenarios and stress testing; and structural fiscal weaknesses, such as sizable nondiscretionary expenditure, a volatile revenue base, and limited institutional capacity for fiscal management.

This paper is informed by these approaches to assessing fiscal vulnerability, and focuses on the evidence from previous financial crises about the relationships between crises and fiscal variables. As such, the study is backward-looking in nature, but it hopefully leads to conclusions that can inform and improve forward-looking assessments of vulnerability and the likelihood of crises.

Conclusions from the Literature

This section summarizes that part of the vast literature on financial crises dealing with fiscal aspects of crises. Only the main conclusions from the literature relating to the fiscal causes of crises and fiscal consequences of crises are reported. A full literature review is provided in Appendix I.

Fiscal Causes of Crises

The theoretical literature suggests the following fiscal causes of crises.

- An overly expansionary fiscal policy—the traditional flow variable channel—can lead to crises in several ways, including through a depletion of reserves eventually leading to a currency crisis; by contributing to a lending boom that leaves the banking sector vulnerable to shocks; or through a consumer boom and consequent current account deficit that becomes unsustainable. Such a policy could show up in the conventional fiscal deficit, or it may only be apparent from some alternative measure of fiscal imbalance; but, in either case, a crisis is likely to manifest itself gradually.

- Bad news about contingent liabilities and/or prospective future deficits could be taken to indicate an increase in inflation or default risk, and hence cause sudden pressure on the exchange rate and/or debt rollover problems for the government. Adverse developments in the government's balance sheet could also undermine confidence in its deposit guarantee and contribute to a bank run. On the asset side, large holdings of government debt can leave banks vulnerable to sovereign default. Again, the underlying fiscal problem may not show up in conventional deficit or debt measures, but in this case a crisis could emerge suddenly.

- For emerging market economies, borrowing short term and in foreign currency are ways of resolving time-inconsistency problems related to the lack of credibility of monetary and fiscal policies. However, the currency and maturity composition of public debt can be critical to investor perceptions of government liquidity, and hence lead to self-fulfilling currency and debt crises.

---

[12]See Hausmann (2002) for a proposal to assess what he calls "fiscal risk" using a balance sheet/VaR approach. Hausmann defines a critical value for debt service as a share of total tax revenue, above which serious payment difficulties would arise, giving rise to a crisis. The probability that the critical value is exceeded would depend on the maturity and currency structure of public debt, and the distribution of shocks to the exchange rate, interest rates, and output, including the covariances among these variables.

II BACKGROUND

Turning to the empirical literature, it is difficult to reach firm conclusions on the causes of crises. This reflects the lack of agreement on the appropriate theoretical model, which in turn is due to the complexity and heterogeneity of financial crises in emerging market economies. It also reflects problems of measurement and collinearity in the data. Nevertheless, there is a large empirical literature on crises, and on currency crises in particular. Much of the recent empirical work takes the form of EWS models, where the focus is on predicting rather than explaining crises (this literature is summarized in Table A1.1 of Appendix I). But the approach can still shed some light on the causes of crises.

Relatively few empirical studies of financial crises focus on fiscal variables. Indeed, many studies omit fiscal variables entirely. This in part reflects the fact that fiscal data are less widely available, especially at monthly or quarterly frequencies and for a long time period, compared with many monetary, financial, and real sector variables.

In empirical studies that do include fiscal variables, the evidence of direct effects of fiscal variables on crises is not strong. Some studies find the deficit (or credit to government) to be significantly correlated with currency crises, but others do not; the same applies to studies that include public debt variables. Some studies of the determinants of crisis severity that include fiscal variables find evidence that a lax fiscal policy is associated with greater pressure in the exchange market during periods of turbulence and contagion. But this finding is not robust, either to the inclusion of nonfiscal explanatory variables or to changes in data and sample period. Empirical studies of banking crises do not generally find a significant role for fiscal variables. The literature review uncovered only one (recent) cross-section study of debt crises, and this finds the deficit to be uncorrelated with debt crises.

Measurement problems associated with most fiscal variables, and the deficit in particular, could play a role in explaining the absence of a strong correlation with crises. Kharas and Mishra (2001) test this possibility by constructing an alternative measure of the fiscal deficit based on the change in the stock of base money plus government debt (which is viewed as a proxy for the change in government net worth). They refer to this measure as the *actuarial deficit*, and find that it significantly outperforms conventional deficit measures in explaining the number of currency crises experienced in a sample of industrial countries and emerging market economies.

There is evidence of a range of indirect means by which fiscal policy can contribute to crises. Several currency crisis studies find that a measure of the fiscal deficit is significant when interacted with the real exchange rate. Two causes of banking crises that are generally deemed robust—rapid domestic credit growth and high real interest rates—could reflect an indirect causal effect from loose fiscal policy. Recent empirical studies have also found that the extent of state ownership of banks is correlated with underdeveloped, poorly functioning—and, by implication, more crisis-prone—banking sectors.

As regards debt crises in particular, there is some support for fiscal policy as a cause of crises via the liquidity channel. Thus Detragiache and Spilimbergo (2001) find that the probability of a debt crisis increases with the proportion of short-term debt (public and private) and debt service falling due. Recent studies of debt crises in Latin America identify several key causes related to fiscal policy. First, in most cases, external debt is concentrated in the public sector and is high relative to exports and tax revenue. This means that devaluation provides a limited boost to activity and hence government revenues, but causes a large increase in debt-service costs. Second, a history of macroeconomic volatility exacerbates liquidity problems and increases default risk. Fiscal policy is an important source of volatility, reflecting a ready willingness to implement discretionary measures and the recognized tendency for fiscal policy in Latin America to be procyclical.

Fiscal Consequences of Crises

There are relatively few empirical studies of the effects of crises on fiscal policy. Green and Campos (2001) find that the Asian crisis resulted in a large fall-off in revenues, due to enterprise insolvency and declining trade and personal incomes; devaluation rapidly increased the domestic cost of external debt service, particularly in those countries with a worse precrisis fiscal situation; and concerns about banking and corporate sector collapse led to massive infusions of public funds. As regards the fiscal costs of crises, Burnside, Eichenbaum, and Rebelo (2001) estimate that 30 percent of the costs of the Mexican crisis in 1994–95 had been paid for through 2000 by a combination of debt deflation, fiscal reform, and seigniorage, and that seigniorage could cover the remaining costs. They also predicted that the costs of the Korean crisis in 1997 would be paid for through future fiscal reform. Other studies have reported the direct costs of resolving banking sector problems, which in some cases exceed 40 percent of GDP.

III Data and Event Studies

To examine the empirical relationships between fiscal variables and emerging market crises, a large fiscal dataset was constructed. This section describes the dataset and an event study analysis of fiscal variables.

Data

The dataset consists of annual observations for 20 or so fiscal variables and three crisis variables for 29 emerging market economies, covering the period 1970 to 2000. The sample of countries and the time period is the same as for the IMF's main EWS model.[13] The 29 countries are Argentina, Bolivia, Brazil, Chile, Colombia, Cyprus, the Czech Republic, Egypt, Hungary, India, Indonesia, Israel, Jordan, Korea, Lebanon, Malaysia, Mexico, Pakistan, Peru, the Philippines, Poland, the Slovak Republic, South Africa, Sri Lanka, Thailand, Turkey, Uruguay, Venezuela, and Zimbabwe. Table A2.1 in Appendix II compares the country and area coverage of a range of empirical studies of emerging market crises.

The IMF's main EWS model is estimated with monthly data. Most of the variables relate to financial or monetary aggregates that are widely available at a high frequency. But almost all the fiscal data available over a long time horizon in existing cross-country databases are only available on an annual basis.

Crisis Variables

Currency Crises

While there is a consensus in the literature on how to define currency crises, the precise specification varies across studies. For purposes of comparability, this study uses the currency crisis variable constructed for the IMF's main EWS model, based on a foreign exchange market pressure (FMP) index.[14]

The FMP index is calculated as the weighted average of month-on-month changes in the exchange rate and in international reserves.[15] Although it would be preferable to include a measure of interest rates in the FMP index, there are insufficient data on short-term market rates for the sample under consideration.[16] A crisis is said to occur if the FMP index in a given month exceeds its mean by more than three standard deviations. An annual version of the crisis variable is used, where a given year is classified as a crisis if it contains one or more crisis months.[17] This definition yields 58 currency crises; Table A2.2 in Appendix II identifies these crises, and Figure 3.1 shows their distribution over time. There is some evidence of a bunching of crises in the early 1980s, around the time of the Latin American debt crisis; in the early 1990s; and in the late 1990s, reflecting the effects of the Asian crisis and its aftermath.

Debt Crises

Unlike currency crises, there are few recent empirical studies of debt crises, and hence less of a consensus on how to define a debt crisis. One possibility would be to use information on sovereign defaults (as in Purcell and Kaufman, 1993). But this study follows Detragiache and Spilimbergo (2001), who define a debt crisis as occurring if either or both of two conditions apply: there are arrears of principal or interest on external private and public debt to commercial creditors (banks or bondholders) of more than 5 percent of total (public and private external) debt

---

[13]This model is discussed in Section V, and more fully explained in IMF (2002a).
[14]See Girton and Roper (1976) for an explanation of the FMP index.
[15]Means, standard deviations, and weights are country-specific. Weights are chosen so that the variance of the exchange rate and reserve components are equal; in this instance, the variance of each series is used as the weight. The weights, means, and standard deviations are calculated separately for periods of hyperinflation, where hyperinflation is defined as the six-month inflation rate exceeding 150 percent.
[16]Data on market-determined short-term interest rates are only widely available for emerging market countries from the mid-to-late 1980s onward.
[17]Crises occurring in successive years are treated as the same crisis for the event studies, to avoid overlapping crisis windows.

III DATA AND EVENT STUDIES

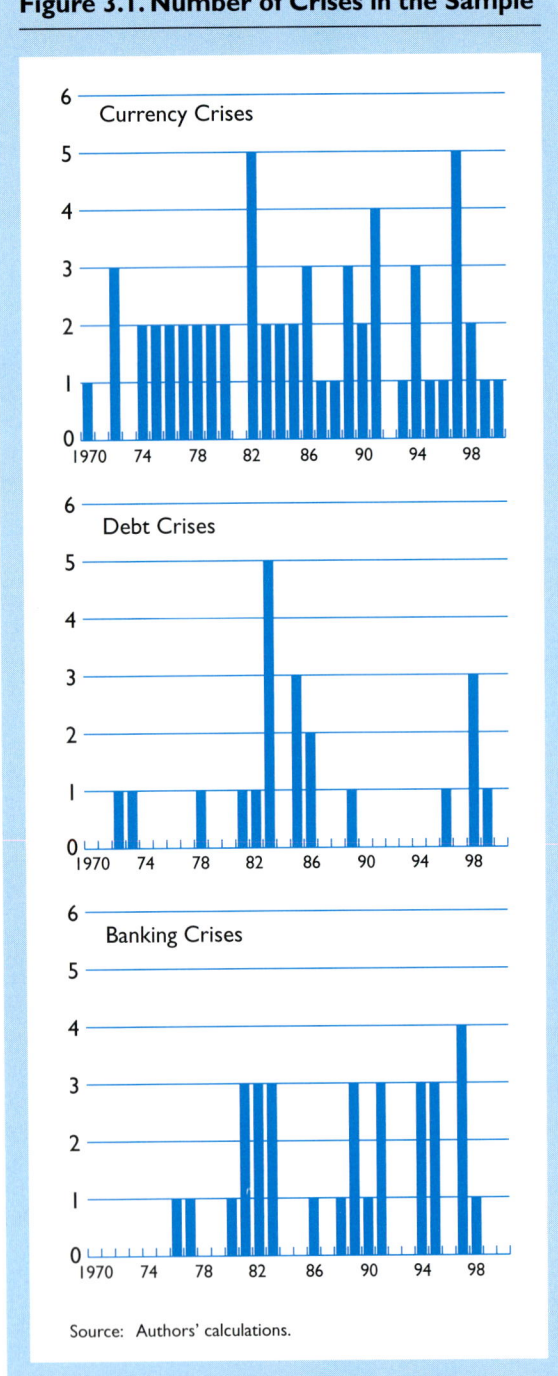

Figure 3.1. Number of Crises in the Sample

Currency Crises

Debt Crises

Banking Crises

Source: Authors' calculations.

outstanding to commercial creditors;[18] and there is a rescheduling or debt restructuring agreement with commercial creditors as listed in the World Bank Global Development Finance (GDF) database.[19] The first criterion is intended to rule out cases where the proportion of debt in arrears is negligible; the second criterion captures countries that are not technically in arrears because they reschedule or restructure their debt before defaulting. A crisis episode is considered to be finished when arrears fall below the 5 percent threshold, but crises beginning within four years of the end of a previous crisis are considered a continuation of the earlier event.[20] This definition yields 21 debt crisis episodes;[21] Table A2.2 in Appendix II identifies these crises, and Figure 3.1 shows their distribution over time. Again, there is some bunching in the early 1980s and in the late 1990s. Episodes of severe external payment difficulties that do not result in arrears or rescheduling, such as the Mexican crisis of 1994–95, are not captured by this definition, even though they are often regarded to be debt crises in the policy debate.

Banking Crises

Defining banking crises requires more judgment than in the case of currency or debt crises. This is because data on which a quantitative definition could be based are difficult to obtain. For instance, although large withdrawals of deposits may have typified banking crises in the past, the widespread existence of deposit insurance means that banking crises are no longer necessarily accompanied by large runs on banks. Another possibility would be to use the performance of bank stocks relative to the overall equity market, but often in emerging market economies many banks are not traded publicly. The approach that has been used most in the empirical literature on banking crises, following Caprio and Klingebiel (1996), is based on data on loan losses and the erosion of bank capital. A systemic banking sector crisis is said to occur when the net worth of the banking system has been almost or entirely eliminated. However, data on nonperforming loans are usually available only at low frequencies, often after considerable lags; even then, official figures typically understate the problem. So data on loan losses and bank capital are supplemented by the judgment of authors and experts familiar with the circumstances of particular countries. More specifically,

---

[18]External debt is defined in the World Bank Global Development Finance database as obligations to nonresidents and repayable in foreign currency, goods, or services.

[19]Note that this information is only available from 1980 onward.

[20]This definition excludes as crisis events Paris Club reschedulings of official debts (i.e., debts to other governments or multilateral institutions), because Detragiache and Spilimbergo (2001) are interested only in defaults with respect to commercial creditors.

[21]This compares with 54 episodes identified in Detragiache and Spilimbergo (2001) using a sample of 69 countries.

> **Box 3.1. Fiscal Variables**
>
> The fiscal variables in the dataset fall into four groups:
>
> - Variables measuring the *deficit and financing*: overall balance; primary balance; actuarial deficit; total financing; and the change in net claims on government (all in percent of GDP).
> - Variables measuring *debt*: total debt; public external debt (including guarantees); short-term debt; long-term debt; foreign debt (all in percent of GDP); and foreign currency debt (in percent of total debt).
> - Variables related to *government expenditure*: total expenditure (in percent of GDP); interest expenditure; defense expenditure; and social expenditure (all in percent of total expenditure).
> - Variables measuring *government revenue*: total revenue (in percent of GDP); international trade taxes; nontax revenue; and grants (all in percent of total revenue); plus two constructed variables, tax buoyancy and revenue buoyancy.[1]
>
> The first two groups of variables correspond to a subset of the "fiscal position indicators" suggested in Hemming and Petrie (2002), which are intended to indicate the strength or weakness of the initial or current fiscal situation as reflected in various measures of the deficit and debt. The expenditure and revenue variables are intended to pick up some of the structural weaknesses discussed in Hemming and Petrie (2002), such as a high proportion of nondiscretionary spending, reflecting either legal or political constraints, or a revenue base dominated by more volatile inflows.
>
> ---
> [1] Defined as the percentage change in tax revenue and total revenue (respectively) divided by the percentage change in nominal GDP.

this study uses the dates of systemic banking crises in Caprio and Klingebiel (1999), which updates, corrects, and expands their earlier list of crises.[22] This gives 32 banking crises; Table A2.2 in Appendix II identifies these crises, and Figure 3.1 shows their distribution over time.

Fiscal Variables

A large number of fiscal vulnerability indicators are used in this paper. The approach taken was to start with the list of suggested indicators in Hemming and Petrie (2002) and to construct as many variables as possible from existing cross-country data sources, including the IMF's International Finance Statistics (IFS) and Government Finance Statistics (GFS) databases, and the World Bank's GDF database. Where possible, the variables refer to general government, although many variables are only available for central government. Box 3.1 lists the fiscal variables. Further details are provided in Table A2.3 in Appendix II.

The availability of fiscal data varies between countries and across variables. Table A2.4 in Appendix II shows the observations available as a percentage of the full sample period (1970 to 2000 inclusive; i.e., 31 observations per country). Coverage is reasonably full for most of the variables related to the deficit and financing, total debt, and total expenditure and revenue, although coverage for the primary balance, the variables capturing the composition of debt, social expenditure, and grants is relatively thin. Country-specific sources are not suitable for filling gaps or extending the range of fiscal vulnerability indicators, due to a lack of comparability with the base data. Overall, the fiscal variables examined are predominantly macroeconomic rather than structural.[23]

Event Studies

Event studies have become an increasingly common approach to analyzing the antecedents and effects of financial crises.[24] The sample is divided between five- or seven-year crisis "windows," and noncrisis or tranquil years. The average values of fiscal variables before, during, and after crises can then be compared to the average during tranquil periods,

---
[22] Caprio and Klingebiel (1999) distinguish between systemic banking crises—when all or most banking system capital is eroded—and borderline or nonsystemic crises, where only a subset of financial intermediaries are affected.

[23] The case studies offer greater scope for examining a wider range of fiscal vulnerability indicators, including indicators of structural aspects of fiscal systems and other more qualitative features. See Section V and Appendix V.

[24] The event study approach was originally developed in the field of finance to determine whether security holders earn abnormal returns in response to news or some well-defined event. One of the first such studies was Fama, Fisher, Jensen, and Roll (1969), which analyzed the reaction of stock prices to stock splits. The first event study of currency crises was Eichengreen, Rose, and Wyplosz (1995); subsequent papers to include event studies of financial crises include Frankel and Rose (1996); IMF (1998); and Aziz, Caramazza, and Salgado (2000).

III DATA AND EVENT STUDIES

in graphical format. Event studies provide a simple and intuitive summary of the univariate relationship between crises and the variables of interest.[25]

The event study approach implicitly treats all crisis and tranquil periods as alike, regardless of country, which raises an issue of the comparability of data across countries. All fiscal variables have been scaled (either by expressing the variable as a share of GDP or as a share of total debt, expenditure, or revenue), which addresses the comparability problem to some extent. But this does not deal with the possibility that some fiscal variables are systematically more volatile in certain countries. Therefore, each variable is further standardized by subtracting the country-specific mean and dividing by the country-specific standard deviation, following the procedure in Aziz, Caramazza, and Salgado (2000). This, however, complicates the interpretation of the results, since differences between tranquil and crisis periods are in terms of country-specific standard deviations from the mean. For this reason, results are presented for both standardized and nonstandardized or "raw" data.

To give an indication of the statistical significance of the difference between crisis and tranquil periods, 95 percent confidence intervals around these differences are shown. These intervals are calculated as twice the combined standard errors for the difference between the estimated crisis and tranquil period means.[26] As such, these confidence intervals reflect the sampling error for both crisis and tranquil periods. Some earlier event studies, such as Frankel and Rose (1996), show confidence intervals based on the standard errors for crisis periods only, implicitly assuming there is no sampling error for tranquil periods.

Averages are computed separately for currency, debt, and banking crises, as well as for all three types of crises pooled together. This indicates whether fiscal variables tend to behave differently before and after each type of crisis. The results are shown in Figures 3.2–3.4 and Figures A3.1–A3.8 in Appendix III (which also includes further guidance on interpreting the figures). These figures relate to slightly more than half the fiscal variables listed in Box 3.1.[27]

The Fiscal Antecedents of Crises

The overall deficit is higher in the run-up to currency crises than in tranquil periods. This is shown in Figure 3.2, and is consistent with the findings in Frankel and Rose (1996) and Aziz, Caramazza, and Salgado (2000). The same is found for debt crises. Thus the overall deficit may be a useful leading indicator of currency and debt crises. The situation is different for banking crises, where the overall deficit has on average been lower in the run-up to a crisis than in tranquil periods. The actuarial deficit rises sharply prior to currency, debt, and banking crises, although its mean value in the two years prior to a crisis is not significantly different from its tranquil period mean. Financing variables tell a similar story to the overall balance. The actuarial deficit, total financing, and the change in net claims on government are shown in Figures A3.1–A3.3 in Appendix III.

All measures of debt increase in the run-up to crises. As shown in Figure 3.3, public external debt increases from a level (two years prior to crises) close to or below the tranquil period mean. The main exception is short-term debt, which Figure 3.4 shows is significantly above the tranquil period mean two (and even three) years prior to currency or debt crises. Perhaps surprisingly, this is not the case for foreign debt, which is shown in Figure A3.4 in Appendix III. This finding is in line with several other studies (e.g., Chang and Velasco, 1999; Bussière and Mulder, 1999), which conclude that indicators related to short-term debt are useful for predicting crises.

Expenditure and revenue variables are not markedly different in the run-up to crises as compared to tranquil periods. However, a few interesting points emerge on the expenditure side from Figures A3.5–A3.7 in Appendix III. Total expenditure increases steadily in the run-up to all three types of crises; interest expenditure is generally lower in the run-up to crises than in tranquil periods, which is unexpected; and social expenditure is above the tranquil period mean prior to currency and debt crises.

On the revenue side, it is notable that international trade taxes, shown in Figure A3.8 in Appendix III, seem to be distinctly higher two years before currency crises than in tranquil periods. This suggests that greater reliance on trade taxes has tended to be associated with higher vulnerability to currency crises, although this may reflect overvaluation of the exchange rate prior to currency crises.

The results from the event studies can also be considered in terms of type of crisis:

- There are four fiscal variables that behave in a consistently abnormal manner in the run-up to currency crises. These are the overall deficit, total financing, the change in net claims on

---

[25] Furthermore, since no parametric structure is imposed on the data and the statistical tests require relatively undemanding distributional assumptions, this technique may be more informative in extracting behavioral patterns over a long time span than more formal econometric procedures (Aziz, Caramazza, and Salgado, 2000).

[26] This assumes that crisis and tranquil periods are independent, and that there is no covariance between them.

[27] The figures for the excluded variables are not particularly revealing.

Event Studies

Figure 3.2. Overall Balance

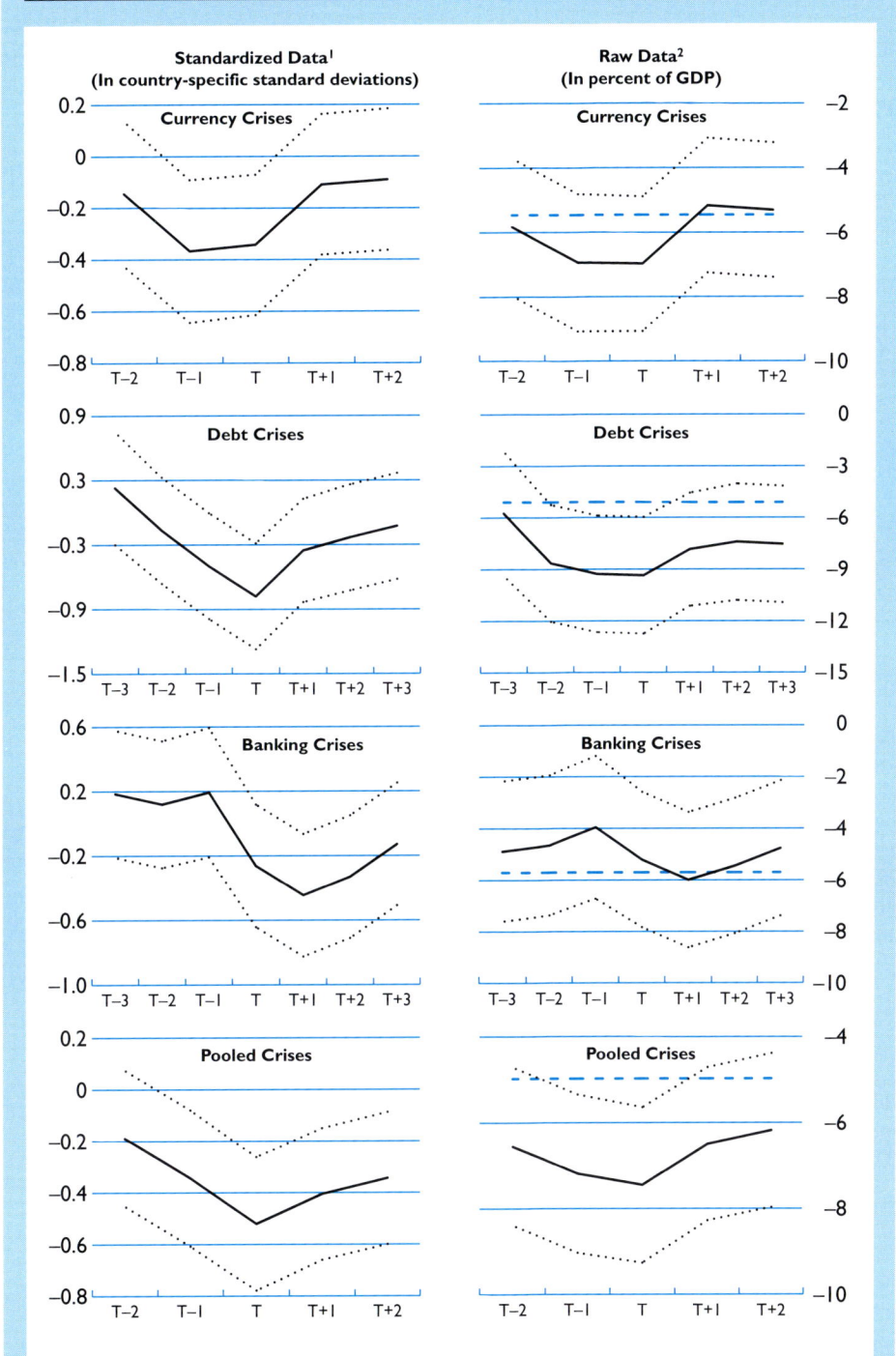

Standardized Data[1]
(In country-specific standard deviations)

Raw Data[2]
(In percent of GDP)

Currency Crises

Debt Crises

Banking Crises

Pooled Crises

Source: Authors' calculations.
[1]In the left-hand column, the solid line shows the difference between the tranquil period mean and the mean in each year of the crisis window, in units of country-specific standard deviations. The dotted lines are two standard errors around the difference in the means, corresponding to a 95 percent confidence interval.
[2]In the right-hand column, the dashed horizontal line shows the tranquil period mean and the solid line shows the crisis period mean, both in percent of GDP (unless otherwise indicated). The dotted lines are two standard errors around the difference in the tranquil and crisis period means.

III DATA AND EVENT STUDIES

Figure 3.3. Public External Debt

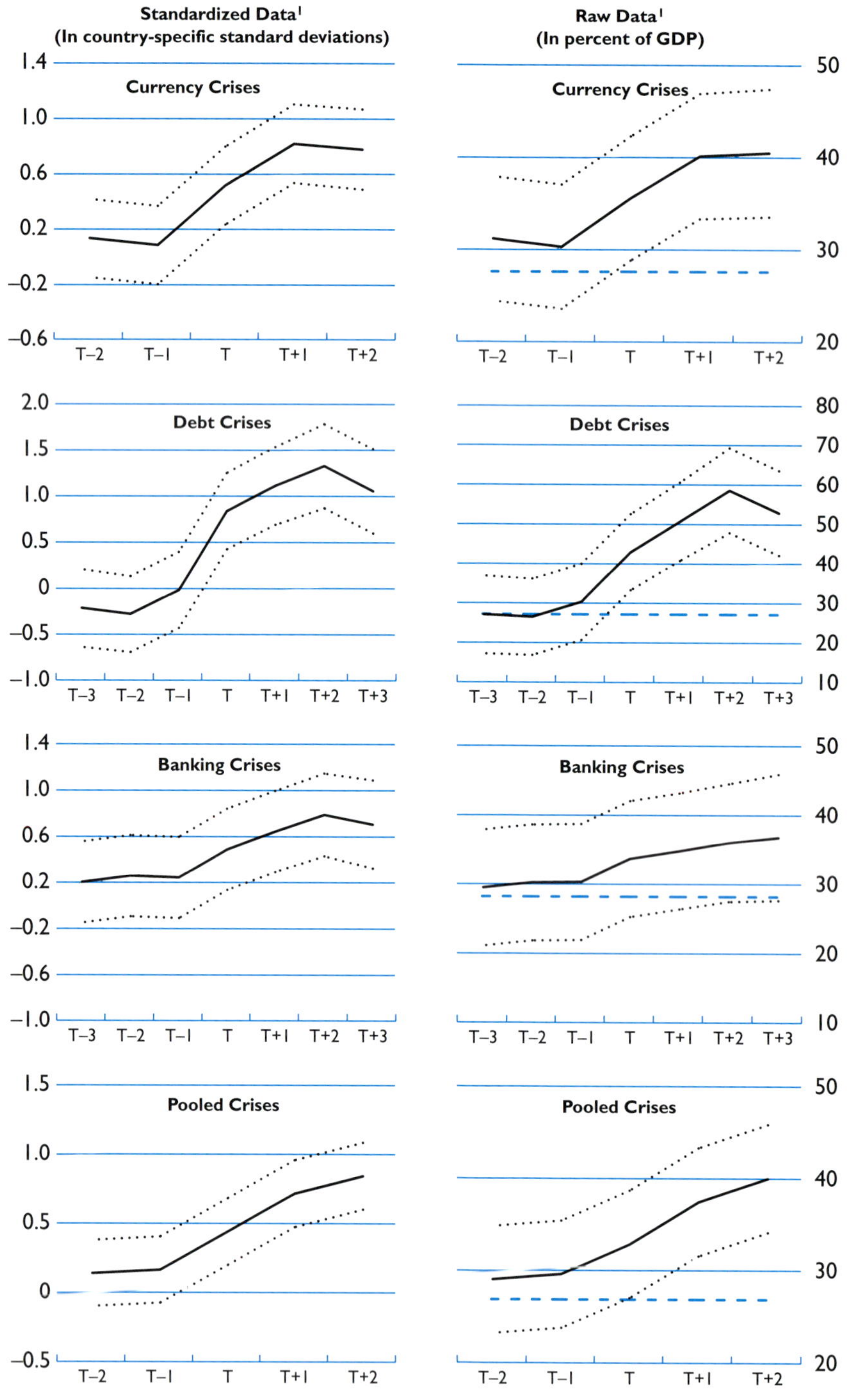

Standardized Data¹
(In country-specific standard deviations)

Raw Data¹
(In percent of GDP)

Currency Crises

Debt Crises

Banking Crises

Pooled Crises

Source: Authors' calculations.
¹See footnotes to Figure 3.2.

Event Studies

Figure 3.4. Short-Term Debt

Standardized Data¹
(In country-specific standard deviations)

Raw Data¹
(In percent of GDP)

Currency Crises

Debt Crises

Banking Crises

Pooled Crises

Source: Authors' calculations.
¹See footnotes to Figure 3.2.

government, and short-term debt. Two other fiscal variables—the actuarial deficit and foreign debt—increase sharply just prior to currency crises, but are less informative as leading indicators.

- With regard to debt crises, short-term debt is the only variable to differ significantly from the tranquil period mean in the two years prior to a crisis. But several variables—the overall deficit, the actuarial deficit, total financing, the change in net claims on government, long-term debt, and foreign currency debt—behave abnormally in the year immediately preceding a crisis.

- There is less evidence of abnormal behavior of fiscal variables in the run-up to banking crises. The only exception is short-term debt. However, a few variables behave differently prior to banking crises compared to currency or debt crises: the overall deficit, for example, is lower than the tranquil period mean in the run-up to banking crises, but higher than the tranquil period mean for debt and currency crises; a similar pattern is apparent for total financing; social expenditure rises in the run-up to banking crises but is falling or stable prior to debt and currency crises; and total revenue is above the tranquil period mean for banking crises but below it for debt and currency crises.

The Fiscal Effects of Crises

The various deficit and financing measures suggest that fiscal policy becomes more restrictive in the two years following currency and debt crises. However, there is evidence that the situation is different following banking crises, with some measures suggesting an increase in the deficit in immediate postcrisis years. As might be expected, debt increases following all types of crises. The increase, relative to tranquil periods, is significant for all three types of crisis when standardized data are considered. There is some evidence of a reduction in short-term debt following currency and debt crises. Foreign debt remains fairly stable in the two years following crises.

Total expenditure generally changes little following currency and debt crises, but in the case of banking crises remains significantly above the tranquil period average. Consistent with the increase in total debt following crises, interest expenditure rises in the years following currency and debt crises, although this is less apparent for banking crises. Social expenditure appears to be somewhat lower on average following currency and debt crises than prior to them; the opposite is true of banking crises. There is very little evidence of major effects of crises on revenue indicators. The big falloff in revenues experienced by some Asian crisis countries during 1997–98 does not appear to be typical of most emerging market crises.[28]

Summary of Findings

The event studies provide some evidence that fiscal variables behave abnormally before and after crises. Some deficit measures have, on average, been significantly higher in the run-up to currency and debt crises than in tranquil periods. This confirms the findings of some other event studies of currency crises, though the results of this study are somewhat clearer, especially when allowance is made for systematic differences in the level and volatility of deficits between countries. By contrast, most measures of debt are not significantly above normal prior to crises. The notable exception is short-term debt, which is significantly higher than usual in the run-up to all three types of crisis, and indeed is the only fiscal variable that behaves abnormally prior to banking crises. Perhaps this is not too surprising, since the ability to borrow long term may begin to diminish at the first sign of problems, no matter what their source. But more generally, there seems to be stronger evidence of abnormal behavior of fiscal variables prior to currency and debt crises, compared with banking crises. The overall deficit tends to narrow immediately following currency and debt crises suggesting that some tightening of policy is the norm; in the case of banking crises, the deficit tends to be reduced only a year or two after the crisis begins (although banking crises are harder to date accurately). Debt typically increases following all types of crises, and there is a shift away from short-term debt.

---

[28]Although the results are not reported in the main text or in Appendix III, the sample of pooled crises was divided into subperiods. This revealed a number of differences between crises in the 1970s, 1980s, and 1990s, the most significant being a suggestion that short-term debt may be a more reliable indicator of crises in the 1980s than in the 1970s and 1990s.

IV   EWS Models and the Severity of Currency Crises

This section summarizes the results of various statistical and econometric analyses of the dataset described in the previous section. First, the extent to which fiscal variables can help to predict crises is examined using two popular EWS models. The second part investigates whether fiscal variables can help to explain the severity of currency crises. Further explanation of the methodologies and detailed results are given in Appendix IV.

Using Fiscal Variables to Predict Crises

EWS models provide a systematic empirical framework for estimating the likelihood of a crisis over a given time horizon based on a combination of vulnerability indicators.[29] The number of EWS models has grown rapidly in recent years, and they have become an important part of IMF work on crisis prevention. The basic approach with EWS models is to determine empirically the relationship between past crises and a range of factors—such as country fundamentals, developments in the global economy and financial markets, and political risks—and then to use the latest values of these variables to predict the probability of future crises. EWS models should be evaluated primarily on the basis of their ability to predict future crises (i.e., out-of-sample testing), rather than on how well the model fits the observations from which it was estimated (i.e., in-sample testing).[30]

EWS models are far from perfect forecasting tools. They have a track record of both missing crises and sending false alarms, and they are certainly not sufficiently accurate to be used as the sole method of predicting crises. But they can contribute to the analysis of vulnerability in conjunction with more traditional surveillance methods and other indicators; in particular, the "mechanical" approach of EWS models can provide a relatively objective and systematic starting point for crisis prediction.[31] Moreover, Berg, Borensztein, and Pattillo (2003) conclude that the best EWS models performed markedly better than other predictors—such as spreads, ratings, and the assessments of market analysts—particularly over the period of the Asian crisis.[32]

The added value of fiscal variables in predicting crises is unclear from the literature. Appendix I includes a survey of the EWS literature, concentrating on those studies that have included at least one fiscal variable. Some EWS models of currency crises find an important role for fiscal variables, but others do not. The evidence from banking crisis EWS models is clearer: fiscal variables do not seem important. However, the range of fiscal variables that have been tested is rather narrow. There do not appear to be any EWS models of debt crises, despite the fact that fiscal variables should be relatively useful in predicting debt crises. More generally, the literature review reveals no EWS studies that have specifically focused on fiscal variables, or indeed tested more than a few standard deficit and debt variables. However, there is sufficient evidence of a role for fiscal variables in predicting crises to merit a more systematic examination of fiscal vulnerability indicators using EWS models.

This study uses two different EWS methodologies—the signals approach and the more widely used probit approach. In the signals approach, the

---

[29]This definition is based on IMF (2002a).

[30]Ideally, the out-of-sample testing would also be "out-of-mind," that is, using a model that was formulated before the sample period, and not merely one estimated on data prior to the sample period. This is to guard against the possibility that the model's structure could have been influenced by considerations that only became apparent after a particular crisis.

[31]The best recent example of the potential value-added of EWS models is given by the Korean crisis of 1997. Despite its long track record of strong performance and sound policies, Korea was exhibiting significant vulnerability to crisis according to a number of EWS models in 1996–97. This was in sharp contrast to the absence of any vulnerability indicated by market participants—perhaps overly influenced by Korea's past performance—prior to the crisis.

[32]On the poor performance of interest rate spreads, see Kaminsky, Lizondo, and Reinhart (1998); on sovereign debt ratings, see Reinhart (2002); and on currency forecasts, see Goldfajn and Valdés (1998).

idea is that when a variable departs significantly from its normal historical behavior, it may be sending a signal of an impending crisis. Historical data are used to assess the accuracy of the signals sent by particular variables prior to actual crises, with the expectation that past relationships will provide a reliable basis for deciding which current signals may be indicating future crises.[33]

The signals approach is closely related to the event study approach. But it extends and refines the event studies by allowing a more precise comparison between variables in terms of their leading indicator properties. In particular, the approach allows the direct comparison and ranking of alternative indicators, in terms of their track record in failing to signal crises (Type I errors) and sending false positives (Type II errors). However, the signals approach is typically univariate, and not amenable to tests of statistical significance.[34]

The probit approach is multivariate and therefore accounts for the correlations and interactions between different variables in forecasting crises. The approach uses probit (or sometimes logit) regressions to identify the factors that jointly explain the occurrence of crises. Latest values of the explanatory variables are then combined with the estimated coefficients to give a predicted probability of a crisis happening during a given window, typically 6, 12, or 24 months ahead. Further details about both the signals and probit approaches are provided in Appendix IV.

Signals EWS Results

Separate signals EWS models are estimated for currency, debt, and banking crises. Detailed results are given in Appendix IV. Table 4.1 summarizes the findings for the six best performing indicators of currency, debt, and banking crises. A signal counts as good when a crisis occurs in either of the two subsequent years (column 2) and as bad when no crisis occurs in either of the two subsequent years (column 3). The ratio of column 3 to column 2 gives the noise-to-signal ratio (column 4), by which indicators are ranked. Other information that can be used to compare indicators is also shown. The main points to note are the following:

- Some fiscal variables are good predictors of currency crises. Short-term debt, foreign currency debt, the overall and primary balances, and some financing variables perform as well as the best indicators of currency crises in other (annual) signals EWS models, such as the current account deficit. These variables are less good, but still useful, predictors of debt crises.

- A few of the expenditure and revenue variables are also useful predictors of currency and debt crises. These include defense and social spending, and international trade taxes. This is in contrast to the findings of the event studies in Section III, but provides some empirical support for the suggestions in Hemming and Petrie (2002) that a high share of expenditure that is nondiscretionary and reliance on volatile revenue sources can add to fiscal vulnerability.

- Fiscal variables have a similar signaling performance overall for banking crises as for debt and currency crises. Despite weaker theoretical links between fiscal policy and banking crises, and the different findings of the event studies, this suggests at least some role for fiscal variables in signaling banking crises.[35]

- However, fiscal variables fail to signal a very high proportion of crises. Even the best performing indicator of currency crises misses around two-thirds of all crises. And the proportion of crises signaled in both years prior to the crisis is very low—just over a quarter for the best performing indicator, and more typically around 10 percent. So fiscal variables, in and of themselves, do not appear to be reliable crisis predictors.

- At the same time, the better performing fiscal variables generally send very few false alarms. This implies that if a fiscal variable does exceed its critical threshold and signals an impending crisis, the warning that is being given should be taken seriously.

Probit EWS Results

The approach taken is to estimate the EWS model developed by the IMF's Developing Countries Studies Division (DCSD), and then add fiscal variables to determine whether this improves the in-sample predictions of the model. The DCSD model predicts currency crises using the crisis definition set out in Section III, with a 24-month-ahead forecasting horizon. The parameters are generated by probit regressions, using monthly data, and there are six explanatory variables—exchange rate overvaluation, measured by the deviation of the real exchange rate from its long-term trend; the current account deficit relative to GDP; reserves growth; export growth; the ratio of

---
[33]The IMF's signaling model based on Kaminsky, Lizondo, and Reinhart (1998) is described in IMF (2002a).
[34]Although Kaminsky (1998) and the IMF's signaling model combine individual indicators into a composite indicator.

[35]Possibly reflecting the fact that banks are often forced to hold large quantities of government securities.

Table 4.1. Summary Results from the Signals Approach

	Percentage of Crises for Which Data Are Available[1] (1)	Good Signals as a Percentage of Possible Good Signals[2] (2)	Bad Signals as a Percentage of Possible Bad Signals[2] (3)	Noise-to Signal Ratio (3)/(2) (4)	Optimal Threshold (Percentile) (5)	Percentage of Crises with No Signal (6)	Percentage of Crises with at Least One Signal (7)	Percentage of Crises with at Least Two Signals (8)
Currency crises								
Primary balance	36	24	10	0.43	90	67	33	14
Short-term debt	86	20	9	0.44	93	70	30	10
Defense expenditure	74	10	4	0.47	98	81	19	0
Social expenditure	50	14	7	0.48	95	72	28	0
International trade taxes	83	7	4	0.54	98	85	15	0
Revenue buoyancy	83	7	4	0.55	98	88	13	0
Debt crises								
Foreign currency debt	43	31	3	0.11	98	44	56	22
Social expenditure	57	13	4	0.31	98	75	25	0
Short-term debt	100	27	9	0.33	91	57	43	10
Revenue buoyancy	81	9	4	0.41	98	82	18	0
Change in net claims on government	95	8	3	0.43	98	85	15	0
Tax buoyancy	81	9	4	0.43	98	82	18	0
Banking crises								
Foreign currency debt	34	25	5	0.22	97	64	36	9
Total debt	56	22	6	0.28	80	67	33	6
Overall balance	88	11	3	0.29	90	79	21	0
Short-term debt	97	34	11	0.33	92	58	42	26
Foreign debt	50	14	5	0.33	95	75	25	0
Grants	53	16	6	0.36	91	71	29	0

Source: Appendix IV.
[1] Out of a maximum of 58 currency crises, 21 debt crises, and 32 banking crises.
[2] See Appendix IV for further explanation.

IV EWS MODELS AND THE SEVERITY OF CURRENCY CRISES

Table 4.2. Summary of Probit EWS Results

	Model 1: Benchmark		Model 2: Best Fiscal Variables		Model 3: Only Fiscal Variables	
Observations	2,289		2,289		2,658	
Pseudo R^2	0.22		0.24		0.17	
Correctly called (percent)						
Crises	81.0		78.0		42.5	
Tranquil periods	89.8		90.5		87.8	
Episodes	89.5		90.1		86.6	
	Coefficient	Wald	Coefficient	Wald	Coefficient	Wald
Exchange rate overvaluation	0.02	10.6	0.02	11.5		
Current account deficit	0.01	7.6	0.01	7.4		
Reserves growth	0.00	2.2	0.00	2.1		
Export growth	0.00	2.6	0.00	2.4		
Short-term debt to reserves	0.01	7.4	0.01	7.1		
M2 to reserves	0.00	1.5	0.00	2.5		
Change in net claims on government			0.00	2.0	0.01	5.8
Foreign currency debt			0.01	6.6	0.01	5.8
Interest expenditure					−0.01	−9.6
Social expenditure					0.01	6.6
Total revenue					0.01	9.3
International trade taxes					0.01	6.8
Constant	−3.92	−18.1	−4.59	−20.7	−3.09	−16.7

Source: Appendix IV.

short-term debt to reserves; and the ratio of M2 to reserves.[36] Fiscal variables have not previously been examined systematically in the context of this model.

The data on which the DCSD model has been estimated cover the same 29 countries and the same period (1970–2000) as the fiscal dataset described in Section II.[37] The DCSD dataset contains mostly financial and monetary variables that are available on a monthly basis, and also some variables available on a quarterly basis, such as the current account balance. All variables have been percentiled to remove country-specific effects. The fiscal variables are, in almost all cases, only available on an annual basis, and therefore have to be converted to a monthly frequency to be used with the DCSD model.

Results are presented for three models. These are the benchmark specification, which includes only the core DCSD variables and no fiscal variables (Model 1); a specification including the DCSD variables plus the two best performing fiscal variables (the change in net claims on government and foreign currency debt) (Model 2); and a specification with only the best performing fiscal variables among each subgroup of deficit, debt, expenditure, and revenue variables (Model 3). Detailed results are presented in Appendix IV. Table 4.2 summarizes the results for each specification.

The main results are as follows:

- All of the deficit and financing variables enter the DCSD model significantly at the 5 percent level and with the expected sign, but none leads to a significant improvement of the model's in-sample predictive power.

- Among the debt variables, only foreign currency debt enters the DCSD model significantly at the 5 percent level and with the expected sign. This tends to confirm the finding of the signals EWS approach that the composition of public debt matters for predicting crises.

- The revenue variables add very little to the model. Two of the six revenue variables—total revenue and international trade taxes—enter the model significantly, but there is no improvement in predictive power.

- The results for the expenditure variables are mixed. Interest expenditure enters significantly

---
[36]See IMF (2002a) for further details.
[37]This results in differences in time period and country coverage compared with the DCSD model. Some other differences are discussed in Appendix IV.

and improves the predictive power of the model. However, the estimated coefficient is not robust. Social expenditure improves the predictive power of the model and enters significantly at the 5 percent level, and this result is stable.

- Of the best performers from each group of fiscal variables, only the change in net claims on government and foreign currency debt are significant and robust. Compared with the DCSD specification, including these two variables marginally reduces the number of correctly called crisis signals, but it improves the model's predictive power for tranquil episodes, and thus its overall predictive power.

- A specification including only fiscal variables performs as well as the DCSD model in terms of calling tranquil periods. This specification performs less well in terms of signaling crises, but still correctly calls around 42 percent of crisis episodes.

Overall, there is robust evidence that currency crises are correlated with some fiscal variables. But in terms of predicting crises, fiscal variables add little to the existing DCSD specification, although they do help signal tranquil episodes.[38] One way of reconciling these findings is to note that the effects of fiscal variables on crisis vulnerability may operate through variables already included in the DCSD model. It seems plausible that loose fiscal policy could lead to overvaluation of the real exchange rate and a wider current account deficit, depletion of reserves, and a buildup of short-term debt. In other words, the findings presented here are consistent with the notion that fiscal variables affect crisis vulnerability indirectly.

Fiscal Variables and the Severity of Currency Crises

In addition to influencing the likelihood and timing of financial crises, a country's fiscal situation could affect the depth or severity of a crisis. For example, a sharp increase in interest rates resulting from pressure on the exchange rate could suddenly worsen public debt dynamics and exacerbate the flight of capital; or a banking crisis could crystallize large contingent liabilities, such as those needed to protect deposits or to recapitalize the banking system, adding to public debt. Alternatively, a weak precrisis fiscal position could make it difficult to respond to a crisis by supporting aggregate demand; conversely, structural fiscal rigidities such as weak capacity for tax administration or budget management could make it hard to tighten fiscal policy quickly and thus restore confidence when a crisis hits.

A number of studies attempt to explain the severity of currency crises conditional on a crisis occurring elsewhere. Sachs, Tornell, and Velasco (1996) (STV) examine the spread of crises during the six months following the onset of the Mexican crisis in December 1994. The severity of crisis is measured using an index of exchange market pressure similar to the FMP variable described in Section III. The explanatory variables are exchange rate overvaluation, measured by the depreciation of the trade-weighted real effective exchange rate; banking sector weakness, proxied by growth of credit to the private sector; and vulnerability to capital inflow reversals, proxied by the ratio of M2 to reserves. STV also include two dummy variables for weak fundamentals and low reserves. STV conclude that their model fits the data well. In addition, they include a measure of government consumption to proxy the extent to which lax fiscal policy prior to the crisis explains the severity of pressure on the exchange rate during the crisis and find that the percentage change in government consumption in the period 1990–94 is statistically significant, but only in countries with weak fundamentals and low reserves. They also find some evidence that lax fiscal policy contributes indirectly to the severity of crises by influencing the degree of exchange rate overvaluation prior to the crisis.

To investigate further the role of fiscal factors in explaining changes in the FMP index, the first step is the estimation of a variant of the STV model to which fiscal variables are added. The sample of countries (the 58 currency crises in the dataset), the fiscal variables, and the currency crisis index are all as described in Section III. Detailed results are given in Appendix IV, but Table 4.3 shows the benchmark specification and various alternative specifications, including the three best performing fiscal variables. While there is evidence that the severity of crisis is positively correlated with the change in net claims on government (Fiscal Models 1 and 2 in Table 4.3), this relationship becomes insignificant when other explanatory variables are included (Fiscal Models 3 and 4). This suggests that, consistent with similar empirical studies using the STV approach, fiscal variables have at most an indirect impact on crisis severity.

As an alternative, panel estimation is used to explain changes in the FMP index over the entire pooled sample of crisis and tranquil periods combined. This

---
[38]Recall, however, that all the probit EWS results have been evaluated in terms of in-sample predictive power. The results could be somewhat different using "out-of-sample and out-of-mind" prediction—that is, how the models estimated in this study perform over the next two years.

IV EWS MODELS AND THE SEVERITY OF CURRENCY CRISES

Table 4.3. Explaining the Severity of Currency Crises (STV Approach)

	Benchmark Model		Fiscal Model 1		Fiscal Model 2		Fiscal Model 3		Fiscal Model 4	
Observations	57		54		54		38		45	
Test for joint significance	$F(3,53)$	27.9	$F(1,52)$	4.9	$F(3,50)$	36.0	$F(5,32)$	17.3	$F(5,39)$	82.2
R^2	0.25		0.06		0.17		0.37		0.27	
Adjusted R^2	0.22		0.06		0.14		0.30		0.20	
	Coefficient	t-ratio	Coefficient	t-ratio	Coefficient	t-ratio	Coefficient	t-ratio	Coefficient	t-ratio
Exchange rate overvaluation (in the previous period)	0.00	8.62			0.00	7.85	0.00	6.80	0.00	7.20
M2 to reserves	0.01	3.15					0.01	2.39	0.01	2.46
Weak fundamentals	1.46	2.29			2.02	3.09	1.91	2.24	1.22	3.33
Change in net claims on government			0.06	2.21	0.06	2.20	0.05	0.75	0.04	1.39
Total debt							–0.00	–0.01		
Long-term debt									0.02	1.19
Constant	0.79	1.39	2.29	9.11	0.38	0.63	0.11	0.14	0.75	2.46

Source: Appendix IV.

is akin to modeling changes in the exchange rate, with all its attendant difficulties; however, it provides a much larger sample for estimation. The methodology and results are discussed in Appendix IV, with the key results shown in Table 4.4. The panel approach finds stronger evidence of a role for fiscal variables in influencing pressure in the foreign exchange market. When the best performers among the fiscal variables are entered jointly in the panel model, elevated deficit, debt, and interest variables all increase pressure in the foreign exchange market, over and above the effect of other factors. The relationships are robust over different specifications, measures of fiscal variables, and sample composition.

Summary of Findings

A thorough examination of the univariate leading indicator properties of a range of fiscal variables finds some that are potentially useful for signaling crises. The best vulnerability indicators—short-term debt, foreign currency debt, and various deficit measures—perform as well as the best (annual) leading indicators in other signals EWS studies. But even the best performing indicators fail to signal around two-thirds of crises, although they send very few false alarms. These findings apply as much to banking crises as currency and debt crises, suggesting that fiscal variables may indeed have a part to play in predicting all three types of financial crisis.

In a multivariate context, there is robust evidence that fiscal variables are correlated with currency crises after controlling for other variables. But in terms of predicting crises, fiscal variables add relatively little to the IMF's main EWS model. It seems plausible that the variables already included in the model are capturing the main fiscal effects on crisis vulnerability—through exchange rate overvaluation, depletion of reserves, buildup of short-term debt, and so on. In probit EWS models, where parsimony is important, it is unlikely that fiscal variables will add sufficient power to the predictions to merit inclusion. This is reinforced by the relatively low frequency and significant time lags associated with most fiscal data. That said, the addition of certain fiscal variables to the probit EWS model does lead to some improvement in its ability to predict tranquil or noncrisis periods.

Finally, fiscal variables have limited value in explaining the severity of currency crises conditional on a crisis having occurred. But when a measure of exchange market pressure is estimated over the entire pooled data sample, there is robust evidence that loose fiscal policy, high public debt, and high interest expenditure are correlated with pressure in the foreign exchange market. This is further evidence that fiscal variables may have a role to play in explaining and predicting tranquil or noncrisis periods in currency markets, albeit indirectly through their effect on the exchange rate and reserves.

Table 4.4. Explaining Changes in the FMP Index (Panel Approach, Fixed Effects)

	Benchmark Model		Fiscal Model 1		Fiscal Model 2		Fiscal Model 3		Fiscal Model 4	
Observations	709		566		559		544		551	
Countries included	29		27		27		27		27	
Per country										
Minimum observations	6		4		4		4		4	
Average observations	24.4		21		20.7		20.1		20.4	
Maximum observations	29		29		29		29		29	
R^2										
Within	0.40		0.42		0.44		0.44		0.43	
Between	0.16		0.12		0.15		0.15		0.11	
Overall	0.38		0.40		0.41		0.41		0.41	
Test for joint significance	$F(6,674)$	73.66	$F(9,530)$	43.43	$F(9,523)$	44.74	$F(9,508)$	44.00	$F(9,515)$	42.67
Hausman test for random effects	$\chi^2(6)$	26.77	$\chi^2(9)$	13.81	$\chi^2(9)$	14.83	$\chi^2(9)$	87.92	$\chi^2(9)$	13.85
Results similar for random effects	Yes		Yes		Yes		Yes		Yes	
	Coefficient	t-ratio	Coefficient	t-ratio	Coefficient	t-ratio	Coefficient	t-ratio	Coefficient	t-ratio
Exchange rate overvaluation (in the previous period)	0.00	2.32	0.00	2.35	0.00	2.35	0.00	2.26	0.00	2.35
Change in M2 to reserves	0.01	14.26	0.01	13.20	0.01	13.39	0.01	13.38	0.01	13.11
Weak fundamentals	0.45	3.62	0.31	2.36	0.31	2.34	0.32	2.36	0.32	2.37
Export growth	−0.02	−7.08	−0.01	−4.92	−0.01	−4.56	−0.01	−4.29	−0.01	−4.68
Short-term debt to reserves	0.00	3.12	0.00	2.75	0.00	2.81	0.00	2.71	0.00	2.78
Real GDP growth	−0.02	−2.63	−0.02	−2.14	−0.02	−2.21	−0.02	−2.15	−0.02	−1.99
Actuarial deficit			0.02	2.67	0.01	1.98	0.02	2.39	0.02	3.12
Public external debt			0.00	1.06					0.00	0.21
Long-term debt					0.01	3.05	0.01	2.88		
Interest expenditure[1]			0.06	2.39	0.05	2.07				
Interest payments[1]							0.05	2.07	0.06	2.64
Constant	−0.15	−1.21	−0.31	−1.92	−0.42	−2.66	−0.44	−2.74	−0.27	−1.67

Source: Appendix IV.

[1] In percent of GDP; interest expenditure from the IMF's Government Finance Statistics (GFS) functional classification and interest payments from the GFS economic classification.

V Case Studies

This section reports the conclusions from case studies of 11 financial crises in emerging market economies in the 1990s. In chronological order, these are Mexico (1994–95), Argentina (1995), Bulgaria (1996–97), the Czech Republic (1997), Thailand (1997), Korea (1997), Pakistan (1998–99), Russia (1998), Ukraine (1998–2000), Brazil (1998–99), and Ecuador (1999). The case studies can be found in Appendix V. These obviously do not cover all emerging market financial crises of recent years, neither are they a random sample. Rather, the cases have been selected to cover a range of different types of financial crisis, some of which have already been extensively analyzed, but others of which are less well known. Each case study covers the background to the crisis; a description of the way in which the crisis manifested itself—currency depreciation, banking system collapse, sovereign debt restructuring or default, the impact on output and inflation, and the immediate policy responses; the causes of the crisis; the evolution of various fiscal vulnerability indicators before, during, and after the crisis; and, finally, the fiscal impact of the crisis and the response of macrofiscal and structural fiscal policies. The main conclusions are organized under three headings: the fiscal causes of crises, fiscal indicators, and fiscal consequences of crises.

Fiscal Causes of Crises

Fiscal vulnerabilities were central in at least 6 of the 11 case studies. Table 5.1 summarizes the main causes, both fiscal and nonfiscal, of the 11 crises. In 4 of the cases examined, public sector solvency and liquidity problems culminated in sovereign debt default (Russia and Ecuador), or negotiated restructuring under the shadow of default (Pakistan and Ukraine). In the other two cases, Bulgaria and Brazil, persistent and growing fiscal deficits were a central cause of pressure on the currency. In nearly all these cases, real interest rates were high and increasing—reflecting the legacy of high inflation and low policy credibility—that increased the debt-service burden and made it very difficult to raise interest rates to defend the currency in response to capital outflows. The underlying structural fiscal problems varied across these countries, but cover all the usual suspects: a high share of nondiscretionary expenditure (e.g., interest payments, social transfers, and intergovernmental transfers), poor expenditure control, overreliance on oil-related revenues, weak tax administration, and a lack of political will to address these problems.

Several of the crises demonstrate the importance of the structure of public debt as source of vulnerability to crisis. While debt-to-GDP ratios were very high in Bulgaria, Pakistan, and Ecuador, in other cases they were comparable to those in noncrisis countries and did not obviously give rise to solvency concerns. But in Mexico, Russia, Ukraine, and Brazil, heavy recourse to short-term and/or foreign currency borrowing increased vulnerability to interest rate and exchange rate shocks, and hence to liquidity or rollover problems. The cases of Russia and Brazil also show how liquidity problems can reflect long-standing fiscal problems, while the crises in Mexico and Ukraine demonstrate how this kind of vulnerability can develop over a short period of time.

Conventional deficit and debt measures can mask severe underlying fiscal vulnerabilities. In the cases of Mexico, Argentina, and the Czech Republic, conventional measures suggested that macrofiscal policy was sustainable in the years preceding the crises; indeed, this led many commentators to discount the role of fiscal vulnerabilities in these crises. But it is apparent—at least with hindsight—that fiscal policy was too expansionary prior to the crises. In the case of Argentina in 1995 and possibly Thailand, unsustainable growth rates meant that the underlying fiscal stance was significantly looser than it appeared. In Mexico and the Czech Republic, the government failed to tighten fiscal policy in the months leading up to the crises, putting an excessive strain on monetary policy and hence the banking system. In Mexico and Argentina there was also "hidden" fiscal expansion: through lending by state-owned banks in the former and through bank financing of provincial deficits in the latter.

Fiscal Causes of Crises

Table 5.1. Causes of Crises

	Mexico, 1994–95	Argentina, 1995	Bulgaria, 1996–97	Czech Republic, 1997	Thailand, 1997
Main underlying vulnerabilities	Pegged exchange rate.	Currency board.	Heavy external borrowing.	Capital inflows/current account deficit.	Pegged exchange rate.
	Current account deficit.	Banking sector weakness.	Failure to carry out structural reforms and address governance problems.	Pegged exchange rate.	Capital inflows/current account deficit.
	Banking sector problems; and weak supervision.	Reliance on short-term external finance.	Banking sector weakness.	Policy mix (loose fiscal policy, tight monetary policy).	Banking/financial sector weakness and weak supervision.
	Public debt management.				Reliance on short-term external borrowing.
How important were fiscal factors?	Contributory factor.	Important contributory factor.	Central.	Important contributory factor.	Marginal.
Main fiscal factors	Switch into short-term government debt.	Growing deficit in 1994 raised sustainability concerns; above-trend growth in early 1990s masked a lax fiscal stance.	Doubts about fiscal sustainability; inability to sufficiently compress discretionary spending.	Failure to tighten fiscal policy despite overheating.	Large contingent liabilities.
	Failure to tighten fiscal policy in 1994.	Bank financing deficits of provincial governments.	Bailing out state-owned banks.	Off-budget spending and implicit liabilities.	Tax distortions encouraged corporate debt.
	"Hidden" fiscal expansion through lending by state-owned banks.	Intergovernmental fiscal relations: flawed revenue-sharing arrangements; excessive provincial wage bills.	Weak revenue collection and secular revenue decline.	Poor governance of state-owned enterprises; high government wages; and high proportion of transfers in total spending.	
	Long-term increase in government expenditure added to real exchange rate appreciation.	Expenditure rigidities; pensions and transfers to provinces accounted for two-thirds of federal expenditure.			

V CASE STUDIES

Table 5.1 (concluded)

	Korea, 1997	Pakistan, 1998–99	Russia, 1998	Ukraine, 1998–2000	Brazil, 1998–99	Ecuador, 1999
Main underlying vulnerabilities	Pegged exchange rate.	Buildup of external and public debt.	Structural fiscal problems.	Persistent budget deficits.	Pegged exchange rate.	Pegged exchange rate.
	Over-leveraged corporate sector.	High interest rates, and growing debt-service burden.	Maturity structure of public debt.	Reliance on short-term external financing.	Current account deficit.	Very high public debt, mainly external.
	Banking sector weakness.		Pegged exchange rate.	Lack of progress in institutional reform and governance.	Increasing fiscal deficit.	Structural rigidities.
	Reliance on short-term external finance.	Narrow production and export base.	Banking sector weakness.	Pegged exchange rate.	Maturity structure of public debt.	Weak macroeconomic policies.
		Governance problems.	Governance problems.			Fractious domestic politics.
						Weak banking sector.
How important were fiscal factors?	Marginal.	Central.	Central.	Central.	Central.	Important contributory factor.
Main fiscal factors	Large contingent liabilities.	High level of public debt, around half external.	Weak tax administration.	Poor debt management.	Doubts about commitment to fiscal adjustment led to debt sustainability concerns.	Heavy reliance on oil-related revenues; extensive earmarking of revenues.
	History of directed lending and government bailouts, contributing to overinvestment.	Low tax ratio because of narrow tax base and weak administration.	Weak expenditure control.	Reliance on netting-out operations.	Expensive public pensions and wages; rigid expenditure structure; and high share of nondiscretionary expenditure.	Low tax yield from non-oil sector (weak administration, extensive exemptions).
		High share of unproductive and inflexible expenditure in total government spending.	High share of non-discretionary expenditure.	Widespread tax exemptions.	Inefficient indirect tax system.	Lack of central government control over expenditure.
			Reliance on short-term financing for public debt.	Slow progress in expenditure rationalization.	Reliance on short-term financing for public debt.	Fiscal factors contributed to the banking crisis: financial transactions tax; cost and sustainability of deposit guarantee scheme.
			Debt dynamics.			
			Parliamentary opposition to measures.			

Source: Appendix V.

The case studies show the different ways in which fiscal policy can contribute to banking sector problems. In Ecuador, the introduction of a financial transactions tax prompted large-scale withdrawals from the banking sector, and doubts about the credibility of deposit guarantees in the face of a deteriorating fiscal situation exacerbated the run on the banks. The main cause of weakness among provincial banks in Argentina was their persistent financing of the deficits of provinces. In Thailand, the government created incentives for banks and companies to borrow abroad through implicit and explicit guarantees and tax breaks. Finally, in Russia and Ecuador, the banks held large amounts of government paper that was rescheduled; this compounded the deterioration in their balance sheets, exacerbating the effects of the sovereign debt crisis on the financial sector and the wider economy.

However, fiscal vulnerabilities were not central to all crises. This contrasts to two other factors—having some form of pegged exchange rate and weaknesses in the banking and financial system—that are critical in explaining almost all the crises examined (with the possible exceptions of Ukraine and Pakistan). But even in Thailand, where the key vulnerabilities were rooted in the private sector, fiscal policy played a role. At the structural level, tax distortions and government guarantees resulted in borrowing that was too high and insufficiently hedged in terms of currency and maturity; at the macroeconomic level, the emergence of large contingent liabilities suddenly raised concerns about sustainability that increased capital account pressures.

Fiscal Indicators

Given the small sample size and difficulties of comparability, the analysis of fiscal indicators in the case studies is more impressionistic than systematic. With that caveat in mind, it is evident that deficit and debt variables gave, at least with hindsight, advance warning of impending problems in five countries. These are Bulgaria, Pakistan, Russia, Brazil, and Ecuador. However, to be useful as warning signals before the event, these indicators need to be compared to a country-specific benchmark or critical threshold, which in turn would need to depend, among other things, on the fiscal history of the country and of similar crises in other countries. However, in other countries, aggregate fiscal variables gave little or no warning of an impending crisis, for a variety of reasons. In Thailand and Korea, the key vulnerabilities were in the private sector; in Mexico and Ukraine, the main fiscal vulnerabilities related to the structure rather than the level of public debt; in several cases—the Czech Republic, Thailand, and Korea—conventional measures failed to capture off-budget activities and contingent liabilities. In other cases, conventional deficits were misleading because they did not adjust for the effects of unsustainably high growth rates (Argentina and Thailand) or because of data quality problems (Pakistan).

Indicators of the maturity and currency structure of public debt are clearly useful for signaling impending problems. This was the case in Mexico, Russia, and Ukraine. But, at present, the coverage and availability of such information varies widely across countries. There is also the problem of defining critical thresholds, and the possibility of apparently perverse developments, such as the lengthening of average maturity of public debt prior to the Russian crisis.

The same observations apply to indicators of structural fiscal vulnerabilities. Indeed, the only useful structural fiscal indicators found for the crises examined here are tax and expenditure arrears in the Czech Republic, Russia, and Ukraine. It is possible that similar indicators could be unearthed for other countries, but these are not easily available. Much work would be needed to construct and maintain a wider set of useful structural fiscal vulnerability indicators, particularly if historical and cross-country comparable series are to be used to determine critical thresholds.

Finally, market indicators typically give little or no advance warning of impending crisis. This confirms the conclusions of other studies that credit ratings in particular seem to be reactive to crises.

Fiscal Consequences of Crises

Crises had wide-ranging effects on public debt. In three cases, there was a large increase in the debt-to-GDP ratio within a year or so of the crisis (by around 20 percentage points of GDP in Mexico and Thailand, and around 15 percentage points of GDP in Korea). In four cases—Argentina, the Czech Republic, Pakistan, and Brazil—the crises resulted in a relatively modest increase in the debt ratio of around 5 percentage points of GDP. In the other four cases—Bulgaria, Russia, Ukraine, and Ecuador—the debt ratio had fallen below precrisis levels within two years of the crisis.

The impact on fiscal sustainability also varied widely. In five cases—Mexico, Bulgaria, Russia, Ukraine, and Ecuador—sustainability improved, albeit for different reasons and to varying extents. In Mexico the stock of debt increased, but became less exposed to currency and interest rate risk; in Bulgaria, Russia, Ukraine, and Ecuador, various combinations of strong fiscal adjustment, higher oil prices, debt restructuring, and an increase in growth

V CASE STUDIES

Table 5.2. Fiscal Consequences of Crises

	Mexico, 1994–95	Argentina, 1995	Bulgaria, 1996–97	Czech Republic, 1997	Thailand, 1997	Korea, 1997
Impact on debt, in percentage points (pps) of GDP, and on sustainability	Large increase (around 20 pps); sustainability subsequently improved.	Modest increase (around 5 pps); sustainability concerns reemerged later.	Modest reduction in 1997; larger reduction in 1998 due to growth and lower interest rates. Progress maintained since.	Modest increase (loan guarantees made explicit); since 1998, deficits and slow growth have led to sustainability concerns.	Large increase (20 pps); sustainability has become a concern.	Moderate increase (by 12 pps); no sustainability concerns.
Stance of fiscal policy following crisis	Original program: 1 pp tightening; first review additional 1 pp tightening. Outturn: 2.7 pps tightening.[1]	Original program: 2 pps tightening. Outturn: ½ pp tightening.[1]	Improvement in primary balance of around 5 pps.	1997 budget projected a 1 pp tightening. Outturn: unchanged deficit implying modest tightening.	Original program: 3 pps tightening. Outturn: 1½ pps tightening.[1]	Original program: 1½ pps tightening. Outturn: 1 pp stimulus.[1]
How achieved/ implemented?	Higher-than-expected oil revenues; delays to investment projects; cuts in social spending and transfers to state-owned enterprises.	Temporary value-added tax (VAT) increase and broad-based central government expenditure cuts.	Rebound in revenues (due to higher wages) and sharp decline in domestic interest payments offset by some recovery of noninterest expenditure.	Weak revenues (due to crisis and floods) offset by large discretionary spending cuts (current and capital).	Large discretionary measures insufficient to offset falling output: increased social spending and public works; tax deferrals.	Mostly discretionary measures: increased expenditure on social safety net, capital projects, and bank restructuring.
Structural fiscal responses	Tax administration reforms introduced 1996–97; targeted social safety net scheme introduced 1997.	No major reforms implemented; some minor reforms to provincial finances (privatization and transferring pensions to federal government).	Improved tax administration and expenditure management; tax base broadened, rates lowered, and other measures to address inflation-induced distortions.	Legal requirement to disclose hidden debts and liabilities; tighter rules for government guarantees.	Expansion of social safety net.	Expansion of social safety net.

Fiscal Consequences of Crises

	Pakistan, 1998–99	Russia, 1998	Ukraine, 1998–2000	Brazil, 1998–99	Ecuador, 1999
Impact on debt, in percentage points (pps) of GDP, and on sustainability	Moderate increase (by 7 pps, between 1998–99 to 2000–01); continued sustainability concerns.	Modest reduction in domestic debt; large reduction in external debt (by 2000); strong growth and exchange rate appreciation also improved debt dynamics.	Initial moderate increase (12 pps) due to fall in exchange rate; subsequent reduction in debt ratio due to fiscal adjustment and growth; sustainability not a major concern.	Modest increase (6 pps); structure of debt improved.	Cost of banking crisis around 20 percent of GDP; debt restructuring and strong recovery in fiscal position reduced sustainability concerns.
Stance of fiscal policy following crisis	Little change in 1999–2000; modest tightening in 2000–01.	General government primary balance improved by 3 pps.	Significant consolidation in 2000; primary balance improved by 1½ pps.	Original program: 3 pps tightening. Outturn: 3 pps improvement in primary surplus.[1]	Original program: 2½ pps improvement in primary surplus. Outturn: 5 pps improvement in primary surplus.
How achieved/implemented?	Expenditure compression (current and capital) in 2000–01.	Growth in tax base as a result of recovery; discretionary tax changes; improved tax compliance; expenditure compression at subnational level.	Discretionary expenditure curbs; enforcing cash payments and eliminating offsets; higher-than-expected growth.	In 1999, mostly at central government level (improved tax administration and expenditure control). In 2000, also at subnational level.	Higher oil revenues; improved tax administration; rebound in activity.
Structural fiscal responses	Tax policy reforms; strengthened fiscal reporting and expenditure management.	Higher export duties; a shift of VAT, profit, and income tax revenues to federal level; improved expenditure control; elimination of offsets at federal level.	Enactment of modern budget code; improved indirect tax enforcement procedures; elimination of noncash offsets.	Fiscal Responsibility Law enacted May 2000; other reforms impeded by Congress.	Financial transactions tax eliminated; VAT rate increased; lower subsidies on fuel; proposal for new oil stabilization fund and Fiscal Prudence and Discipline Law.

Source: Appendix V.
[1] See Ghosh and others (2002).

improved the medium-term fiscal outlook. In three cases, the crisis had little impact on sustainability in the short run: in the Czech Republic and Korea this was because of the low precrisis level of debt (though subsequently sustainability concerns have emerged in the Czech Republic because of stagnant growth and growing deficits); the crisis in Argentina also had little immediate impact on fiscal sustainability, although it is clear with hindsight that the underlying fiscal problems were not resolved following that crisis. Finally, in only two cases—Thailand and Pakistan—did the crisis result in a deterioration in fiscal sustainability. Table 5.2 summarizes the impact of the crises on the fiscal situation in each country, and the fiscal policy response in terms of the fiscal stance planned and achieved in the first year following the crises and the structural fiscal reforms implemented.

In terms of the response of fiscal policy to crises, the six countries where sustainability improved implemented a large fiscal tightening in the year following the crises. In each case this was based on improved tax collections, but not necessarily on expenditure cuts: Bulgaria used some of the room created by lower interest payments to increase social spending; Argentina and the Czech Republic implemented a modest discretionary tightening based mostly on expenditure reductions; and in Thailand and Korea, there was some offset from discretionary fiscal stimulus. In three of these countries—the Czech Republic, Thailand, and Korea—the initial fiscal tightening was reversed. In the Asian countries this followed the much larger-than-expected decline in output, and indications that fiscal tightening was reducing rather than bolstering confidence, both domestically and internationally. In the Czech Republic, the reversal came somewhat later, although also as a response to slower-than-anticipated recovery in growth.

The successful implementation of discretionary tightening in Mexico, Bulgaria, Russia, Ukraine, Brazil, and Ecuador contrasts with the difficulties of implementing an expansionary fiscal policy in Korea and Thailand. The latter was due to a combination of a tradition of fiscal conservatism, capacity constraints, and budget management problems. The experience of Korea, in particular, shows that the capacity for fiscal policy to support recovery following a capital account crisis depends on structural features of the tax and spending systems, as well as the precrisis debt-to-GDP ratio.

In many cases, the crisis proved to be a decisive catalyst for significant structural fiscal reforms. Notable in this regard are improved tax administration and expenditure management (Bulgaria, Russia, Ukraine, Brazil); a significant expansion of the social safety net (Thailand, Korea); and enhanced fiscal transparency (Czech Republic, Brazil). However, crises do not always result in the degree of structural reform necessary to address fundamental fiscal problems; Argentina is a case in point.

VI Conclusions

What Are the Fiscal Causes of Crisis?

A review of the theoretical literature suggests three main ways in which fiscal policy can cause a financial crisis. These are through an overly expansionary fiscal stance, leading to a lending and/or consumption boom; through concerns about sustainability, which could be triggered by news about contingent liabilities or by a shift in expectations about the government's commitment to fiscal adjustment; and through the maturity and currency structure of public debt, which can be critical to perceptions of government liquidity, and hence increase vulnerability to self-fulfilling crises.

Conclusive evidence on the causes of crises is hard to find. In particular, most existing empirical studies of crises are more relevant to the issue of correlation than causation. That said, the evidence on fiscal variables is mixed. Some studies find the deficit and debt variables to be significantly correlated with crises, others do not. But very few studies conclude that fiscal variables provide the main "explanation" of crises. The empirical analysis of a large sample of emerging market economies finds robust evidence that a few fiscal variables are correlated with crises and with pressure in the foreign exchange market. There is also evidence suggesting that fiscal effects operate indirectly, through variables such as the exchange rate or the current account.

In contrast, the 11 case studies of financial crises in the 1990s suggest a direct and important role for fiscal policy in causing crises. In six countries—Bulgaria (1996–97), Pakistan (1998–2000), Russia (1998), Ukraine (1998–99), Brazil (1998–99), and Ecuador (1999)—fiscal problems were clearly central to, and arguably the single most important cause of, the crises. In three countries—Mexico (1994–95), Argentina (1995), and the Czech Republic (1997)—fiscal problems contributed to the crisis, but were probably not the most important factor. In the other two countries—Thailand and Korea—the key vulnerabilities were rooted in the private sector, but fiscal policy still played a role in the Thai crisis.

Several of the case studies confirm the importance of the structure of public debt as a source of vulnerability to crisis. The most obvious example is the Mexican government issuing large amounts of short-term dollar-denominated debt in 1994, but a similar reliance on short-term domestic and external financing—and low policy credibility—led to the rollover problems that precipitated the crises in Russia and Ukraine. When external public debt is high relative to tax revenue and exports, the public finances are vulnerable to a fall in the exchange rate, which increases debt-service costs without having a large positive effect on growth.

The case studies also show how fiscal policy can contribute to financial sector vulnerabilities. On the asset side, this could come through banks holding significant amounts of government paper that is restructured (Russia, Ecuador), or by contributing to nonperforming loans as a result of directed lending (Bulgaria), financing the deficits of provincial governments (Argentina), or through implicit government guarantees and tax breaks contributing to balance sheet vulnerabilities in the corporate and financial sectors (Thailand). On the liability side, banks in Ecuador suffered deposit runs as a result of tax changes prompting large-scale withdrawals, and due to a widening fiscal deficit undermining the credibility of deposit guarantees.

Which Fiscal Vulnerability Indicators Help to Predict Crises?

A number of fiscal variables are potentially useful as univariate leading indicators for signaling crises on an annual basis. The best indicators—short-term debt, foreign currency debt, and various deficit measures—perform as well as the best (annual) leading indicators in other signals EWS studies. While even the best performing indicators fail to signal around two-thirds of crises, these indicators send very few false alarms, and therefore warnings about an impending crisis should be heeded. These findings apply as much to banking crises as currency and debt crises, suggesting that fiscal variables may

VI   CONCLUSIONS

indeed have a part to play in predicting financial sector crises. This is somewhat surprising, given the absence of a role for fiscal variables in most other EWS models of banking crises.

In a multivariate context, fiscal variables appear to add relatively little to the IMF's main EWS model. Bearing in mind the relatively low frequency of most fiscal data, and the premium on high-frequency data for EWS models, this suggests that fiscal variables are of limited use in parsimonious probit EWS models. But there is evidence from both the signals and probit EWS models that fiscal variables help more to identify tranquil or noncrisis periods than to signal crisis episodes.

Regarding particular types of fiscal indicators, the main findings are as follows:

- Deficit and financing variables can certainly send clear signals of impending crisis. This was the case in the crises in Bulgaria, Pakistan, Russia, Ukraine, Brazil, and Ecuador in the late 1990s. But in other crises, as mentioned above, standard measures of the deficit did not send a clear signal in advance. The evidence from the event studies is that deficits are significantly higher, on average, in the two years prior to currency and debt crises than in noncrisis periods.

- Total debt does not seem to add much to crisis prediction. In the event studies, most debt variables are no different, on average, prior to a crisis than in noncrisis periods; they rank poorly among fiscal variables in the signals EWS approach; and they are insignificant or have perverse signs when included in probit EWS models.

- Some variables relating to the composition of debt emerge as useful predictors of crises. The event studies show that short-term debt is significantly higher in the run-up to crises; indeed, this is the only variable examined that is systematically "abnormal" prior to banking crises. Short-term debt also comes out as one of the best predictors of currency, debt, and banking crises according to the signals EWS approach. However, the fact that available cross-country data on short-term debt do not distinguish public from private sector debt limits the usefulness of the result.

- There is little evidence that expenditure and revenue variables help to predict crises. None of these variables adds to the predictive power of the IMF's main EWS model, and the event studies fail to find any expenditure or revenue variables, which differ systematically in the run-up to crises compared with noncrisis periods.

Can Fiscal Variables Explain the Severity of Currency Crises?

Using the standard approach in the literature, some deficit and financing variables are found to be weakly correlated with the severity of currency crises. However, this correlation is not robust, being dominated by other variables. Using a panel data approach, the picture changes somewhat. Deficit, debt, and interest expenditure variables are important for explaining changes in the foreign exchange market pressure index, in both crisis and noncrisis periods. This provides more support for the conclusion noted above, namely that fiscal variables help explain relatively tranquil periods better than crisis periods. It also suggests that there is an important indirect impact of fiscal policy on currency crises, operating through the real exchange rate appreciation.

What Are the Fiscal Consequences of Crises?

The event studies show that the deficit declines on average in the two years following currency and debt crises. Given that crises will typically result in a slowdown in growth, an improvement in the conventional deficit implies discretionary fiscal tightening, on average, following currency and debt crises. This will often be inevitable when a crisis hits. However, there is some evidence that the situation is different following banking crises, with some deficit variables pointing to fiscal loosening following a crisis. The appropriateness of a fiscal loosening will depend not only on the type of crises, but also its underlying cause, the precrisis fiscal position, and the response of the domestic economy and international investors to the crises.

On average, the debt-to-GDP ratio increases significantly following all types of crises. While there is some evidence of a reduction in short-term debt following currency and debt crises, foreign debt remains fairly stable in the two years following crises. The case studies show how these averages can conceal wide variations; indeed in 4 of the 11 cases, debt fell following the crisis, due to a combination of debt restructuring, fiscal adjustment, and real exchange rate appreciation.

The event studies suggest that total expenditure changes little, on average, following currency and debt crises, but remains significantly above the tranquil period average in the case of banking crises. Consistent with the increase in total debt stocks following crises, interest expenditure rises in the years following currency and debt crises, offset by lower social expenditure. The event studies imply that the big falloff in revenue experienced by some Asian crisis countries during 1997–98 is not typical of most emerging market economies following financial crises.

Finally, the case studies demonstrate that crises can catalyze significant structural fiscal reforms. In particular, they allow political barriers to reform to be overcome. Clearly, if crises clear the way to undertake much-needed structural reform, full advantage should be taken of this opportunity.

Appendix I Literature Review

The literature on fiscal aspects of financial crises in emerging market economies is organized under five headings: the fiscal causes of crises; predicting crises using early warning system models; fiscal factors explaining the severity of currency crises; the fiscal consequences of crises.

Fiscal Causes of Crises

Theoretical Literature

The following concentrates on the subset of theoretical models of financial crises in which fiscal factors are emphasized. Although in much of the recent theoretical work on financial crises the distinction between currency, debt, and banking crises is becoming less clear, treating them separately is useful in linking the theoretical and empirical literature.

Currency Crises

In "first-generation" models of currency crises, expansionary fiscal policy that is inconsistent with an exchange rate peg is typically the root cause of crises. This could be evident: in an increasing (recorded) fiscal deficit (Krugman, 1979); in the issuance of domestic debt in an attempt to hide the depletion of reserves (Calvo, 1995); or in an unrecorded deterioration of the net asset position, for example, due to quasi-fiscal activities or contingent liabilities (Dooley, 1998). Calvo (1995) also shows how an exchange rate crisis can be consistent with a sound fiscal position in the run-up to a crisis, while the underlying fiscal imbalances are masked by an unsustainable consumer boom (due to an expectation of a future devaluation).

In "second-generation" models, crises are not inevitable or predicated on policy inconsistencies; rather, they result from a switch between good and bad equilibria. Multiple equilibria result from nonlinearities in government behavior, such as when policy reacts to changes in private decisions or when the government faces a trade-off between the exchange rate peg and other objectives. In such models, fiscal policy is not necessarily central, but could contribute to a crisis in various ways. One possibility is that the government's commitment to its exchange rate peg could be conditional on its debt-service obligations, in that the higher the debt stock, the greater the costs of defending the exchange rate peg by raising interest rates (Obstfeld, 1994).

"Third-generation" models, developed in the light of the Asian crises, take various forms, but tend to stress balance sheet problems. Third-generation models allow for both self-fulfilling nonfundamentals- and fundamentals-driven crises. Most of these models focus on private sector vulnerabilities, with fiscal factors playing only a limited role. Some models emphasize structural fiscal problems. For example, Corsetti, Pesenti, and Roubini (1999) have government guarantees, subsidies, and directed lending causing moral hazard in the corporate and financial sectors, leading to an excessive buildup of external debt. Although deficits may not be high before a crisis, the eventual refusal of foreign creditors to refinance a country's debt forces the government to step in and guarantee the outstanding debt. To remain solvent, the government must undertake fiscal adjustment and/or resort to seigniorage. Expectations of inflationary financing cause a collapse of the currency and are the prelude to a banking crisis. Other models focus on new information or changes in market sentiment about fiscal policy as the cause of crises. For example, contingent liabilities and large prospective deficits associated with the bailout of failing banks—as in Burnside, Eichenbaum, and Rebelo (1999) and Corsetti and Mackowiak (2001)—cause a sudden change in investor expectations about the financing of future deficits, leading to massive capital outflows and a collapse of the currency.

Kopits (2000) argues that vulnerability to a currency crisis in second- and third-generation models often depends on perceived fiscal sustainability. An attack takes place when investors obtain new information that the government's net liabilities exceed a certain threshold, or decide that the government's optimal choice is to inflate away debt, instead of undertaking fiscal adjustment, to meet its intertemporal budget constraint.

Debt Crises

In principle, external debt default and crises could reflect a permanent problem of solvency—the present value of a country's prospective resources is insufficient to meet its external obligations—or a more temporary problem of illiquidity, where lending is withdrawn even though the country is technically solvent. It is now widely recognized that in very few cases, if ever, has the level of external indebtedness reached the point where the country as a whole is insolvent. In the face of this empirical fact, theoretical models of debt crises have taken three approaches, with somewhat different implications for the role of fiscal policy.

Most models analyze debt default as a "willingness-to-pay" problem where the borrower is solvent, but chooses not to repay after weighing the costs and benefits of default. Although such models are often (implicitly or explicitly) about sovereign debt—repayment of which often cannot be legally enforced, in contrast to commercial debt—the analysis typically does not consider the underlying (fiscal) causes of the debt buildup, in part because these models tend to focus on explaining the decisions of lenders—why lend when repayment cannot be legally enforced?—rather than borrowers.

An alternative approach, less favored in the theoretical debt crisis literature, sees debt default as an "ability-to-pay" problem, but on the part of the government rather than the country as a whole. The public sector is perceived as solvent as long as its net worth—comprehensively defined to include existing assets and liabilities, and the present value of all future flows of receipts and payment obligations—is positive. But a shock, such as an increase in interest rates, a slowdown in growth, or the appearance of significant new liabilities, can cause perceptions of solvency to change rapidly, leading to the withdrawal of new lending and capital flight. Some have explained the debt crisis of the early 1980s in these terms: a period of negative real interest rates in the 1970s encouraged government borrowing, without solvency concerns on the part of lenders, but this was reversed by the sharp increase in global interest rates in the early 1980s (Agénor and Montiel, 1999). More recent models that emphasize the public sector balance sheet and the vulnerability of public sector solvency to shocks are often couched in terms of a currency crisis rather than a debt crisis—such as the models of Burnside, Eichenbaum, and Rebelo (1999) and Corsetti and Mackowiak (2001), discussed above—but they still emphasize the source of the crisis being the public sector.

A third class of models explains how it is possible for a solvent country or government to suffer a liquidity crisis due to self-fulfilling expectations on the part of lenders. Creditors do not lend because they think the government will fail to repay; without the possibility of rolling over, the debtor ends up defaulting, validating the pessimistic expectations. This process can work through risk premia, as pessimistic expectations push up interest rates, which in turn increases the probability of default (see Calvo, 1988); or it can work through liquidity effects, pessimistic expectations reduce lending, which reduces liquidity and investment, and hence future output, which increases the chances of default (see Detragiache, 1996). If lenders can coordinate, these bad equilibria can be avoided; but if lenders are numerous and uncoordinated—as is typically the case with bond finance—then creditor runs can result. However, such models can still have an important role for (fiscal) fundamentals. The self-fulfilling debt crisis model of Cole and Kehoe (2000) shows how fundamentals such as the level and composition of government debt can lie in a "crisis zone" where multiple equilibria are possible. The policy response is to reduce the level of debt or lengthen its maturity structure.

Related to this third strand of the literature are a series of models that attempt to explain the composition of public debt. Calvo and Guidotti (1990) argue that government debt denominated in domestic currency gives rise to a time-inconsistency problem because of the incentive to generate inflation to reduce the real debt burden. Borrowing in dollars removes this problem, but full dollarization may not be optimal if there are shocks to government expenditure and the government cannot issue bonds contingent on those shocks.[39] Jeanne (2000) attempts to explain why so much emerging market external (sovereign) debt is short term, and hence why rollover or liquidity crises have been so common in the 1990s. His argument is that when government solvency deteriorates, short-term debt becomes cheaper or more accessible than long-term debt because the former imposes a more effective constraint on the government's future fiscal policy. The currency and maturity composition arguments are brought together in explanations of "original sin"—that is, the inability of emerging market economies to borrow long term in domestic currency (Eichengreen and Hausmann,

---

[39]There are also a number of papers explaining why the private sector borrows in foreign currency, related to bailout guarantees, lack of domestic financial development, or commitment problems at the level of domestic entrepreneurs. This is relevant to fiscal vulnerability because large increases in the domestic currency cost of foreign debt can lead to the assumption of private debt by the government, as happened in several countries during the Asian crisis.

1999; and Hausmann, 2002). This arises not only from lack of policy credibility on the part of emerging market governments, but also as a result of economies of agglomeration in international capital markets, and rapidly diminishing returns from portfolio diversification.

Banking Crises

Among the many theories of banking crises, some have a role for fiscal factors, but the linkages are usually indirect. Some theories emphasize the inherent instability of banking systems as a result of credit risk (i.e., the unpredictability of the value of bank assets). Expansionary fiscal policies could be the driving force behind a lending boom, which drives up asset prices; when the bubble eventually bursts, bank borrowers cannot service their loans, and a banking crisis ensues (see Demirgüç-Kunt and Detragiache, 1998, for further details). Other theories emphasize maturity mismatch as the key source of banking sector vulnerability. In these models, a sharp increase in short-term interest rates—which could, for example, be the result of the central bank responding to lax policy on the part of the fiscal authorities—reduces bank profitability and triggers a crisis. Velasco (1987) sees government guarantees of bank liabilities as the source of financial crises. This creates rapid credit expansion that eventually triggers a currency crisis, along the lines of first-generation models.

Diamond and Dybvig (1983) show how banking crises can be the result of self-fulfilling prophesies. Bank runs can occur simply because depositors believe other depositors are withdrawing their funds, even in the absence of a deterioration in a bank's balance sheet. In the Diamond and Dybvig model, if the government announces a guarantee of deposits, no bank run occurs. However, as Calvo and Reinhart (2000) point out, for this to be credible the government has to be able to raise sufficient revenue to finance the resulting liability. So fiscal problems could undermine the credibility of government deposit guarantees and increase the likelihood of a self-fulfilling bank run.

Some more recent work examines how currency crises—which could be driven by fiscal factors—can lead to banking crises (e.g., Goldfajn and Valdés, 1998; and Kaminsky and Reinhart, 1999). There are two main ways a currency crisis could lead to a banking crisis. First, a large loss in reserves could, if not sterilized, result in a sharp decline in credit, leading to bankruptcies among firms borrowing from banks. Indeed, if depositors participate in the run against central bank reserves, they may force banks to suspend the convertibility of deposits, or reduce lending abruptly and force the liquidation of profitable investments. Second, devaluation could create insolvencies among banks that have large foreign exchange exposures.

Other possible fiscal factors that could contribute to vulnerability in the banking sector include budgetary stress that can be used as an excuse for deferring action to strengthen banks' balance sheets (Lindgren, Garcia, and Saal, 1996); failure to control the deficit that may be a serious obstacle to financial liberalization (McKinnon, 1991); state-owned banks and/or state-influenced lending for political objectives rather than maximizing the return on bank capital, which can be a source of banking sector problems (Eichengreen and Rose, 1998); and large-scale holdings of government debt that can make bank balance sheets vulnerable to sovereign debt problems and crises (Enoch, Gulde, and Hardy, 2002).

Empirical Evidence

It is intrinsically difficult to reach firm empirical conclusions on the causes of financial crises. This reflects the lack of agreement on the appropriate theoretical model, which in turn indicates the complexity and heterogeneity of financial crises in emerging market economies. It also indicates problems of measurement and collinearity in the data (Stone and Weeks, 2001). Nevertheless, there is a large empirical literature on crises, and currency crises in particular, and some general conclusions have emerged.

There are broadly two types of empirical approaches. The first is to use statistical and econometric analyses of a large cross section of countries; this approach has grown in popularity recently, particularly in the form of early warning system (EWS) models, which focus more on predicting rather than explaining crises. But bearing in mind the dangers of inferring causality from correlation, the EWS approach can still shed some light on the causes of crises. The second empirical approach focuses on particular crises or groups of crises, either testing a particular model or using a descriptive, case study approach. This literature is not comprehensively reviewed here, although the country-specific literature on several crises of the 1990s is reviewed in Appendix V.

A subset of the empirical literature on crises, namely those studies that include at least one fiscal variable, is summarized in Table A1.1. Most follow the EWS approach, but some papers using event and case study approaches are also included.

Currency Crises

Despite the clear importance of fiscal factors in Krugman's seminal currency crisis model, relatively few empirical studies actually focus on fiscal

Appendix I

Table A1.1. Literature Review: Empirical Studies of Financial Crises

Study	Approach	Sample	Fiscal Variable Measure	Fiscal Variable Significant?	Other Variables	Findings
Currency Crises						
Brüggemann and Linne (2002)	Signal–individual indicators and index.	16 EU accession countries; 1999–2000; monthly data.	Fiscal deficit (monthly data as a linear interpolation of quarterly data).	Yes (noise-to-signal ratio=0.13).	M2 multiplier, domestic credit, assets of the domestic banking sector, exports, imports, real effective exchange rate (REER), international reserves, M2/reserves, interest differential, U.S. interest rate, external debt, short-term external debt, capital flight, industrial production, deposit rate, lending rate.	EWS performs well in anticipating crisis. The fiscal deficit is an important component of the EWS.
Moreno (1995)	Nonparametric test of differences between quiet periods and periods of speculative pressure.	7 Asia-Pacific basin countries; 1980–94; monthly and quarterly data.	Fiscal deficit as a ratio of expenditure relative to the United States.	Yes.	Exchange rate, net foreign assets, log interest rate, central bank domestic credit, narrow and broad money, inflation, deviation of output growth from mean, exports/imports—all variables relative to the United States.	Expansionary fiscal policy and growth in monetary aggregates are associated with depreciation periods. Internal imbalances are also associated with depreciation periods.
Osband and Van Rijckeghem (2000)	Identification of "safety zones" through univariate and multivariate filtering.	31 emerging market economies, 1985–98; monthly, quarterly, and annual data.	Fiscal deficit, domestic credit to the government, share of official debt in total debt.	Important.	Reserves/imports, reserves/broad money, reserves/short-term debt, domestic credit to private sector, exchange rate, current account, exports, terms of trade, foreign direct investment (FDI), portfolio investment, debt-service/exports, external debt/exports, real growth, industrial production, export diversification.	Fiscal variables are important filters, by themselves and in combination with others.
Caramazza, Ricci, and Salgado (2000)	Likelihood of financial crisis (probit).	61 industrial and emerging market countries; 1990–98.	Fiscal deficit.	Only when interacted with real exchange rate.	REER, current account, exports, GDP growth, unemployment rate, banking crisis, trade linkages, short-term debt/reserves, M2/reserves, financial market linkages, short-term share of debt to Bank for International Settlements member banks, stock market variability, exchange rate regime, capital controls.	Trade spillovers and financial linkages play an important role after controlling for domestic and external fundamentals. Exchange rate regimes and capital controls do not play a significant role.

APPENDIX I

Table A1.1 (continued)

Study	Approach	Sample	Fiscal Variable Measure	Fiscal Variable Significant?	Other Variables	Findings
Eichengreen, Rose, and Wyplosz (1996)	Likelihood of a currency crisis (probit).	20 industrial countries; 1959–93; quarterly data.	Fiscal deficit.	In some specifications.	Nongold reserves, exchange rate, short-term interest rate, exports, imports, long-term government bond yields, stock market index, domestic credit, M1, M2, CPI, real GDP, REER, total employment, unemployment rate, business sector wage rate, indicator for electoral victories and defeats, exchange rate regime.	Contagion plays an important role after controlling for an array of other factors.
Glick and Rose (1998)	Likelihood of a currency crisis (probit), index of exchange market pressure (OLS).	Annual data in 161 countries from five episodes of widespread currency instability (1971, 1973, 1992–93, 1994–95, 1997–98).	Fiscal deficit.	No.	Trade linkages, credit expansion, current account, real growth, M2/reserves, inflation, degree of exchange rate misalignment.	Contagion through trade linkages is important, macroeconomic controls are mostly insignificant.
Kamin and Babson (1999)	Likelihood of currency crisis (probit).	Argentina, Brazil, Chile, Colombia, Mexico, and Venezuela; 1981–98; annual data.	Fiscal deficit.	In some specifications.	Real GDP growth, domestic bank loan growth, REER, export growth, current account, reserves/imports, M2/reserves, external debt, reserves/short-term debt, terms of trade, U.S. treasury bill rate, industrial country GDP growth.	Domestic policies are mostly responsible for Latin American currency crises, exogenous external factors have played only a secondary role.
Ötker and Pazarbaşıoğlu (1995)	Likelihood of currency crisis (probit).	Monthly data for Mexico, October 1982–December 1984.	Fiscal deficit.	No.	Central bank credit to banks, REER, current account, inflation, share of foreign currency debt, reserves, output growth, U.S. money market rate, upper bound of exchange rate.	Economic fundamentals drive the likelihood of currency crises in Mexico, in particular, inflation differential, REER appreciation, reserve loss, expansionary monetary and fiscal policy. But 1994–95 crisis was not the result of fiscal imbalances.
Milesi-Ferretti and Razin (2000)	Likelihood of current account reversals (probit), event study; likelihood of currency crisis (probit), event study.	105 low- and middle-income countries; 1970–96; annual data.	Fiscal deficit, share of public debt in external debt.	Debt: yes; deficit: no.	Growth, real consumption, investment, per capita GDP, current account, REER, real exchange rate overvaluation, openness, external official transfers, external debt, debt service, share of concessional debt, share of short-term debt, share of multilateral debt, FDI, M2, domestic	Currency crises and current account reversals are distinct events.

Appendix I

Study	Methodology	Sample	Fiscal variable	Fiscal significant?	Other variables	Conclusions
Nitithanprapas and Willett (2000)	Exchange market pressure by OLS.	26 emerging market economies involved in the Mexican (1994) and Asian crises.	Fiscal deficit.	Yes.	Current account, real exchange rate, FDI, domestic credit growth, reserves/imports, short-term debt/reserves.	Economic fundamentals and their interactions matter. Composite indicators appear more useful than single indicators. Absence of fiscal deficit does not ensure absence of crises.
Edwards and Santaella (1992)	Event study of devaluation episodes in the Bretton Woods era.	48 episodes of major devaluations by developing countries 1948–71.	Fiscal deficit, domestic credit to the government.	Yes.	Domestic credit, real exchange rate, current account, net foreign assets/money supply, history of exchange rate changes, parallel markets.	Expansionary policies often precede a depreciation; particularly clear for fiscal policy indicators.
Eichengreen, Rose, and Wyplosz (1995)	Event study of currency crisis and likelihood of currency crisis (multinomial logit).	20 industrial countries, 1959–93; quarterly data.	Fiscal deficit.	Barely.	Reserves, exports, imports, current account, credit growth, M1, REER, interest rate, government bond yield, stock market index, CPI, wage rate, unemployment rate, employment, real output growth.	Currency crises are associated with external and internal imbalances. Expansionary policy often precedes crisis. But "good" policies do not guarantee insulation from speculative attack.
Ghosh and Ghosh (2002)	Binary recursive tree techniques.	40 industrial and emerging market countries, 1987–99.	Fiscal deficit.	No.	4 macroeconomic indicators (real exchange rate (RER) appreciation, current account, growth of banking system credit, total external debt/reserves); 6 "rule of law" indicators; 8 shareholders' rights indicators; 5 indicators of creditors' rights; firm level debt/equity data.	Macroeconomic imbalances, especially a large current account deficit, are often the trigger of crisis. But weak public sector and corporate governance increase vulnerability to macroeconomic imbalances. The interaction between structural vulnerabilities and macroeconomic imbalances is highly complex.
Frankel and Rose (1996)	Event study of currency crisis, and likelihood of currency crisis (multinomial logit).	105 developing and emerging market countries for the period 1971–92; annual data.	Fiscal deficit, government external debt.	Debt: yes; deficit: no.	Domestic credit, reserves/imports, current account, real per capita output growth, degree of overvaluation, external debt, REER, debt/GNP, debt lent by commercial banks, concessional debt, variable rate debt, short-term debt, FDI, OECD output growth, foreign interest rate.	Currency crisis occurs when FDI dries up, reserves are low, domestic credit growth is high, world interest rate rises, and the real exchange rate is overvalued.
Dornbusch, Goldfajn, and Valdés (1995)	Case studies of currency crises.	Chile, 1978–92; Mexico, 1978–82; Finland, 1988–92; Mexico, 1990–94.	Fiscal deficit, public external debt.	No.	GDP growth, inflation, depreciation, current account, real exchange rate, real interest rate, terms of trade, external debt, saving, investment, net exports, imports, foreign reserves, unemployment rate.	Real exchange rate matters most and is usually a policy variable. Overly accommodating capital market aggravates misaligned exchange rate policy. Inflation has been overemphasized as a policy target.

APPENDIX I

Table A1.1 (continued)

Study	Approach	Sample	Fiscal Variable — Measure	Fiscal Variable — Significant?	Other Variables	Findings
Milesi-Ferretti and Razin (1996)	Case studies of persistent current account deficits.	9 episodes: Australia, Chile, Ireland, Israel, Malaysia (2), Mexico (2), Korea.	Fiscal deficit.	No.	Saving, investment, growth, openness, trade, composition of external liabilities, financial structure, capital account regime, exchange rate regime, political uncertainty and credibility, market expectations.	Size of current account deficit matters only in conjunction with other factors such as exchange rate policy, openness, saving and investment, and the health of the financial system. Absence of large fiscal deficits ex ante does not imply that current account deficits will be sustainable.
Kumar, Moorthy, and Perraudin (2002)	Likelihood of currency crash (logit).	32 developing and emerging market countries; January 1985–October 1999; monthly and annual data.	Fiscal deficit (annual data interpolated by cubic spline). Official debt as a share of the total debt.	Marginally.	Real GDP, REER, exports, FDI, portfolio investment, reserves, global liquidity indicators, commodity prices, capital account liberalization dummy, high-inflation regime.	Most important variables are declining reserves, exports, and activity; contagion also important.
Kharas and Mishra (2001)	Ordered probit to explain number of currency crises.	32 emerging market and industrial countries; 1980–97 (1992–97 for transition economies).	Actuarial deficit	Yes.	Number of banking crises, change in real exchange rate, change in reserves.	Actuarial deficits are more closely linked to currency crises than conventional measures of the deficit.

Severity of Currency Crises

Study	Approach	Sample	Fiscal Variable — Measure	Fiscal Variable — Significant?	Other Variables	Findings
Sachs, Tornell, and Velasco (1996) (STV)	Explaining severity of currency crisis following Mexican crisis in 1994, by OLS and case study.	20 emerging market economies, excluding transition economies, covering period of the crisis (November 1994–June 1995).	Government consumption/GDP average and percentage change (1990–94); insufficient data to use fiscal deficit.	Only when reserves and fundamentals are weak.	RER, lending boom, M2/reserves, capital inflows/GDP, short-term capital inflows/GDP, current account deficit/GDP.	Main determinants of severity of crisis are M2/reserves, a high initial real exchange rate, and a bank lending boom. Some evidence that change in government consumption has additional explanatory power, but only when resources and fundamentals are weak. Some evidence from case studies that fiscal policy influenced extent of real appreciation prior to crisis.
Tornell (1999)	Explaining severity of crises during Tequila and Asian crises, using OLS, and fixed and random effects models.	As STV, but including Poland and Hungary (22 European Union (EU) countries in total); data around the Mexican and Asian crises.	Government consumption (average level and growth prior to crisis).	Only if lending boom and exchange rate variables are excluded.	Lending boom, real exchange rate, M2/resources, capital inflows, current account.	Fundamentals—lending booms, real exchange rate overvaluation, and reserves—explain the severity of crises across countries. Excessive government consumption correlated with more severe crises, but this works indirectly through the impact of lending booms and the real exchange rate.
Bussière and Mulder (1999)	As above, but also covering the Russian crisis.	As above.	Ratios of credit to government reserves.	Only for crises in 1998.	Overvaluation of real exchange rate, current account deficit, short-term debt/reserves,	The first three variables, plus a dummy for IMF programs, explain the severity of crises across countries, and predict

Appendix I

Study	Purpose/Method	Sample	Fiscal variable	Significant?	Other variables	Conclusions
Gupta, Mishra, and Sahay (2003)	Explaining the impact on growth of currency crises, by OLS.	195 currency crisis episodes in 91 developing countries, 1970–98; annual data.	Budget deficit in year following crisis; change in deficit pre- and postcrisis.	Former significant; latter insignificant.	20 or 80 variables, money motivated; domestic control variables, global control variables, and monetary policy.	Most important explanatory variables are the size of private capital flows prior to the crisis; liberalization of capital and current accounts; size of precrisis business cycle boom and per capita income. Tight fiscal policy after a crisis is positively associated with growth.
Bordo, Eichengreen, Klingebiel, and Martinez Peria (2001)	Determinants of occurrence of crises (multinomial logit) and severity of crises in terms of lost output (tobit).	21 industrial and emerging market countries, 1880–1998; 56 economies, 1973–98; annual data.	Government surplus/GDP.	Only for currency crises; not for banking and twin crises. Insignificant for explaining severity of currency crises.	Inflation, capital controls, M2/reserves, GDP/capita; GDP growth.	Crises have become more frequent in the post–Bretton Woods era, but not more severe.
Debt Crises						
Cohen (1997)	Likelihood of debt rescheduling (probit).	Approximately 100 industrial, developing, and market economies, 1970–90; annual data.	Debt-to-tax ratio.	Yes.	Debt-to-GDP, debt-to-exports, liquidity, degree of openness, Latin American dummy.	Debt-to-GDP is the best conditional predictor of debt crises, controlling for liquidity, openness, and Latin American dummy. Debt-to-tax and debt-to-exports are best unconditional predictors.
Detragiache and Spilimbergo (2001)	Likelihood of defaulting on external debt (probit).	69 emerging market and developing countries, 1971–98; annual data.	Fiscal surplus.	No.	Short-term debt, debt service due, reserves, total debt, variable share, concessional share, multilateral share, interest rates, FDI, current account, income growth, credit growth, OECD growth, overvaluation, openness.	Liquidity (measured by short-term debt, debt repayment due, and reserves) matters most for default.
Banking and Currency Crises						
Brüggemann and Linne (1999)	Signal—individual indicators and index for currency and banking crises.	Czech Republic, Hungary, Romania, Russia, and Bulgaria, 1991–98; annual and monthly data.	Fiscal deficit.	Yes.	M2 multiplier, domestic credit, bank deposits, current account, imports, real exchange rate, reserves, M2/reserves, real interest differential, external debt, capital flight, short-term external debt, output, domestic real interest rate, ratio of lending to deposit rate.	Good indicators are exports, real exchange rate, fiscal deficit.

(continued from previous page: ...credit to the banking sector; presence of IMF program.) the 1998 crisis out-of-sample. Credit to government is important in the 1998 crises, but not those in 1994 and 1997.

APPENDIX I

Table A1.1 (concluded)

Study	Approach	Sample	Fiscal Variable Measure	Significant?	Other Variables	Findings
Goldstein, Kaminsky, and Reinhart (2000)	Signal—individual indicators and index for currency and banking crises.	25 emerging market and smaller industrial countries, 1970–95; monthly and annual data.	Fiscal deficit, central bank credit to public sector, government consumption, net credit to public sector.	Deficit: yes; others: less so.	Bank deposits, credit rating, current account, domestic credit, interest rate differential, excess M1 balances, exports, FDI, imports, lending-deposit interest rate, M2 multiplier, M2/reserves, output, real exchange rate, real interest rate, reserves, short-term capital inflows, stock prices, terms of trade.	Good indicators are appreciation of real exchange rate, decline in stock prices, fall in exports, high M2/reserves, M2 multiplier, rise in real interest rate, recession, current account deficit, short-term capital inflow.
Aziz, Caramazza, and Salgado (2000)	Event study of currency and banking crises.	20 industrial and 30 developing countries, 1975–97; monthly and annual data.	Fiscal deficit.	No.	REER, export growth, trade balance, terms of trade, inflation, M1 growth, M2 growth, domestic credit growth, interest rate, change in stock prices, change in reserves, M2/reserves, M2/M1, output growth, world interest rate, unemployment rate, current account.	Typically, precrisis, economies were overheated, inflation was high, the domestic currency was overvalued, and monetary aggregates grew strongly.
Banking Crises						
Eichengreen and Arteta (2000)	Event studies and likelihood (probit) of banking crises.	75 developing and emerging market countries, 1975–97; annual data.	Fiscal deficit/GNP.	No.	Macroeconomic indicators (total external debt, reserves, current account balance, RER overvaluation, domestic credit growth, output per capita growth, M2/reserves); external factors; exchange rate regime; external shocks; financial liberalization; institutional variables.	Perverse sign on budget deficit, but due to correlation with debt/GNP and current account. Robust causes of banking crises include rapid domestic credit growth and large bank liabilities relative to reserves.
Demirgüç-Kunt and Detragiache (1998)	Likelihood of banking crises (logit).	65 developing, emerging market, and industrial countries, 1980–94; annual data.	Fiscal deficit.	No.	GDP growth, terms of trade, exchange rate depreciation, real interest rate, inflation, M2/reserves, private debt, domestic credit growth, banks' cash and reserves/assets, deposit insurance, quality of legal system and contract enforcement.	Low GDP growth, excessively high real interest rates, and high inflation increase the likelihood of a banking crisis.

Appendix I

Hutchison and McDill (1999)	Event study and likelihood of banking crises (probit) highlighting Japan.	97 developing, emerging market, and industrial countries, 1995–97; annual data.	Fiscal deficit.	No.	Real GDP growth, real credit growth, interest rates, inflation, stock prices, M2/reserves, exchange rate depreciation, explicit deposit insurance, financial liberalization, moral hazard, central bank independence.	Institutional variables important, including independence of central bank (lowering moral hazard). Real interest rates and stock prices are reliable macro leading indicators.
Eichengreen and Rose (1998)	Event study of banking crises.	105 developing countries, 1975–92.	Fiscal deficit; public external debt.	Deficit marginally significant; perverse sign.	Reserves, external debt, current account, real exchange rate overvaluation, domestic credit growth, growth of GDP per capita, growth of real GDP in OECD countries, G-7 interest rates.	The most important domestic imbalances are an overvalued exchange rate and slowing output growth; credit booms are less important. Changes in global financial conditions are the most important factor in precipitating banking crises. Some evidence that the probability of banking crises increases with a larger fiscal surplus.
Sharp Reversal of Capital Flows						
Rodrik and Velasco (1999)	Likelihood of reversal of net private capital flows (of 5 percentage points of GDP or more); severity of crisis (change in growth rate).	32 emerging market economies, 1988–98; annual data.	Debt-to-GDP ratio; budget deficit.	Debt ratio: yes; deficit: no.	Short-term debt owed to banks, other short-term debt, medium- and long-term debt, current account deficit, real exchange rate, M2/reserves, change in credit-GDP ratio.	Short-term debt to reserves is a robust predictor of financial crises, greater short-term debt exposure is associated with more severe crises when capital flows reverse.

variables. Indeed, many studies omit fiscal variables entirely. To some extent, this reflects the fact that fiscal data are less widely available, and certainly at monthly or quarterly frequencies, compared with many other monetary, financial, and real sector variables. And particularly in EWS models, there is a premium on high-frequency data.

In those empirical studies of currency crises that do include fiscal variables, the findings are mixed. Some studies find the deficit (or credit to government) to be significantly correlated with currency crises, but others do not; similarly with studies that include public debt variables. It is possible, however, that fiscal policy is causing crises indirectly, through its effects on other variables that are more systematically correlated with crises, such as overvaluation of the real exchange rate (Caramazza, Ricci, and Salgado, 2000).

The well-known measurement problems associated with most fiscal variables, and the deficit in particular, could also obscure the role they play in explaining crises. Kharas and Mishra (2001) explicitly test this possibility by constructing an alternative measure of the fiscal deficit—the actuarial deficit—based on the annual change in the stock of debt and stock of base money (i.e., a measure of the total stock of government liabilities, the change in which is a proxy for the change in government net worth). They find that this measure significantly outperforms conventional deficit measures in explaining the number of currency crises experienced in industrial and emerging market economies.

Debt Crises

There are very few (recent) cross-section studies of debt crises. Cohen (1997) explains whether a country defaulted in the 1970s or 1980s in terms of a few fiscal variables (such as ratios of debt-to-GDP, debt-to-exports, and debt-to-tax revenue, and proxies for the degree of trade liberalization) in the context of attempting to explain the poor growth performance of Latin America. He finds that all three debt ratios are good predictors of default. Detragiache and Spilimbergo (2001) find that the probability of a debt crisis increases with the proportion of short-term debt (public and private) and debt service coming due, and decreases with foreign exchange reserves, which provides some support for the "liquidity channel" of fiscal policy as a cause of crises. A debt variable for the fiscal surplus was included in their regressions but was found to be insignificant.[40]

---

[40]See also Calvo (1995) and Chang and Velasco (1999).

Two recent studies (IMF, 2002b; and Hausmann, 2002) analyze the possible causes of the relatively high frequency of debt crises in Latin America. They identify a number of key factors, most of which are related to fiscal policy. First, by international standards, total external debt is not high relative to GDP, but is high relative to exports; external debt is also concentrated in the public sector. This means that devaluation provides a limited boost to activity and hence government revenues, but causes a large increase in debt-service expenditure. Second, debt is also high relative to tax revenue. The third factor is a history of macroeconomic volatility. This exacerbates liquidity problems and increases default risk given that credit markets are not perfect. One important source of this volatility is fiscal policy, reflecting both discretionary actions and the recognized tendency for fiscal policy in Latin America to be procyclical. This latter characteristic is due in part to features of the tax system (a reliance on cyclically sensitive revenue sources such as indirect taxes, and weak tax administration that cannot offset the rise in incentive to evade taxes during downturns) but more fundamentally reflects the weakness of fiscal institutions in containing government spending during "good times." A high debt-service burden also makes it difficult to use fiscal policy countercyclically. The fourth factor is that emerging markets in general and Latin American emerging markets in particular suffer from "original sin." Borrowing tends to be in foreign currency and at short maturities, which exposes the country to real exchange rate and interest rate risk; both of these risks, moreover, tend to be positively correlated with adverse domestic developments (i.e., in "bad times," the real exchange rate falls and real interest rates rise).

Banking Crises

Empirical studies of banking crises do not generally find an important role for fiscal variables. This is consistent with theoretical models of banking crises that typically assign a marginal or indirect role to fiscal factors. Indeed, only 5 of the 14 studies surveyed in Eichengreen and Arteta (2000) include any fiscal variables, and in each case the sole variable is the deficit. Eichengreen and Arteta conduct a battery of sensitivity tests across different samples (based on different definitions of banking crises) and find, like some other studies, that the deficit variable is significant but has the wrong sign. They argue that this is driven by collinearity with other regressors (such as external debt and the current account) and find that eliminating these regressors "corrects" the sign on the deficit variable. However, one cause of banking crises that they deem robust—rapid domestic credit growth—could imply an indirect channel for loose fiscal policy to contribute to banking crises. A second survey of recent empirical studies, Bell (2000), notes that high real interest rates are typically correlated with banking crises, which suggests another indirect causal link from fiscal policy to banking crises.

Brixi and Schick (2002) argue that the financial sector offers the largest scope for "fiscal opportunism"—financing various projects and programs off-budget through banks and other financial intermediaries; however, those liabilities often end up as a call on government resources, and hence as a source of fiscal vulnerability. While privatization and a reduction of the explicit role of the state in the financial sector may have allowed a reduction in budgeted expenditures, it also required explicit or implicit government guarantees that subsequently became a significant source of fiscal risk. There are also political economy explanations for the buildup of contingent government liabilities in the financial sector, namely to avoid difficult and painful structural reforms such as the closure of loss-making enterprises, and for off-budget funding as a way to reduce scrutiny.[41] Two recent empirical studies have found that the extent of state ownership of banks is correlated with an underdeveloped, poorly functioning—and, by implication, more crisis-prone—banking sector (see La Porta, Lopez-de-Silanes, and Shleifer, 2000; and Barth, Caprio, and Levine, 2000).

Fiscal Variables in EWS Models

The number of surveys of the literature on EWS models has also grown rapidly, so here the focus is on the subset of EWS models that include fiscal variables.[42] Most EWS studies follow a similar approach. First, crisis episodes are identified within a sample of countries.[43] Second, a forecast horizon is chosen. Third, predictions are generated, using a variety of approaches, from a set of variables suggested by theory, casual observation, or other studies. Fourth, the model is evaluated based on some combination of in-sample goodness-of-fit and out-of-sample predictive accuracy.

Regarding the definition of crises, the main point to note is that any definition will be arbitrary to some extent, and it is important in interpreting results from various empirical studies that the crisis definition should be well understood. Currency crises are generally identified using quantitative criteria (such as changes in exchange rates relative to recent trend and reserves), although some studies rely on journalistic and academic histories to identify crisis episodes (e.g., Glick and Rose, 1998). The lack of historical data on market-determined interest rates means that most studies of currency crises in emerging market economies fail to capture crises where the main instrument for fending off speculative attack has been an increase in domestic interest rates, such as the Argentine crisis of 1995. Kamin and Babson (1999) look at alternative measures of currency crises and find that the crises identified by all definitions tend to cluster together, though there is some dispersion. Hence, they argue for robustness checks based on alternative definitions. Dating banking crises is less straightforward, and typically relies on judgment as well as data. Various recent papers have compared the crises identified by different studies, and found a high degree of correlation.[44]

The forecast horizon varies widely, depending on the use of the model. For some private sector EWS models, intended to guide investment strategies, the forecast horizon is very short, ranging from one to six months ahead. The IMF's main EWS model predicts two years ahead, reflecting an emphasis on signaling the need for policy changes.

Once crisis episodes have been identified, most EWS studies use one of two main approaches:[45]

- The *signals approach* analyses the ability of individual indicators to predict a crisis. For each indicator, a threshold is determined beyond which the indicator is said to signal a crisis. Thresholds are typically set to minimize the noise-to-signal ratio (i.e., the number of false signals relative to the number of correct signals of past crises). Indicators are then ranked according to their noise-to-signal ratios and the lead with which the first signal is emitted.

- The *probit approach* uses probit (or sometimes logit) regressions to identify the factors that help

---

[41]Brixi and Schick (2002) point out that similar fiscal risks in the form of implicit contingent liabilities and off-budget activity can arise via state-owned enterprises, subnational governments, and public pension and health schemes, as well as the financial sector.

[42]Wider discussions of other empirical studies are provided in Kaminsky, Lizondo, and Reinhart (1998) and IMF (2002a).

[43]A notable exception is Osband and Van Rijckeghem (2000) who attempt to predict "safe or near-safe" zones for fundamentals under which currency crises are unlikely to occur.

[44]See Eichengreen and Arteta (2000) and Bell (2000).

[45]More recent EWS models have been based on different methodologies. Osband and Van Rijckeghem (2000) use a process of univariate and multivariate filtering to identify values of fundamentals consistent with tranquil periods; Ghosh and Ghosh (2002) use a decision-theoretic classification approach known as a binary recursive tree, which they argue is well-suited to situations in which threshold effects and interactions between explanatory variables may be important.

APPENDIX I

explain the probability of a crisis. Rival explanatory variables can be tested against each other using standard statistical methods.

Table A1.1 summarizes the results of recent EWS studies that include fiscal variables. Two general points to note are, first, that many EWS studies omit fiscal variables entirely. This reflects, at least in part, the fact that fiscal data are less widely available, and certainly at monthly or quarterly frequencies, than many other monetary, financial, and real sector variables, and in many EWS models there is a premium on high-frequency data. But it may also reflect a belief that fiscal indicators will add little to other variables in predicting crises. A second general point is that the majority of EWS studies focus on currency crises, in part because currency crises lend themselves more readily to definition using objective quantitative criteria.

Currency Crises

No single variable stands out as being an important factor in a majority of studies of currency crises listed in Table A1.1. This may not be surprising given that individual studies look at different country groups or crisis episodes, depending in part on their timing. Moreover, the work by Berg and Pattillo (1999) suggests that results are sensitive even to data revisions.[46] That said, the studies covered in Table A1.1 find that currency crises tend to be associated with expansionary policy and high growth in monetary aggregates; internal imbalances such as downturns or overheating are also associated with currency crises. Some studies find evidence for contagion after controlling for internal and other external factors (e.g., Glick and Rose, 1998).

Fiscal variables included in these studies are the fiscal deficit, credit to government, public external debt, the share of public debt in external debt, and government consumption. The results are mixed:

- The fiscal deficit is the only variable included in all studies surveyed here. In the signals approach, the fiscal deficit is typically found to be among the better indicators (e.g., Brüggemann and Linne, 1999 and 2002; and Goldstein, Kaminsky, and Reinhart, 2000). In the probit approach, the fiscal deficit sometimes enters significantly (e.g., Kamin and Babson, 1999; Bordo and others, 2001), but more often is found to be insignificant (e.g., Glick and Rose, 1998; Kumar, Moorthy, and Perraudin, 2002; Frankel and Rose, 1996; Ghosh and Ghosh, 2002).

- Credit to government could be viewed as a proxy for the fiscal deficit (and one that may be available at a higher frequency). Goldstein, Kaminsky, and Reinhart (2000) find credit to government to be a less useful indicator than the deficit in their signals EWS model. However, Osband and Van Rijckeghem (2000) find credit to government to be an important filter for identifying tranquil periods.

- Public external debt or the share of public debt in total external debt is included in some studies. Typically, public external debt is found to be a significant factor predicting currency crisis, even when the deficit variable is insignificant (e.g., Milesi-Ferretti and Razin, 2000; Frankel and Rose, 1996; Kumar and others, 2002).

- Government consumption is only included in the signals EWS model in Goldstein, Kaminsky, and Reinhart (2000). They find that the variable is not a reliable indicator.

Banking Crises

The two signals EWS models of banking crises in Table A1.1 find some evidence of the deficit being a useful leading indicator. But probit EWS studies of banking crises do not find an important role for fiscal variables.

Fiscal Variables and the Severity of Currency Crises

Several studies have attempted to explain the depth of currency crises as measured by the change in the foreign exchange market pressure (FMP) index during a period of high volatility. The seminal paper explaining crisis severity in terms of the change in an FMP index is Sachs, Tornell, and Velasco (1996) (STV), which examines the spread of crises following the onset of the Mexican crisis in December 1994. The explanatory variables are real exchange rate overvaluation, measured by the depreciation of the trade-weighted real effective exchange rate; banking sector weakness, proxied by credit growth to the private sector; and vulnerability to capital inflow reversals, proxied by the M2 to reserves ratio. They also include two dummy variables for countries with weak fundamentals and low reserves.[47] The model is estimated for a sample of emerging market crises during 1994–95;

---

[46]When the authors attempt to replicate results presented in other studies using revised data for the same sample they find some significant divergence.

[47]Weak fundamentals are defined as a real exchange rate depreciation in the lowest three quartiles or credit growth to private sector in the highest three quartiles. Low reserves are defined as a ratio of reserves to M2 in the lowest quartile.

the regression results are therefore conditional on a crisis having occurred. STV conclude that their model fits the data well. In addition, they include a measure of government consumption to proxy the extent to which lax fiscal policy prior to the Mexican crisis explains the severity of pressure on the exchange rate during the crisis, and find that the percentage change in government consumption in the period 1990–94 is statistically significant, but only in countries with low reserves and weak fundamentals. They also find some evidence that lax fiscal policy contributed indirectly to the severity of crises by influencing the degree of exchange rate overvaluation prior to the crisis.

Several studies have reestimated the STV model with revised data, for a slightly modified list of countries, and for an extended sample that includes the Asian and other crises. Berg and Pattillo (1999) show that the STV results are very sensitive to data revisions and sample coverage. Furman and Stiglitz (1998) conclude that the basic STV specification (i.e., excluding any fiscal variables) cannot explain cross-country variation in the FMP index during the Asian crisis. On the other hand, Tornell (1999) finds that the basic STV specification does explain the cross-country variation in exchange market pressure during the Asian crisis. He also finds that government consumption (during a four-year period prior to the crisis) is significantly correlated with the change in the FMP index, but only if variables for a lending boom and real exchange rate appreciation are excluded; when the latter are included the fiscal variable is no longer significant. Tornell interprets this as evidence that fiscal policy affects the severity of crisis indirectly, through its effects on levels of credit and the real exchange rate. Bussière and Mulder (1999) extend the STV approach to the 1998 crises triggered by the Russian debt default. They include a variable for the growth in net credit to government and find that it is significant in explaining movements in the FMP index during the crises of 1998, but not for the Asian and Mexican crises.

Glick and Rose (1998) look at contagion in the STV framework. They use data for 161 countries for five crisis episodes: the breakdown of the Bretton Woods system (1971), the collapse of the Smithsonian agreement (1973), the European Monetary System crisis (1992/93), the Mexican crisis (1994/95), and the Asian crisis (1997/98). They find some evidence for crisis severity being correlated with the budget deficit for the 1971 and 1973 crises, but not the more recent episodes.

A few more recent studies have attempted to explain the severity of crises as measured by the impact on output growth. Calvo and Reinhart (2000) and Bordo and others (2001) find that a measure of the budget deficit is not significantly correlated with the output loss resulting from currency crises.

Gupta, Mishra, and Sahay (2003) find that tight fiscal policy following a crisis has a positive and significant association with short-run growth during crises. Rodrik and Velasco (1999) find a significant correlation between the collapse in growth following a crisis and the ratio of short-term external debt to reserves.

Overall, therefore, the existing literature on the determinants of crisis severity finds some evidence that a lax fiscal stance is associated with greater pressure in the exchange market during periods of contagion and severe turbulence. But this finding is not robust, either to the inclusion of nonfiscal explanatory variables or to changes in data and sample.

Fiscal Consequences of Crises

Costs

Currency crises in emerging market economies have been shown to be very costly. Calvo and Reinhart (2000) estimate that growth falls by 2 percentage points comparing the year before and the year after a currency crisis (compared to 0.2 percentage points—insignificantly different from zero—for advanced economies). In terms of cumulative output decline, IMF (1998) estimates that emerging market economies suffer on average an 8 percent cumulative loss in real output, relative to trend during a severe currency crisis. Caprio and Klingebiel (1999) have produced a comprehensive list of banking crises between 1980 and 1997. They find at least 20 emerging market banking crises with public sector resolution costs in excess of 10 percent of GDP, and 5 with costs in excess of 40 percent of GDP. The cost of resolving the banking sector problem resulting from the Asian crisis is also enormous: of the order of 58 percent of GDP in Indonesia, 30 percent of GDP in Thailand, and 16 percent of GDP in Korea (World Bank, 2000).

Impact on Fiscal Policies

Green and Campos (2001) is one of the few studies to look in detail at the impact of the Asian crisis on fiscal policy. The general points that emerge are:

- The crises resulted in a big fall in revenues, due to enterprise insolvency and declining trade and personal incomes. In Indonesia, the Philippines, and Thailand this was exacerbated by a fall in tax collection effort.

- Devaluation rapidly increased the domestic cost of external debt service, particularly in those countries with a worse precrisis fiscal situation (Indonesia, the Philippines, and Thailand).

APPENDIX I

- Concerns about banking and corporate sector collapse led to massive infusions of public funds. The exception was the Philippines, which had learned the lessons of the 1980s and reduced exposure to foreign currency risk and the real estate sector.

- In principle, this increase in public debt was offset by a transfer of assets from the private sector. But the latter was not generally included in net public debt figures; in any case, the value of these assets was subject to considerable uncertainty.

Burnside, Eichenbaum, and Rebelo (2001) analyze the factors that influence which combination of strategies will be used to meet the fiscal costs of banking and currency crises (i.e., explicit fiscal reform based on higher taxes or lower spending; explicit default on outstanding debt; printing money to generate seigniorage; creating inflation to reduce the real value of nominal debt; and implicit fiscal reform by deflating certain government outlays that are fixed temporarily in nominal terms, such as civil service wages). Using a model to interpret the crises in Mexico in 1994–95 and Korea in 1997, they estimate that the Mexican government has (up to 2000) paid for about 30 percent of the total cost of the crisis through a combination of debt deflation, fiscal reforms, and seigniorage, and that the rest can be paid for by seigniorage revenue if inflation persists at historically normal rates. By contrast, their model predicts that most of the fiscal cost of the Korean crisis will be financed by (future) explicit and implicit fiscal reforms.

Appendix II Country and Area Coverage and Data Availability

Table A2.1. Countries and Areas Included in EWS and Event Studies[1]

	KLR	BP	FR	STV	ACS	IMF	HKS
Algeria			x				
Argentina	x	x	x	x	x	x	x
Australia					x		
Austria					x		
Bangladesh					x		
Belgium					x		
Bolivia	x	x	x	x		x	x
Botswana			x				
Brazil	x	x	x	x	x	x	x
Canada					x		
Chile	x	x	x	x	x	x	x
China					x		
Colombia	x	x	x	x	x	x	x
Costa Rica			x		x		
Côte d'Ivoire			x				
Cyprus						x	x
Czech Republic						x	x
Denmark	x				x		
Dominican Republic			x				
Ecuador			x		x		
Egypt			x		x	x	x
El Salvador			x				
Finland	x				x		
France					x		
Greece					x		
Guatemala			x				
Hungary			x			x	x
Iceland					x		
India		x	x	x	x	x	x
Indonesia	x	x	x	x	x	x	x
Ireland					x		
Islamic Republic of Iran			x				
Israel	x	x		x	x	x	x
Italy					x		
Jamaica			x		x		
Japan					x		
Jordan		x		x		x	x
Korea		x	x	x	x	x	x
Lebanon						x	x
Malaysia	x	x	x	x	x	x	x
Mauritius			x				
Mexico	x	x	x	x	x	x	x
Morocco			x				
Netherlands					x		
New Zealand					x		

APPENDIX II

Table A2.1 *(concluded)*

	KLR	BP	FR	STV	ACS	IMF	HKS
Nigeria					x		
Norway	x				x		
Oman			x				
Pakistan		x	x	x	x	x	x
Panama			x				
Paraguay			x		x		
Peru	x	x	x	x	x	x	x
Philippines	x	x	x	x	x	x	x
Poland						x	x
Portugal			x		x		
Romania			x				
Singapore					x		
Slovak Republic						x	x
South Africa		x		x	x	x	x
Spain	x				x		
Sri Lanka		x	x	x	x	x	x
Sweden	x				x		
Switzerland					x		
Syrian Arab Republic			x				
Taiwan Province of China		x		x	x		
Thailand	x	x	x	x	x	x	x
Trinidad and Tobago			x				
Tunisia			x				
Turkey	x	x	x	x	x	x	x
United Kingdom					x		
Uruguay	x	x	x	x	x	x	x
Venezuela	x	x	x	x	x	x	x
Zimbabwe		x	x	x	x	x	x
Total	20	23	41	23	50	29	29

Source: Authors' calculations.

[1] KLR: Kaminsky, Lizondo, and Reinhart (1998); BP: Berg and Pattillo (1999); FR: Frankel and Rose (1996); STV: Sachs, Tornell, and Velasco (1996); ACS: Aziz, Caramazza, and Salgado (2000); IMF: IMF's main EWS model, see IMF (2002a); HKS: Hemming, Kell, and Schimmelpfennig (this paper).

Table A2.2. Dates of Crisis Episodes

	Currency Crises	Debt Crises	Banking Crises
Argentina	1975, 1982, 1989	1983	1980, 1989, 1995
Bolivia	1982, 1985	1981	1986, 1994
Brazil	1979, 1982, 1990, 1999	1983	1990, 1994
Chile	1972, 1974	1973, 1983	1976, 1981
Colombia	1985, 1995, 1998	1985	1982
Cyprus	1978, 1991		
Czech Republic			1989, 1997
Egypt	1979, 1989, 1991	1972, 1986	1982
Hungary			1991
India	1991, 1993		
Indonesia	1978, 1986, 1998	1998	1997
Israel	1974, 1977, 1983		1977
Jordan	1988	1989	
Korea	1980, 1997	1998	
Lebanon	1990	1985	1988
Malaysia	1997		1997
Mexico	1976, 1982, 1984	1982	1981, 1995
Pakistan	1972	1999	
Peru	1976, 1987	1983	1983
Philippines	1983, 1986, 1997	1986	1983, 1998
Poland			1991
Slovak Republic			1991
South Africa	1975, 1984		
Sri Lanka	1977	1996	1989
Thailand	1997	1998	1983, 1997
Turkey	1970, 1980, 1994		1982
Uruguay	1972, 1982	1983	1981
Venezuela	1984, 1986, 1989, 1994, 1996	1985	1994
Zimbabwe	1991, 1997, 2000	1978	1995
Total	58	21	32

Source: Authors' calculations.

APPENDIX II

Table A2.3. Description and Sources of Fiscal Variables

Variable Name	Description	Source[1]
Overall balance	General government overall balance, in percent of GDP	WEO
Primary balance	General government primary balance, in percent of GDP	WEO
Actuarial deficit	Change in currency in circulation plus public sector and publicly guaranteed debt, in percent of GDP[2]	IFS, GDF
Total financing	Central government total financing, in percent of GDP	GFS
Change in net claims on government	Change in net claims of the banking sector on central government, in percent of GDP	IFS
Total debt	Central government total debt (short and long term, domestic and foreign), in percent of GDP	GFS
Public external debt	Public sector and publicly guaranteed long-term external debt, in percent of GDP	GDF
Short-term debt	Short-term public and private debt, in percent of GDP	GDF
Long-term debt	Variable rate long-term public and private debt, in percent of GDP	GDF
Foreign debt	Central government debt held by nonresidents, in percent of GDP	GFS
Foreign currency debt	Central government foreign currency debt, in percent of total debt	IFS
Total expenditure	Central government total expenditure and net lending, in percent of GDP	GFS
Interest expenditure	Central government interest expenditure, in percent of total expenditure	GFS
Defense expenditure	Central government defense expenditure, in percent of total expenditure	GFS
Social expenditure	Central government social security and welfare expenditure, in percent of total expenditure	GFS
Total revenue	Central government total revenue and grants, in percent of GDP	GFS
International trade taxes	Central government revenue from international trade taxes, in percent of total revenue	GFS
Nontax revenue	Central government nontax revenue, in percent of total revenue	GFS
Grants	Central government grants, in percent of total revenue	GFS

[1]WEO: World Economic Outlook database; IFS: International Financial Statistics database; GDF: Global Development Finance database; GFS: Government Finance Statistics database.
[2]See text and Kharas and Mishra (2001) for further details.

Appendix II

Table A2.4. Data Availability
(In percent of potential observations available, 1970–2000)

	Overall Balance	Primary Balance	Total Financing	Change in Net Claims on Government	Average Across Deficit and Financing Variables
Argentina	100	26	61	100	72
Bolivia	61	52	45	100	65
Brazil	65	35	52	100	63
Chile	65	45	90	100	75
Colombia	61	29	90	87	67
Cyprus	100	0	94	100	73
Czech Republic	68	26	23	23	35
Egypt	100	55	71	100	81
Hungary	100	55	61	58	69
India	100	32	84	100	79
Indonesia	84	84	90	100	90
Israel	65	68	90	100	81
Jordan	100	35	84	100	80
Korea	100	84	90	100	94
Lebanon	100	35	23	100	65
Malaysia	52	0	84	100	59
Mexico	100	35	87	100	81
Pakistan	100	26	87	100	78
Peru	100	32	97	100	82
Philippines	100	0	90	100	73
Poland	65	55	35	68	56
Slovak Republic	68	26	13	23	32
South Africa	68	68	90	94	80
Sri Lanka	100	48	97	100	86
Thailand	100	0	90	100	73
Turkey	45	45	94	100	71
Uruguay	48	48	90	100	72
Venezuela	42	42	97	100	70
Zimbabwe	65	65	71	68	67

	Total Debt	Public External Debt	Short-Term Debt	Long-Term Debt	Foreign Debt	Foreign Currency Debt	Average Across Debt Variables
Argentina	81	97	84	81	13	0	59
Bolivia	19	97	19	19	19	0	29
Brazil	23	97	23	23	23	0	31
Chile	42	97	42	42	42	42	51
Colombia	19	97	19	19	19	0	29
Cyprus	94	0	0	58	94	94	56
Czech Republic	23	61	23	0	23	23	25
Egypt	0	97	0	0	0	0	16
Hungary	52	74	52	52	52	29	52
India	84	97	84	84	84	84	86
Indonesia	90	97	90	90	90	90	91
Israel	90	0	0	0	90	90	45
Jordan	90	97	90	74	90	84	88
Korea	90	97	90	90	90	90	91
Lebanon	23	97	23	23	23	19	34

APPENDIX II

Table A2.4 (continued)

	Total Debt	Public External Debt	Short-Term Debt	Long-Term Debt	Foreign Debt	Foreign Currency Debt	Average Across Debt Variables
Malaysia	77	97	77	77	77	77	81
Mexico	87	97	87	87	87	77	87
Pakistan	81	97	81	81	81	81	83
Peru	32	97	32	32	32	0	38
Philippines	90	97	90	90	90	74	89
Poland	19	61	19	19	19	19	26
Slovak Republic	13	61	13	13	13	13	21
South Africa	94	19	19	19	94	94	56
Sri Lanka	94	97	94	77	94	0	76
Thailand	97	97	94	94	97	97	96
Turkey	87	97	87	87	87	0	74
Uruguay	74	97	74	74	74	74	78
Venezuela	55	97	55	55	55	0	53
Zimbabwe	71	97	68	65	71	71	74

	Total Expenditure	Interest Expenditure	Defense Expenditure	Social Expenditure	Average Across Expenditure Variables
Argentina	68	58	61	0	57
Bolivia	45	45	45	45	48
Brazil	61	55	52	52	57
Chile	90	84	90	90	84
Colombia	94	68	48	48	64
Cyprus	94	94	94	94	95
Czech Republic	23	23	23	23	32
Egypt	74	74	71	71	78
Hungary	61	61	58	58	68
India	84	84	84	0	70
Indonesia	90	90	87	19	74
Israel	90	90	90	90	86
Jordan	84	84	81	0	70
Korea	90	90	90	90	92
Lebanon	23	23	23	23	38
Malaysia	84	84	65	65	70
Mexico	90	90	84	84	90
Pakistan	87	84	32	0	61
Peru	97	97	58	0	70
Philippines	90	90	90	0	74
Poland	35	35	19	19	35
Slovak Republic	13	13	13	13	24
South Africa	90	90	6	0	51
Sri Lanka	97	97	97	87	95
Thailand	94	94	90	90	74
Turkey	94	94	94	94	84
Uruguay	90	90	90	90	82
Venezuela	97	97	55	0	58
Zimbabwe	71	71	61	61	66

Table A2.4 (concluded)

	Total Revenue	International Trade Taxes	Nontax Revenue	Grants	Tax Buoyancy	Revenue Buoyancy	Average Across Revenue Variables
Argentina	68	58	61	0	65	65	59
Bolivia	48	48	48	45	45	45	49
Brazil	61	55	55	52	48	48	55
Chile	90	90	90	29	87	87	77
Colombia	94	94	94	71	90	90	85
Cyprus	94	94	94	87	90	90	93
Czech Republic	23	23	23	13	19	19	27
Egypt	74	74	74	71	71	71	76
Hungary	61	61	61	32	58	58	62
India	84	84	84	84	81	81	85
Indonesia	90	90	90	16	87	87	78
Israel	90	90	90	87	87	87	86
Jordan	84	84	84	84	81	81	85
Korea	90	90	90	23	87	87	81
Lebanon	23	23	23	13	19	19	31
Malaysia	84	84	84	52	81	81	74
Mexico	90	90	90	3	87	87	78
Pakistan	87	84	84	77	77	84	85
Peru	97	97	97	29	94	87	86
Philippines	90	90	90	90	87	87	91
Poland	35	35	35	26	29	29	36
Slovak Republic	13	13	13	13	10	10	20
South Africa	90	90	90	90	87	87	86
Sri Lanka	97	97	97	97	90	90	95
Thailand	94	94	94	94	90	90	79
Turkey	94	94	94	39	87	87	77
Uruguay	90	90	90	3	87	87	71
Venezuela	97	97	97	52	94	94	82
Zimbabwe	71	71	71	55	68	68	67

Source: Authors' calculations.

Appendix III　　Event Studies

Figures 3.2–3.4 in Section III and Figures A3.1–A3.8 in this appendix depict the behavior of selected fiscal variables during windows around currency, debt, banking, and pooled crises across the full sample. The figures on the right use the nonstandardized or "raw" data: the dashed horizontal line shows the mean value of the variable for tranquil periods; the dark solid line shows the mean for each of the years in the crisis window (with "T" corresponding to the year of the crisis, "T–2" corresponding to two years before the crisis, and so on); and the dotted lines show the 95 percent confidence interval for the difference between the means in the tranquil and crisis periods. Thus for the overall balance, the top right-hand chart of Figure 3.2 in Section III shows that the overall deficit in tranquil times is on average around 5½ percent of GDP; two years before a currency crisis it is higher, at around 6 percent of GDP, rising to 7 percent in the year before the crisis, remaining at 7 percent in the crisis year, and then declining to marginally less than the tranquil period mean in the two years following a currency crisis. However, at no point in the crisis window is the crisis mean significantly different from the tranquil period mean at the 95 percent confidence level.

The corresponding findings for the standardized version of the variables are shown in the figures on the left. Thus in the top left chart of Figure 3.2 (Section III), the general government overall deficit is, on average, around 0.1 standard deviations higher than the tranquil period mean two years before a crisis, rising to 0.3 standard deviations higher than the tranquil period mean in the year before the crisis and in the year of the crisis, then falling back to around 0.1 standard deviations greater than the tranquil period mean in the two years following crises. Note that standardizing this variable has the effect that the difference between the tranquil period mean and the mean in years T–1 and T is significant at the 95 percent level.

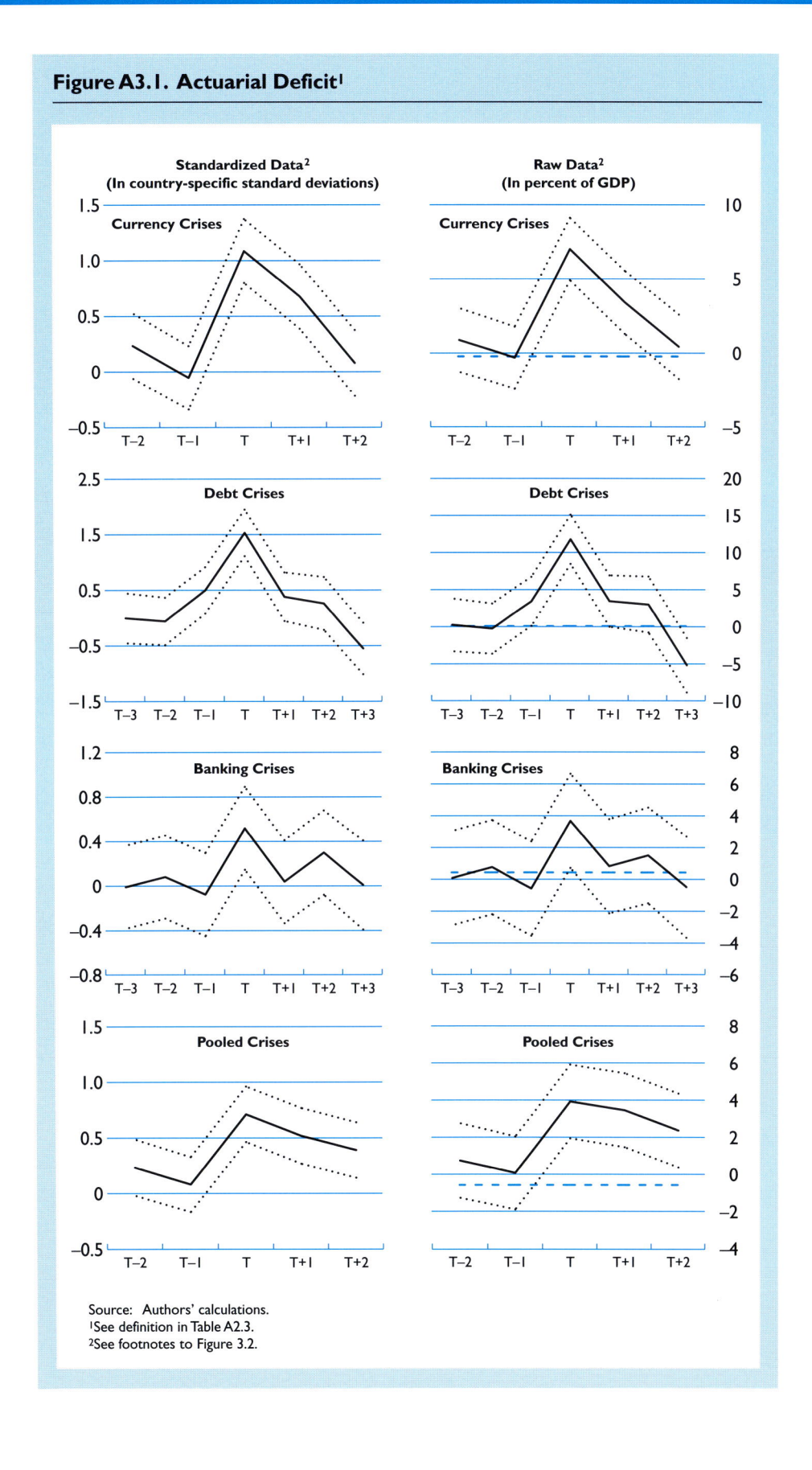

Appendix III

Figure A3.1. Actuarial Deficit[1]

Standardized Data[2]
(In country-specific standard deviations)

Raw Data[2]
(In percent of GDP)

Currency Crises

Debt Crises

Banking Crises

Pooled Crises

Source: Authors' calculations.
[1]See definition in Table A2.3.
[2]See footnotes to Figure 3.2.

Figure A3.2. Total Financing

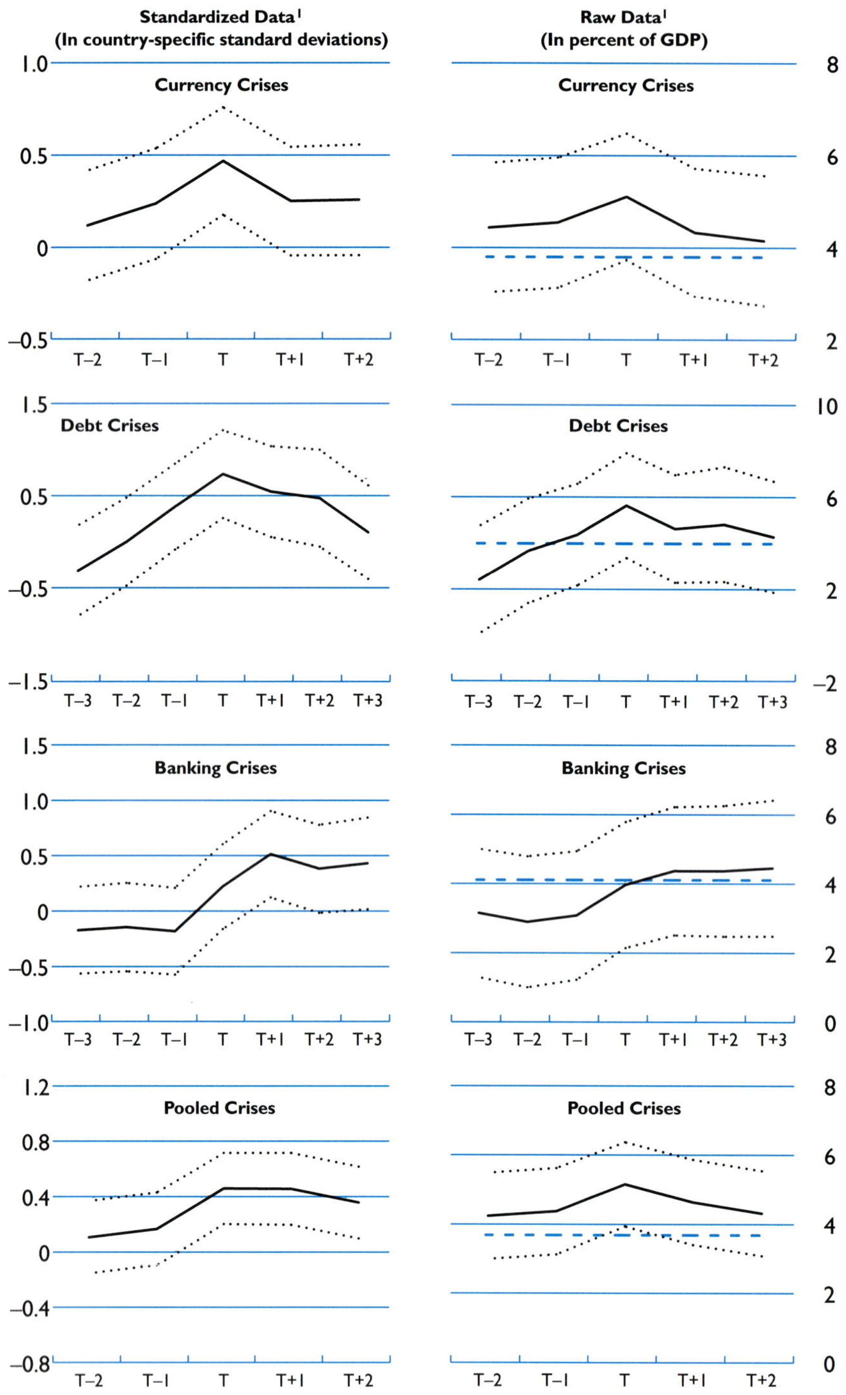
Standardized Data[1]
(In country-specific standard deviations)
Raw Data[1]
(In percent of GDP)
Currency Crises
Currency Crises
1.0
0.5
0
–0.5
8
6
4
2
T–2
T–1
T
T+1
T+2
Debt Crises
Debt Crises
1.5
0.5
–0.5
–1.5
10
6
2
–2
T–3
T–2
T–1
T
T+1
T+2
T+3
Banking Crises
Banking Crises
1.5
1.0
0.5
0
–0.5
–1.0
8
6
4
2
0
Pooled Crises
Pooled Crises
1.2
0.8
0.4
0
–0.4
–0.8
8
6
4
2
0

Source: Authors' calculations.
[1]See footnotes to Figure 3.2.

Appendix III

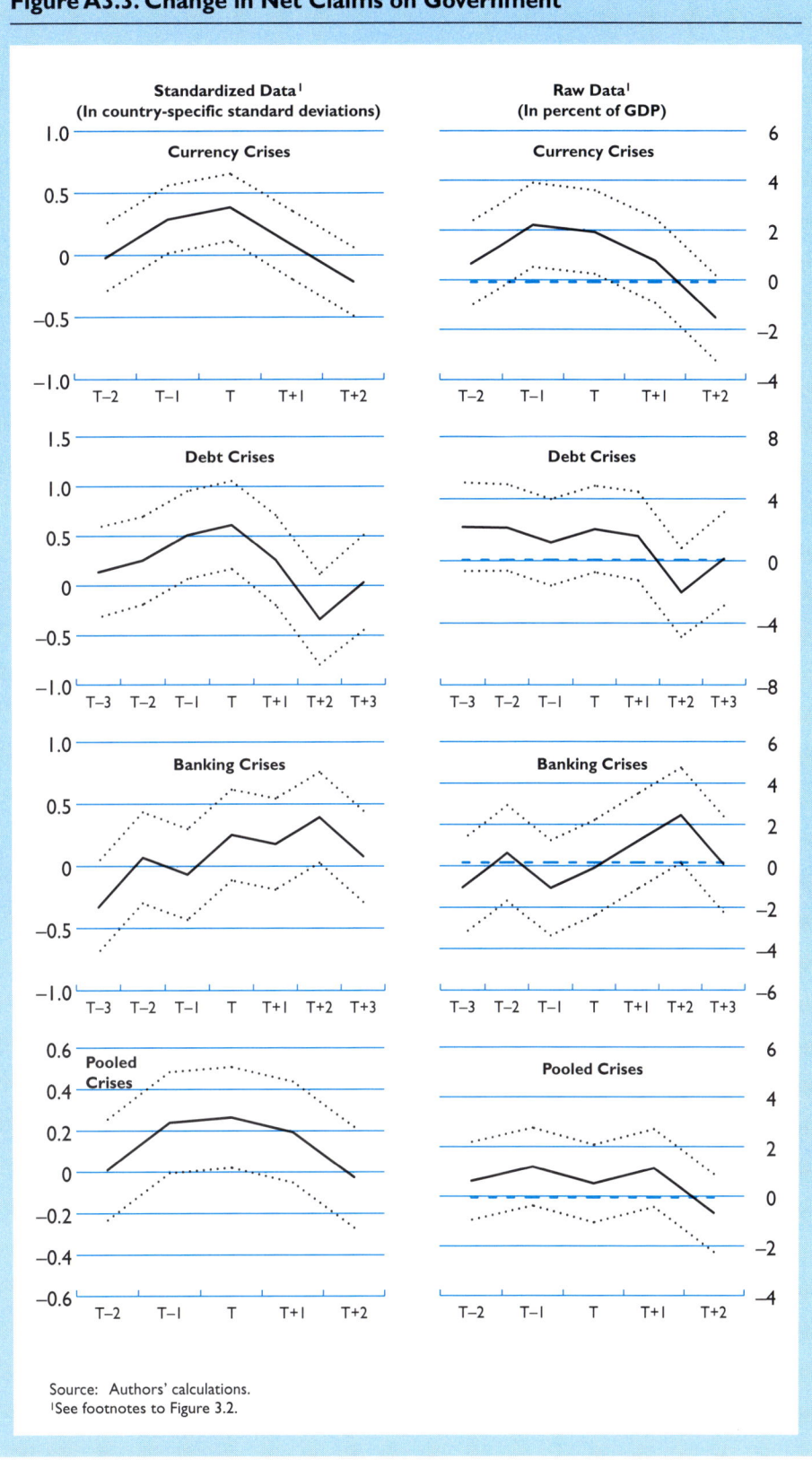

Figure A3.3. Change in Net Claims on Government

Standardized Data¹
(In country-specific standard deviations)

Raw Data¹
(In percent of GDP)

Currency Crises

Debt Crises

Banking Crises

Pooled Crises

Source: Authors' calculations.
¹See footnotes to Figure 3.2.

APPENDIX III

Figure A3.4. Foreign Debt

Source: Authors' calculations.
[1]See footnotes to Figure 3.2.

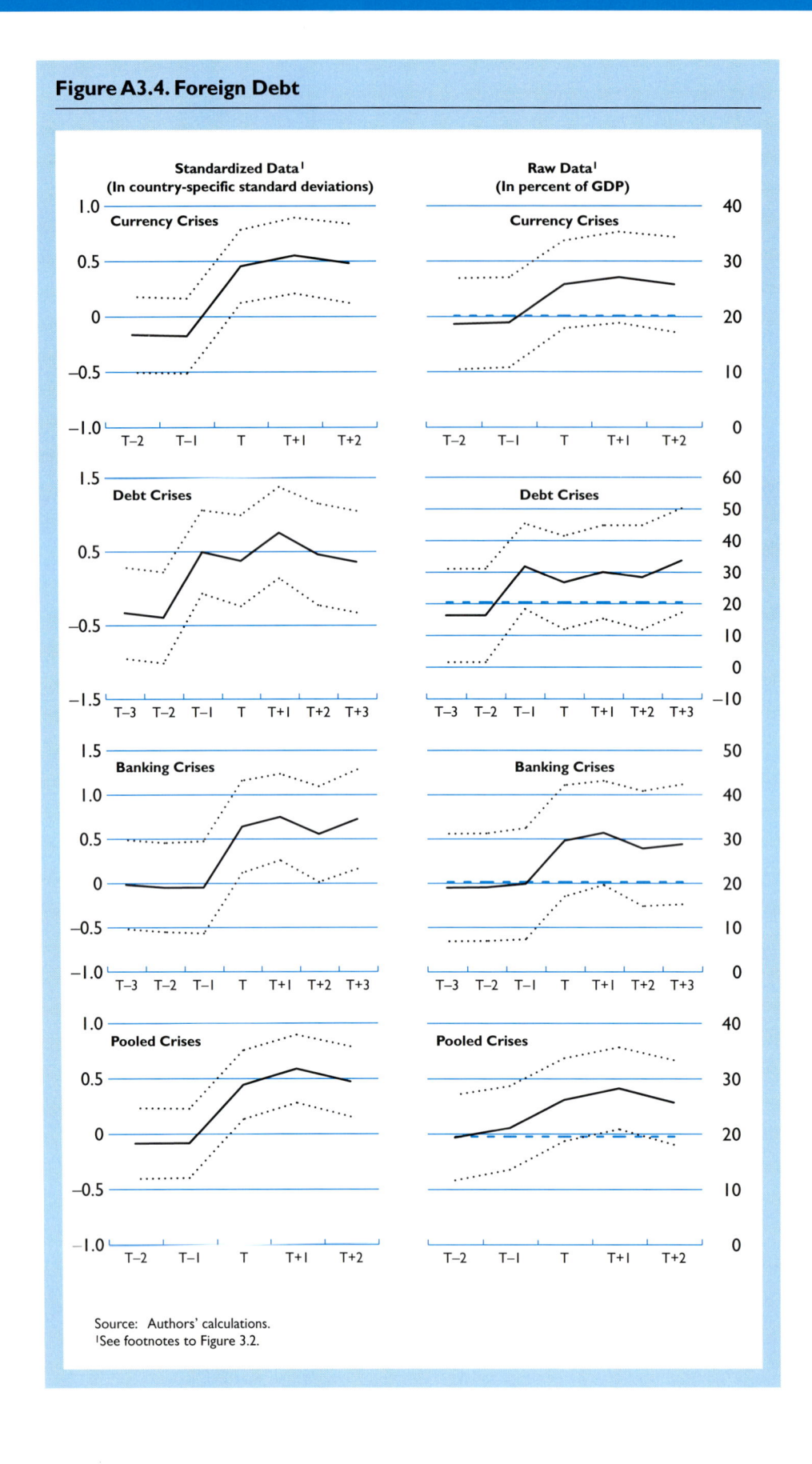

Figure A3.5. Total Expenditure

Standardized Data¹
(In country-specific standard deviations)

Currency Crises

Debt Crises

Banking Crises

Pooled Crises

Raw Data¹
(In percent of GDP)

Currency Crises

Debt Crises

Banking Crises

Pooled Crises

Source: Authors' calculations.
¹See footnotes to Figure 3.2.

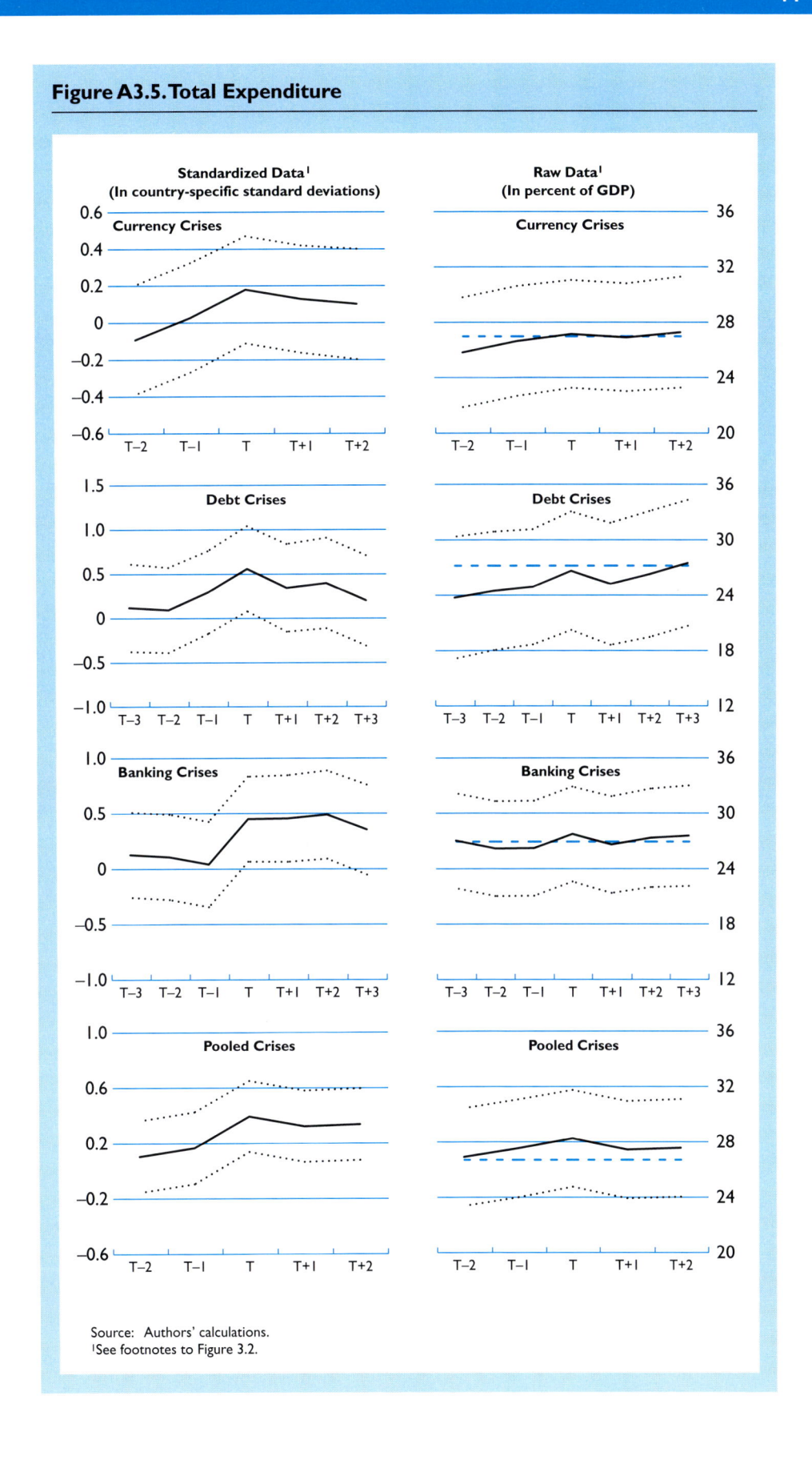

APPENDIX III

Figure A3.6. Interest Expenditure

Standardized Data[1]
(In country-specific standard deviations)

Raw Data[1]
(In percent of total expenditure)

Currency Crises

Debt Crises

Banking Crises

Pooled Crises

Source: Authors' calculations.
[1] See footnotes to Figure 3.2.

Appendix III

Figure A3.7. Social Expenditure

Standardized Data¹
(In country-specific standard deviations)

Raw Data¹
(In percent of total expenditure)

Currency Crises

Debt Crises

Banking Crises

Pooled Crises

Source: Authors' calculations.
¹See footnotes to Figure 3.2.

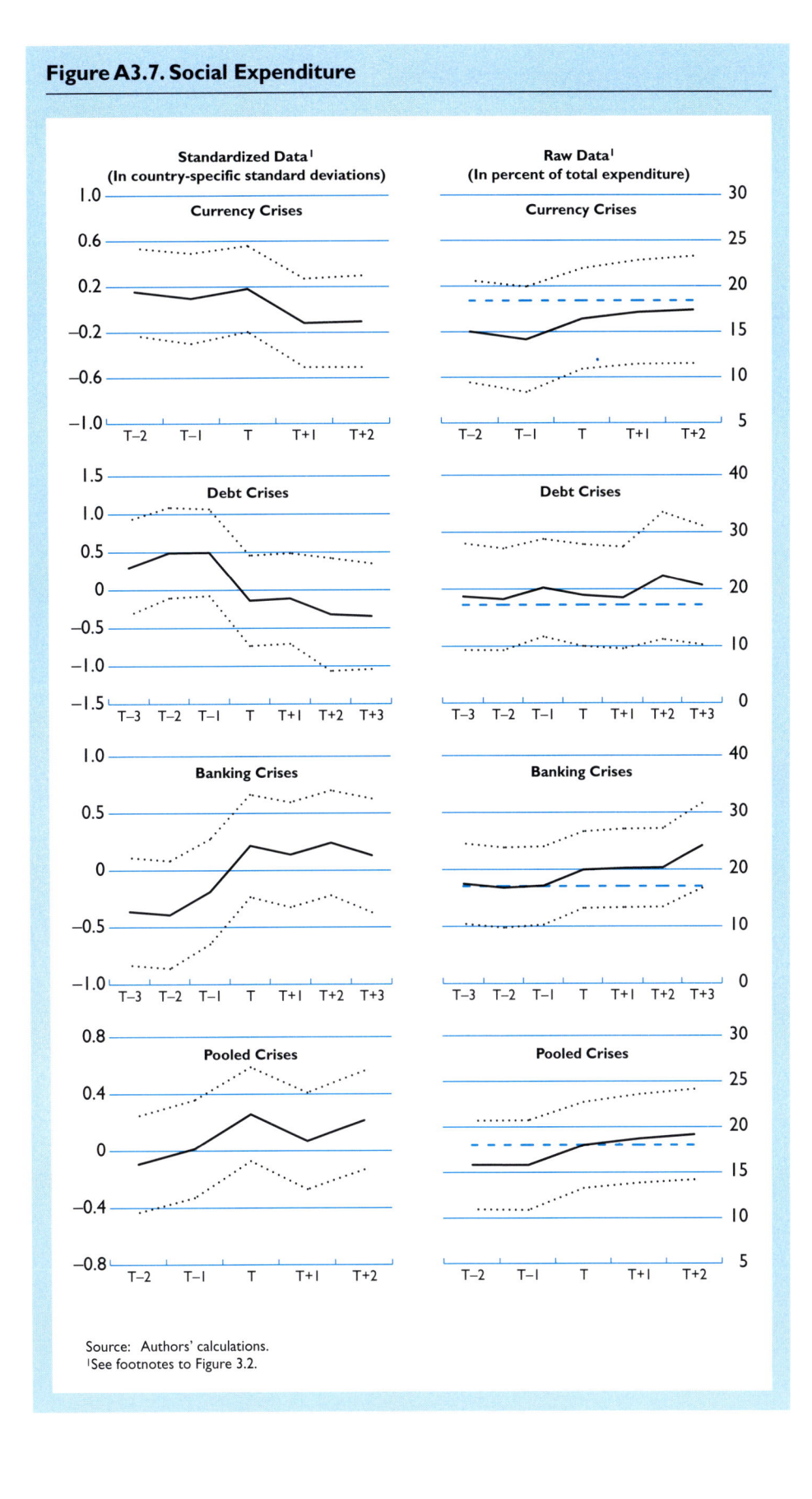

APPENDIX III

Figure A3.8. International Trade Taxes

Standardized Data[1]
(In country-specific standard deviations)

Raw Data[1]
(In percent of total revenue)

Currency Crises

Currency Crises

Debt Crises

Debt Crises

Banking Crises

Banking Crises

Pooled Crises

Pooled Crises

Source: Authors' calculations.
[1]See footnotes to Figure 3.2.

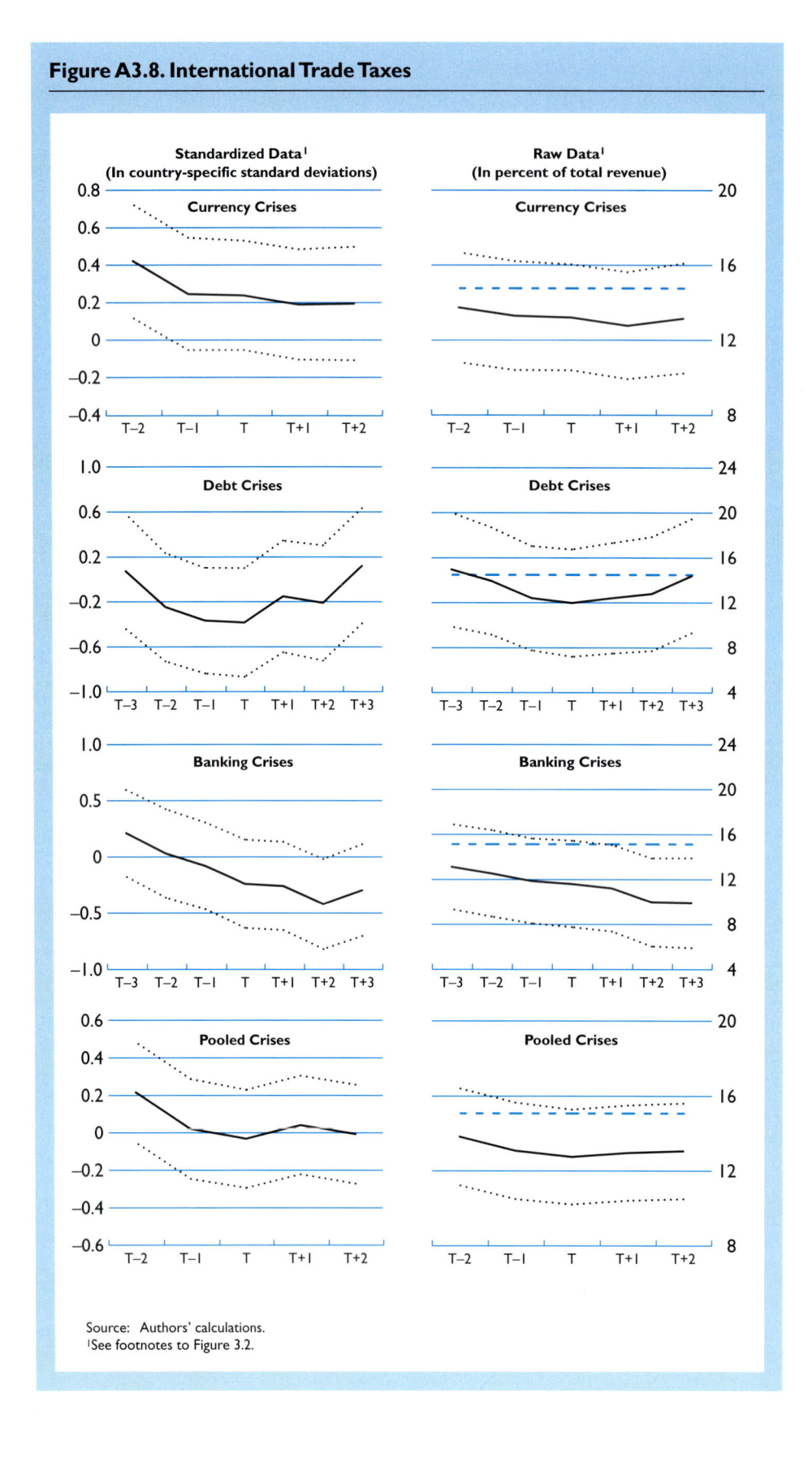

Appendix IV   EWS Models and the Severity of Currency Crises

This appendix explains the methodology and results of the econometric analyses discussed in Section IV. The first section describes the role of fiscal variables in predicting currency, debt, and banking crises using a univariate approach. The second section examines the role of fiscal variables in predicting currency crises using a multivariate framework. The third section discusses the results of including fiscal variables in models designed to explain the severity of currency crises.

Predicting Crises—the Signals Approach

The basic idea of the signals EWS approach is that when a variable departs significantly from its "normal" behavior, it may be sending a signal of an impending crisis. Historical data are used to assess the accuracy of the signals sent by particular variables prior to actual crises, with the expectation that past relationships will provide a reliable basis for deciding which current signals may be indicating future crises. The results presented here extend existing EWS studies using the signals approach in two ways. First, debt crises are analyzed, in addition to the currency and banking crises covered in other studies. Second, while most other studies have considered a wide range of potential signaling variables, this study examines only fiscal variables. This allows consideration of a much wider range of possible fiscal vulnerability indicators than the two or three covered by other studies.

Operationalizing the Signals Approach

Currency, debt, and banking crises are considered separately, using the definitions described in Section III. To ensure a sufficiently large sample, the observations for each variable are pooled across countries. To remove country-specific effects and make the data comparable across countries, the observations for each variable for each country are converted to percentiles. The signaling time frame is set at two years, so that a signal followed by a crisis in either the following or subsequent year is considered to be "good signal," and a signal not followed by a crisis within two years is classified as a "false alarm" or "noise." In the case of banking crises, where dating is less precise than for currency or debt crises, an alternative two-year signaling window (covering the year before the crisis and the year of the crisis) is also examined.

A signal is deemed to be delivered when a variable exceeds a critical threshold. The threshold has to balance two considerations: the lower it is set, the more likely it is that a subsequent crisis will be signaled, but at the cost of sending more false alarms; the higher the threshold is set, the fewer are false alarms, but also the more crises that will be missed. The threshold is set at different points in the percentile range, constrained to be constant across countries, and a "noise-to-signal" ratio is computed for each threshold (as described below). The threshold that produces the lowest noise-to-signal ratio is the preferred or optimal threshold for that variable. To give an example: suppose the lowest noise-to-signal ratio for the level of total debt occurs when the signaling threshold is set at the eighty-seventh percentile of the distribution. Although this threshold is then common to all countries in percentile terms, it corresponds to different levels of debt depending on each country's history for that variable.

Once the optimum threshold for each variable has been determined, the signaling qualities of the variables can be compared in terms of different criteria, as described below. The better performing indicators can also be combined to form composite indicators, with weights reflecting the relative reliability of the individual indicators. This approach can be viewed as controlling for country-specific effects.

Results

The findings for currency, debt, and banking crises are shown in Tables A4.1, A4.2, and A4.3, respectively. To evaluate the findings for each variable

APPENDIX IV

and across different thresholds, it is useful to consider the following matrix.

	Crisis occurs in the following two years	No crisis occurs in the following two years
Signal	A	B
No signal	C	D

Each (annual) observation can be classified into one of four possible categories: those that correspond to a good signal, that is, one that is followed by a crisis within two years, are classified "A"; false alarms, when a signal is emitted but there is no crisis within two years, are classified "B"; missing signals, when no signal is emitted but a crisis occurs within the following two years, correspond to "C;" and an observation is classified as a "D" when no signal is emitted and no crisis follows during the crisis window. A perfect indicator would produce observations only in cells A and D, and none in cells B and C.

For each variable, a number of summary measures of performance can be derived based on this classification. In Tables A4.1–A4.3, column 2 shows the number of good signals expressed as a percentage of the total number of good signals that could have been sent, A/(A+C) in terms of the matrix above. An indicator that issues a signal in each of the two years before every crisis would score 100 percent on this measure. Column 3 gives the number of bad signals (false alarms) expressed as a percentage of the total number of bad signals that could have been issued, B/(B+D) in terms of the matrix. A perfect indicator would score zero on this measure. Column 4 combines these two measures in what Kaminsky, Lizondo, and Reinhart (1998) call an "adjusted noise-to-signal ratio," which is column 3 divided by column 2. The lower this number, the better the indicator. A purely random signal would produce a noise-to-signal ratio of unity (with a sufficiently large sample); so a variable with a ratio of more than one is worse than random and should be discarded, while a ratio of less than one implies that the variable contains some predictive power (at least in-sample, and hopefully out-of-sample).

Signaling ability can be considered in another way. Column 5 shows the probability of crisis conditional on a signal being emitted, A/(A+B). Column 6 shows the difference (in percentage points) between this conditional probability and the unconditional probability of crisis, which is (A+C)/(A+B+C+D). To the extent the variable has useful signaling qualities, the conditional probability should exceed the unconditional probability; hence a negative number in column 6 implies that the variable should be discarded, while a positive number implies a potentially useful indicator.[48] The last three columns present the signaling performance of the variables in a slightly different form, namely the percentage of crises missed entirely (column 7), the percentage of crises with a signal in at least one of the two years prior to the crisis (column 8), and the percentage of crises with a signal in both years prior to the crisis (column 9).

Currency Crises

Table A4.1 shows the (in-sample) performance of the fiscal variables in signaling currency crises, ranked by noise-to-signal ratio. The best performing variable, in terms of noise-to-signal ratio, is the primary balance, although data on this variable are available for less than 50 percent of the crises in the sample. Short-term debt has a noise-to-signal ratio that is only marginally higher, but is available for 50 of the 58 crises in the sample. The noise-to-signal ratios for these two variables are very similar to the best performing annual indicator of currency crises in Goldstein, Kaminsky, and Reinhart (2000), namely, the current account balance as a share of GDP, and somewhat better than for the three fiscal indicators in that study. Short-term debt was also one of the four fiscal variables that appeared to behave "abnormally" prior to currency crises in the event studies discussed in Section IV. The other three variables identified as potentially good leading indicators of currency crises in the event studies—the overall balance, total financing, and the change in net claims on government—also score relatively highly in Table A4.1. It is interesting to note, however, that some variables—such as defense and social expenditure—rank highly in Table A4.1 but did not appear to be good leading indicators judged by the event studies approach.

Several of the variables perform very badly, with a noise-to-signal ratio exceeding unity, including two indicators—the actuarial deficit and foreign debt—which looked reasonably promising from the event studies. Moreover, note that even the best performing variables in Table A4.1 signal only around a third of currency crises in either of the two prior years, and send a signal in both years prior to the crisis in only 10–15 percent of crisis episodes. Again, these findings are comparable to those for the fiscal

---

[48]Kaminsky, Lizondo, and Reinhart (1998) note that the two conditions—a noise-to-signal ratio of less than one and the conditional probability exceeding the unconditional probability—are equivalent.

Appendix IV

Table A4.1. Performance of Indicators of Currency Crises Using the Signals Approach

	Number of Crises for Which Data Are Available[1] (1)	Good Signals as a Percentage of Possible Good Signals (2)	Bad Signals as a Percentage of Possible Bad Signals (3)	Noise-to-Signal Ratio (Adjusted) (4)	Probability (Crisis/Signal) (5)	Probability (Crisis/Signal)/ Probability (Crisis) (6)	Percentage of Crises with No Signal (7)	Percentage of Crises with at Least One Signal (8)	Percentage of Crises with Two Signals (9)
Primary balance	21	24	10	0.43	26	13	67	33	14
Short-term debt	50	20	9	0.44	27	13	70	30	10
Defense expenditure	43	10	4	0.47	28	13	81	19	0
Social expenditure	29	14	7	0.48	26	12	72	28	0
International trade taxes	48	7	4	0.54	24	10	85	15	0
Revenue buoyancy	48	7	4	0.55	24	9	88	13	0
Overall balance	45	10	6	0.63	20	6	82	18	2
Foreign currency debt	25	12	8	0.65	18	6	84	16	8
Change in net claims on government	57	15	10	0.65	22	6	75	25	5
Total financing	48	12	8	0.65	21	6	81	19	4
Tax buoyancy	48	9	6	0.72	20	5	85	15	2
Nontax revenue	48	9	7	0.75	19	4	88	13	6
Grants	28	9	8	0.80	15	3	86	14	4
Public external debt	50	12	10	0.83	16	2	82	18	6
Total revenue	48	16	13	0.86	16	2	77	23	8
Total debt	36	11	11	1.00	13	0	83	17	6
Long-term debt	49	15	16	1.01	14	0	78	22	8
Foreign debt	35	4	4	1.03	13	0	91	9	8
Actuarial deficit	50	13	14	1.04	14	−1	74	26	0
Total expenditure	48	18	21	1.18	13	−2	71	29	6
Interest expenditure	47	6	8	1.21	12	−2	91	9	4

Source: Authors' calculations.
[1]Out of a maximum of 58 crises.

APPENDIX IV

Table A4.2. Performance of Indicators of Debt Crises Using the Signals Approach

	Number of Crises for Which Data Are Available[1] (1)	Good Signals as a Percentage of Possible Good Signals (2)	Bad Signals as a Percentage of Possible Bad Signals (3)	Noise-to-Signal Ratio (Adjusted) (4)	Probability (Crisis/Signal) (5)	Probability (Crisis/Signal)/ Probability (Crisis) (6)	Percentage of Crises with No Signal (7)	Percentage of Crises with at Least One Signal (8)	Percentage of Crises with Two Signals (9)
Foreign currency debt	9	31	3	0.11	28	24	44	56	22
Social expenditure	12	13	4	0.31	17	11	75	25	0
Short-term debt	21	27	9	0.33	16	10	57	43	10
Revenue buoyancy	17	9	4	0.41	12	7	82	18	0
Change in net claims on government	20	8	3	0.43	12	6	85	15	0
Tax buoyancy	17	9	4	0.43	12	6	82	18	0
Foreign debt	12	9	4	0.47	9	4	83	17	0
Nontax revenue	18	20	10	0.48	10	5	67	33	6
Total debt	13	8	5	0.54	8	4	85	15	0
Defense expenditure	17	15	8	0.54	10	4	76	24	6
Overall balance	16	16	9	0.56	8	3	81	19	13
Primary balance	5	10	6	0.57	6	2	80	20	0
Grants	10	11	6	0.59	7	3	80	20	0
Actuarial deficit	21	22	13	0.61	10	4	62	38	5
Long-term debt	19	13	9	0.67	8	3	79	21	5
Total financing	18	6	4	0.68	8	2	89	11	0
Total revenue	18	9	6	0.71	7	2	94	6	0
International trade taxes	18	11	8	0.74	7	2	83	17	6
Total expenditure	18	20	16	0.81	6	1	67	33	6
Interest expenditure	17	15	13	0.87	6	1	82	18	12
Public external debt	21	5	21	4.37	1	–4	90	10	0

Source: Authors' calculations.
[1] Out of a maximum of 21 crises.

Appendix IV

Table A4.3. Performance of Indicators of Banking Crises Using the Signals Approach

	Number of Crises for Which Data Are Available[1] (1)	Good Signals as a Percentage of Possible Good Signals (2)	Bad Signals as a Percentage of Possible Bad Signals (3)	Noise-to-Signal Ratio (Adjusted) (4)	Probability (Crisis/Signal) (5)	Probability (Crisis/Signal)/ Probability (Crisis) (6)	Percentage of Crises with No Signal (7)	Percentage of Crises with at Least One Signal (8)	Percentage of Crises with Two Signals (9)
Foreign currency debt	11	25	5	0.22	19	14	64	36	9
Total debt	18	22	6	0.28	18	12	67	33	6
Overall balance	28	11	3	0.29	22	15	79	21	0
Short-term debt	31	34	11	0.33	22	13	58	42	26
Foreign debt	16	14	5	0.33	14	9	75	25	0
Grants	17	16	6	0.36	18	11	71	29	0
Change in net claims on government	30	15	6	0.41	17	9	73	27	3
Actuarial deficit	29	22	10	0.43	18	9	59	41	3
Primary balance	13	20	9	0.46	15	8	62	38	0
Total revenue	28	15	7	0.49	15	7	75	25	4
Defense expenditure	27	20	10	0.50	16	7	70	30	7
Total financing	28	8	4	0.54	14	6	86	14	0
Total expenditure	28	7	4	0.54	14	6	86	14	0
Long-term debt	30	17	10	0.61	13	5	73	27	7
Public external debt	31	29	19	0.66	12	4	65	35	23
International trade taxes	27	6	4	0.74	10	2	89	11	0
Social expenditure	21	28	22	0.77	12	3	57	43	10
Interest expenditure	27	13	11	0.80	10	2	81	19	7
Nontax revenue	28	9	10	1.09	7	−1	86	14	4
Tax buoyancy	28	17	18	1.10	8	−1	71	29	4
Revenue buoyancy	28	17	18	1.10	8	−1	71	29	4

Source: Authors' calculations.
[1]Out of a maximum of 32 crises.

variables reported in Goldstein, Kaminsky, and Reinhart (2000), but not very encouraging in terms of using fiscal variables to predict crises. On the other hand, the Type II errors (column 3) are much lower, averaging just 9 percent. This implies that although fiscal indicators tend to miss many currency crises, they send few false alarms.

Debt Crises

It is probably not surprising that several of the debt variables do well in signaling debt crises. Table A4.2 shows that foreign currency debt has a very low noise-to-signal ratio, and that it is considerably better than the best performing annual indicators for currency and banking crises, although data are available for only a third of all debt crises in the sample. This result supports the finding in IMF (2002b) that a high proportion of sovereign debt denominated in foreign currency has been a major source of external vulnerability in Latin America. The short-term debt variable also performs relatively well, corresponding to the findings of the event study analysis in Section III. It is notable how poorly the public external debt variable performs in signaling debt crises, having by some distance the worst noise-to-signal ratio in Table A4.2. Recall from the event study (Figure 3.3) that, before debt crises, public external debt is on average no different from tranquil periods, but then rises steadily in the years after a crisis; this suggests that once the level of debt exceeds the threshold value to send a signal, it will usually continue sending signals after the crisis has begun, which in this methodology are counted as false signals and increase the noise-to-signal ratio. Overall, the findings suggest that it is the composition of debt, and not the level, that is important for signaling crises.

It should also be noted that the change in net claims on government is the best performing deficit and financing variable, and unexpectedly, interest expenditure is one of the weakest performing variables; as with currency crises, the social expenditure variable is one of the best in terms of signaling performance, contrary to the conclusion of the event studies.

Banking Crises

Table A4.3 shows the results for a two-year signaling window that covers the year before and the year of the crisis; the corresponding results for a signaling window of two years prior to the crisis are similar, but with somewhat poorer predictive ability. In contrast to the findings of the event studies, Table A4.3 indicates that fiscal variables overall do about as well in signaling banking crises as they do for currency and debt crises, with almost all of the fiscal variables having some information content for signaling crises (i.e., a noise-to-signal ratio of less than one). As with debt crises, foreign currency debt has a very good noise-to-signal ratio, and one that is considerably lower than the best performing annual indicator of banking crises in Goldstein, Kaminsky, and Reinhart (2000), but once again the indicator still misses a high proportion of crises. Other debt variables perform relatively strongly, as does the overall balance.

Optimum Thresholds

For those fiscal variables that have some marginal predictive power (i.e, those with a noise-to-signal ratio less than one) Tables A4.4, A4.5, and A4.6 show the country-specific values corresponding to the optimum percentile thresholds for currency, debt, and banking crises, respectively. There is wide variation in these critical thresholds across countries: thus in the case of Korea, a currency crisis signal would be sent if the overall deficit exceeded 3 percent of GDP, whereas for Lebanon a signal would be sent only when the deficit exceeded 37 percent of GDP. This latter example highlights a problem with the thresholds shown in the tables. When a country has undergone dramatic regime shifts over the last three decades, such as moving between periods of very high and moderate inflation, this will distort the thresholds and make them less useful. Similarly, significant changes in sources of external finance over the sample period make it hard to compare crises across time: a debt level that may have prompted a crisis in 1975 might not be seen as problematic in a period of high capital flows such as the mid-1990s. On the other hand, restricting the time period of the sample will reduce the number of crisis episodes and increase the sampling variability of the results. Even using the full sample—a maximum of 31 observations for each variable per country—there will be a wide margin of error around the value corresponding to a particular percentile in the distribution (even though it is not possible to formally test the statistical significance of the thresholds). The thresholds in Tables A4.4–A4.6 should therefore be seen only as a starting point, and would need to be considered in the light of individual country circumstances before being used as an input into formulating policy advice.

Predicting Crises—A Multivariate EWS Approach

This section examines the performance of fiscal indicators in predicting currency crises using a multivariate probit EWS model. The starting point is the

Appendix IV

Table A4.4. Country-Specific Thresholds for Currency Crises[1]

	Overall Balance	Primary Balance	Total Financing	Change in Net Claims on Government	Public External Debt	Short-Term Debt	Foreign Currency Debt	Defense Expenditure	Social Expenditure	Total Revenue	International Trade Taxes	Nontax Revenue	Grants	Tax Buoyancy	Revenue Buoyancy
Noise-to-signal	0.63	0.43	0.65	0.65	0.83	0.44	0.65	0.47	0.48	0.86	0.54	0.75	0.80	0.72	0.55
Optimal threshold Percentile	5	10	94	85	90	93	94	98	95	89	98	95	97	97	98
Country-specific thresholds[2]															
Argentina	−8.7	−0.9	6.7	3.2	38.6	11.0		11.7	27.6	15.6	20.7	22.2	19.6	3.8	4.1
Bolivia	−20.0	−2.6	2.6	2.1	90.0	16.8		15.3	33.5	20.1	17.9	35.5	1.5	2.6	2.5
Brazil	−7.9	−0.1	15.2	6.9	30.1	9.1		3.8		31.0	5.6	38.3		1.6	2.0
Chile	−3.5	−0.5	4.5	7.2	56.7	12.8	42.9	13.7	44.9	31.4	13.2	23.3	6.3	1.9	2.8
Colombia	−6.0	−1.4	4.9	1.2	35.3	10.1		15.0	19.1	13.7	23.2	17.4	6.0	1.8	1.9
Cyprus	−4.9		7.3	3.8			60.2	8.6	24.5	31.4	29.9	26.6	18.4	2.5	1.9
Czech Republic	−3.2	−2.5	1.6	1.6	24.4	13.4	37.6	6.7	38.2	36.9	4.0	7.8		2.4	2.4
Egypt	−23.1	−18.4	17.5	2.9	78.3	18.0		16.6	11.6	45.9	30.4	36.7	8.8	2.5	3.2
Hungary	−8.2	−2.1	6.5	4.3	53.5	15.9	10.2	7.5	38.9	49.5	9.9	15.5	4.9	2.9	2.1
India	−11.0	−4.4	8.2	1.6	26.4	2.6	27.2	19.4		14.1	28.3	25.2	2.8	1.7	1.6
Indonesia	−3.1	−0.4	3.3	2.1	46.4	14.2	99.3	17.6	6.5	19.7	18.6	24.0	1.2	2.1	2.3
Israel	−14.7	−3.4	22.7	12.6			43.6	46.6	26.6	66.7	19.6	15.8	26.0	2.2	3.1
Jordan	−27.8	0.3	12.9	5.4	134.7	20.3	122.4	37.5		41.1	32.8	28.8	54.4	3.4	8.3
Korea	−3.0	0.5	3.2	1.2	27.1	14.7	74.9	31.7	9.1	18.9	18.0	13.5	6.0	1.5	1.5
Lebanon	−37.3	−12.1	23.2	13.8	14.9	27.3	19.1	14.8	8.2	18.7	46.0	31.1	16.2	4.4	7.1
Malaysia	−6.8		12.3	2.0	42.2	11.0	36.1	16.3	6.7	28.1	36.8	31.7	0.4	2.2	2.2
Mexico	−15.9	1.0	12.6	3.3	44.4	9.8	71.4	4.6	26.1	15.9	14.1	16.4		1.4	1.6
Pakistan	−8.7	−1.5	8.1	2.7	43.9	7.1	65.3	32.1		16.6	39.9	29.1	5.6	1.7	2.1
Peru	−7.1	−0.4	6.3	2.7	45.1	18.1		26.5		16.3	28.3	15.3	1.5	1.5	2.3
Philippines	−4.6		4.4	1.3	55.3	29.8	56.9	19.7		18.9	36.4	15.8	2.0	2.5	2.5
Poland	−7.8	−4.6	2.3	5.6	58.7	13.5	62.9	4.6	53.3	45.9	8.1	10.4	1.2	1.0	0.9
Slovak Republic	−12.0	−3.7	4.3	0.5	21.5	9.3	40.7	5.7	27.3	40.2	5.7	14.5	0.1		
South Africa	−8.8	−3.3	7.8	1.1	7.9	9.6	8.6			26.6	8.3	12.7	1.6	1.7	1.9
Sri Lanka	−13.4	−4.5	12.7	2.8	61.1	5.8		17.6	25.6	24.3	48.3	15.0	16.5	3.2	4.0
Thailand	−6.2		7.0	2.3	25.3	25.0	62.2	22.5	4.4	18.7	30.9	11.5	3.7	6.1	6.2
Turkey	−12.6	−4.3	8.6	2.9	33.7	10.6		16.9	8.9	19.4	16.6	25.0	5.7	1.7	1.5
Uruguay	−3.9	−1.4	5.2	2.2	49.5	12.9	77.1	14.3	61.8	29.4	14.0	10.5		1.3	1.4
Venezuela	−10.9	−5.4	4.5	1.8	48.1	20.6		9.5		27.2	17.9	32.4	1.9	10.8	18.9
Zimbabwe	−10.1	−4.6	10.9	2.6	48.9	11.4	60.8	23.8	10.8	30.3	19.5	18.0	8.3	4.6	5.9

Source: Authors' calculations.
[1]Variables with noise-to-signal ratio less than one.
[2]Missing values due to insufficient observations.

APPENDIX IV

Table A4.5. Country-Specific Thresholds for Debt Crises[1]

	Overall Balance	Primary Balance	Actuarial Deficit	Total Financing	Change in Net Claims on Government	Total Debt	Short-Term Debt	Long-Term Debt
Noise-to-signal	0.56	0.57	0.61	0.68	0.43	0.54	0.33	0.67
Optimal threshold Percentile	7	3	88	98	98	98	91	94
Country-specific thresholds[2]								
Argentina	−8.7	−1.0	6.6	7.3	8.6	63.8	11.0	38.5
Bolivia	−20.0	−3.3	9.0	2.9	6.8	59.0	16.8	40.2
Brazil	−7.9	−0.8	4.1	15.6	16.9	16.8	9.1	32.2
Chile	−3.5	−1.3	11.4	5.4	16.4	85.0	12.8	76.4
Colombia	−6.0	−2.0	3.1	6.1	2.1	28.3	10.1	19.8
Cyprus	−6.9			8.5	5.1	59.1		
Czech Republic	−3.2	−3.1	2.7	1.6	2.7	18.2	13.4	13.7
Egypt	−23.1	−18.8	11.5	20.4	7.8		18.0	5.2
Hungary	−7.8	−3.4	7.5	6.6	7.9	87.3	15.9	33.0
India	−10.9	−4.5	3.0	8.6	1.7	53.8	2.6	6.1
Indonesia	−3.1	−0.8	5.4	3.6	4.8	63.8	14.2	29.5
Israel	−14.7	−6.3		25.5	19.2	452.0		
Jordan	−27.7	−1.6	12.4	17.8	8.9	146.2	20.3	54.8
Korea	−3.0	0.1	3.7	3.6	1.6	17.0	14.7	18.2
Lebanon	−35.8	−17.2	9.6	25.1	25.2	131.9	27.3	6.4
Malaysia	−4.2		7.3	15.5	2.5	103.4	11.0	33.9
Mexico	−12.9	0.7	13.4	13.7	6.4	69.8	9.8	47.2
Pakistan	−8.6	−1.6	3.7	8.4	3.6	78.1	7.1	14.4
Peru	−6.8	−0.8	9.7	7.0	3.6	81.1	18.1	25.2
Philippines	−4.5		8.7	4.8	3.1	66.7	29.8	30.6
Poland	−7.8	−6.6	8.5	2.3	12.6	66.3	13.5	40.2
Slovak Republic	−12.0	−3.8	2.6	4.3	1.7	30.1	9.3	21.6
South Africa	−8.8	−4.6	0.7	8.9	1.9	51.2	9.6	6.6
Sri Lanka	−12.7	−6.1	6.9	14.0	3.3	104.9	5.8	7.1
Thailand	−6.1		3.6	9.4	3.2	33.6	25.0	33.9
Turkey	−12.3	−5.0	3.8	10.8	7.4	49.8	10.6	15.9
Uruguay	−3.6	−2.0	2.6	7.6	5.1	40.8	12.9	35.2
Venezuela	−9.7	−6.8	10.5	4.8	2.7	37.1	20.6	49.2
Zimbabwe	−10.1	−6.7	6.8	11.1	4.1	69.9	11.4	13.5

Source: Authors' calculations.
[1]Variables with noise-to-signal ratio less than one.
[2]Missing values due to insufficient observations.

IMF's main EWS model, the Developing Countries Studies Division (DCSD) model. The model predicts currency crises using the crisis definition set out in Section III and has a 24-month-ahead forecasting horizon. The parameters are generated by probit regressions, using monthly data. With a deliberate emphasis on parsimony, the model is specified with only six explanatory variables—exchange rate overvaluation measured by the deviation of the real exchange rate from its long-term trend, the current account deficit relative to GDP, reserves growth, export growth, the ratio of short-term debt to reserves, and the ratio of M2 to reserves. Fiscal variables have not previously been examined systematically in the context of this model.[49]

---
[49]For further details on the DCSD model, see Berg, Borensztein, and Pattillo (2003); and IMF (2002a).

Appendix IV

Foreign Debt	Foreign Currency Debt	Total Expenditure	Interest Expenditure	Defense Expenditure	Social Expenditure	Total Revenue	International Trade Taxes	Nontax Revenue	Grants	Tax Buoyancy	Revenue Buoyancy
0.47	0.11	0.81	0.87	0.54	0.31	0.71	0.74	0.48	0.59	0.43	0.41
98	98	86	89	95	98	97	94	91	98	98	98
35.5		17.6	14.3	9.2		15.8	16.0	22.2		4.8	4.1
47.5		22.8	9.5	14.7	28.1	20.9	15.3	35.5	22.0	3.0	2.5
3.2		38.1	48.8	3.8	34.0	33.1	4.2	38.3	1.6	1.8	2.0
62.4	79.4	30.3	9.7	13.0	45.3	33.2	11.6	23.3	7.2	3.1	2.8
14.4		15.7	12.4	14.6	19.2	14.8	22.5	17.4	13.1	1.8	1.9
29.5	60.6	34.1	15.2	8.3	24.5	31.7	27.3	26.6	20.2	3.8	1.9
6.9	38.2	35.5	3.9	6.7	38.4	37.5	4.0	7.8		2.6	2.4
		57.0	20.7	16.1	12.0	47.7	24.5	36.7	9.9	2.8	3.2
9.2	12.9	52.5	19.8	6.9	39.1	50.1	9.1	15.5	5.1	3.1	2.1
9.4	27.7	21.8	23.0	17.9		14.2	28.1	25.2	2.9	1.8	1.6
62.8	99.7	21.1	13.3	16.9	6.6	19.9	12.7	24.0	1.3	2.2	2.3
172.0	46.2	82.5	23.2	40.7	26.8	75.0	15.8	15.8	26.2	2.6	3.1
113.9	147.8	49.1	14.6	29.4		42.3	32.0	28.8	54.7	3.7	8.3
10.9	76.2	20.0	6.2	30.7	9.1	20.1	16.8	13.5	6.2	1.5	1.5
32.3	21.6	39.0	40.2	14.4	8.3	19.3	45.9	31.1	17.3	4.7	7.1
37.1	37.2	34.6	20.6	16.2	6.9	30.0	33.0	31.7	0.4	2.2	2.2
38.6	77.6	24.8	51.2	4.4	26.1	16.2	11.6	16.4		1.6	1.6
46.7	67.4	23.7	25.5	30.8		17.2	34.9	29.1	5.7	1.7	2.1
135.4		18.4	24.4	25.8		16.7	27.4	15.3	1.5	2.2	2.3
28.0	60.5	19.1	30.8	19.2		19.4	29.8	15.8	2.1	2.7	2.5
42.0	63.3	45.6	9.4	4.6	53.5	46.1	7.9	10.4	1.6	1.0	0.9
12.3	41.0	43.1	7.6	5.6	27.3	41.5	5.7	14.5	0.1		
4.0	10.2	31.0	17.8			28.6	6.2	12.7	1.7	1.8	1.9
58.2		34.5	22.7	17.4	25.9	25.5	41.4	15.0	16.9	4.2	4.0
9.2	77.1	20.5	15.5	21.2	4.7	19.0	27.3	11.5	4.0	9.7	6.2
23.7		24.5	19.7	16.0	9.1	24.2	15.9	25.0	7.1	1.8	1.5
25.4	78.2	30.6	8.0	13.2	61.9	30.0	13.6	10.5		1.4	1.4
26.9		27.5	18.9	9.5		31.1	17.6	32.4	2.0	11.9	18.9
37.3	62.3	36.3	20.2	20.5	14.6	31.7	19.0	18.0	8.7	5.3	5.9

Estimation

The data on which the DCSD model has been estimated cover the same 29 countries and the same period (1970–2000) as the fiscal dataset used in this paper. The DCSD dataset contains mostly financial and monetary variables that are available on a monthly basis, and also some variables available on a quarterly basis, such as the current account balance. Altogether, the database covers 9,263 monthly observations across the 29 countries. All variables have been percentiled to remove country-specific effects.

The fiscal variables are, in almost all cases, only available on an annual basis, and therefore have to be converted to a monthly frequency to be used with the DCSD model. Monthly fiscal data are interpolated from annual observations by means of a

APPENDIX IV

Table A4.6. Country-Specific Thresholds for Banking Crises[1]

	Overall Balance	Primary Balance	Actuarial Deficit	Total Financing	Change in Net Claims on Government	Total Debt	Public External Debt	Short-Term Debt
Noise-to-signal	0.29	0.46	0.43	0.54	0.41	0.28	0.66	0.33
Optimal threshold								
Percentile	1	6	91	98	95	97	83	90
Country-specific thresholds[2]								
Argentina	−12.1	−1.0	9.6	7.3	3.2	54.5	33.2	10.4
Bolivia	−23.0	−2.6	10.3	2.9	2.1	58.7	86.5	16.2
Brazil	−10.0	−0.5	4.7	15.6	6.9	16.7	28.8	9.0
Chile	−3.5	−0.9	11.8	5.4	7.2	85.0	42.1	12.6
Colombia	−6.4	−1.7	3.2	6.1	1.2	28.3	34.0	9.8
Cyprus	−6.9			8.5	3.8	58.7		
Czech Republic	−4.7	−2.8	2.7	1.6	1.6	18.2	21.4	13.3
Egypt	−24.3	−18.6	11.5	20.4	2.9		74.3	17.5
Hungary	−9.2	−2.2	7.6	6.6	4.3	87.3	52.2	14.9
India	−11.2	−4.4	3.5	8.6	1.6	53.3	22.8	2.3
Indonesia	−3.7	−1.0	7.8	3.6	2.1	55.2	41.9	14.2
Israel	−19.0	−3.9		25.5	12.6	448.8		
Jordan	−30.1	−1.0	15.6	17.8	5.4	134.7	109.3	19.3
Korea	−3.8	0.3	3.7	3.6	1.2	16.8	26.8	14.7
Lebanon	−48.8	−15.5	12.2	25.1	13.8	95.3	13.9	27.1
Malaysia	−9.5		7.6	15.5	2.0	103.4	38.2	10.4
Mexico	−20.7	0.7	13.7	13.7	3.3	66.9	39.8	9.3
Pakistan	−8.9	−1.5	4.0	8.4	2.7	76.8	40.3	6.7
Peru	−7.5	−0.7	10.4	7.0	2.7	116.3	43.1	17.3
Philippines	−5.1		9.0	4.8	1.3	66.3	52.4	28.4
Poland	−13.1	−5.3	10.5	2.3	5.6	66.3	54.3	13.0
Slovak Republic	−15.0	−3.8	2.6	4.3	0.5	30.1	21.0	9.3
South Africa	−9.9	−4.2	0.6	8.9	1.1	51.0	7.8	9.6
Sri Lanka	−18.2	−5.3	7.3	14.0	2.8	101.2	58.4	5.7
Thailand	−7.2		4.8	9.4	2.3	33.6	21.5	23.4
Turkey	−13.1	−4.6	3.9	10.8	2.9	46.1	29.1	10.3
Uruguay	−4.2	−1.7	3.9	7.6	2.2	40.8	39.0	10.8
Venezuela	−13.2	−6.1	11.3	4.8	1.8	37.1	44.9	18.4
Zimbabwe	−12.7	−6.4	7.8	11.1	2.6	69.9	42.1	10.9

Source: Authors' calculations.
[1] Variables with noise-to-signal ratio less than one.
[2] Missing values due to insufficient observations.

cubic spline function, designed to lay a smooth curve through the annual data points.[50]

The specification strategy is to examine the fiscal variables in four groups: variables reflecting deficits

---

[50] More formally, the spline function fits a third-order polynomial to every two adjacent annual observations. The polynomials are chosen so that the first and the second derivative of adjacent observations (January/December) are equal. Spline functions have the advantage of producing interpolated series with lower volatility than other interpolation methods. Some other EWS studies that have included fiscal variables have followed a different method. They simply set the monthly observations for a year equal to the value of the annual observation. The method could be justified if information on fiscal variables changes only with the release of the annual numbers. However, while official data may become available only once a year, related information or coincidental indicators become available on a continuous basis so that the public will likely have a more frequently changing perception of the fiscal variables that interpolation using the spline function is intended to capture. Indeed, transforming annual data into monthly data may represent the fiscal situation more accurately than an actual monthly series. Fiscal data are typically subject to pronounced seasonal effects. Expenditure is bulky (e.g., debt service, wage bonuses, and investment projects) while revenue tends to be more smooth. Hence,

Appendix IV

Long-Term Debt	Foreign Debt	Foreign Currency Debt	Total Expenditure	Interest Expenditure	Defense Expenditure	Social Expenditure	Total Revenue	International Trade Taxes	Grants
0.61	0.33	0.22	0.54	0.80	0.50	0.77	0.49	0.74	0.36
91	98	97	98	91	93	80	95	98	98
35.2	35.5		19.9	14.4	9.0		15.6	20.7	
39.7	47.5		23.2	9.7	14.4	25.3	20.6	17.9	22.0
30.3	3.2		43.2	53.4	3.8	27.7	31.5	5.6	1.6
72.6	62.4	67.3	31.7	9.9	12.9	37.3	32.6	13.2	7.2
19.5	14.4		18.1	12.6	14.4	17.6	14.4	23.2	13.1
	29.5	60.4	36.8	15.3	8.2	22.6	31.6	29.9	20.2
12.8	6.9	38.0	35.7	4.3	6.7	37.1	37.3	4.0	
5.2			63.2	21.2	15.9	10.4	47.5	30.4	9.9
32.4	9.2	12.0	53.2	20.2	6.9	37.8	49.9	9.9	5.1
6.0	9.4	27.7	22.6	23.4	17.1		14.2	28.3	2.9
26.8	62.8	99.5	23.7	14.1	16.5	6.0	19.8	18.6	1.3
	172.0	45.1	99.0	23.8	40.0	24.3	74.3	19.6	26.2
50.8	113.9	125.3	54.1	15.3	28.1		41.8	32.8	54.7
18.0	10.9	75.0	21.5	6.3	30.6	8.4	19.6	18.0	6.2
6.1	32.3	20.8	41.9	40.3	13.6	7.8	19.1	46.0	17.3
31.9	37.1	36.1	42.5	23.1	16.1	5.9	29.3	36.8	0.4
42.8	38.6	75.8	29.6	51.8	4.3	23.0	16.1	14.1	
10.8	46.7	66.2	25.1	25.5	29.6		17.0	39.9	5.7
24.9	135.4		19.3	24.7	25.8		16.5	28.3	1.5
28.9	28.0	59.5	20.1	31.3	19.0		19.2	36.4	2.1
39.1	42.0	63.2	47.4	9.4	4.5	52.2	46.0	8.1	1.6
18.4	12.3	41.0	43.1	7.6	5.6	27.2	41.3	5.7	0.1
6.3	4.0	9.5	33.4	18.3			28.1	8.3	1.7
6.9	58.2		39.9	22.8	17.4	22.7	25.1	48.3	16.9
28.2	9.2	77.1	25.3	15.7	20.9	3.7	18.9	30.9	4.0
14.3	23.7		35.6	22.8	15.7	3.9	23.1	16.6	7.1
34.1	25.4	78.2	32.3	8.0	13.1	59.8	30.0	14.0	
44.3	26.9		30.2	19.0	9.5		30.1	17.9	2.0
13.4	37.3	62.3	41.5	22.8	20.3	6.7	30.5	19.5	8.7

and financing; variables reflecting debt; variables reflecting expenditure; and variables reflecting revenue. Within each group, one variable at a time is included in the DCSD specification to see which variable is best suited. This is done for a joint sample so that the results are not driven by sample composition effects. The different specifications are compared based on the in-sample prediction, significance tests, and, to a lesser extent, the pseudo R^2. For those variables that appear promising, the model is reestimated for the maximum sample available.

Results

As a benchmark, the DCSD specification is reestimated for the sample used in this study (Table A4.7). Data are available for 4,254 observations. All variables are significant at the 5 percent level. The model's predictive power is evaluated in-sample by comparing predicted signals to the actual signals: the estimated model correctly calls 64 percent of all cri-

---
monthly data may significantly overstate the volatility of the true fiscal situation, and thus the market's perception.

Table A4.7. Regression Results for the DCSD Specification (Maximum Sample)

Observations	4,254	
Log likelihood	−1,567	
Pseudo R^2	0.15	
Percent of cases correctly called[1]		
Crisis	63.64	
Tranquil periods	85.90	
Episodes	85.21	

	Coefficient	Wald
Exchange rate overvaluation	0.013	12.4
Current account deficit	0.006	5.8
Reserves growth	0.005	5.2
Export growth	0.002	2.3
Short-term debt to reserves	0.014	12.7
M2 to reserves	0.002	1.9
Constant	−3.199	−26.9

Source: Authors' calculations.
[1] A crisis is called if the predicted probability is greater than 50 percent.

sis signals, 86 percent of all tranquil signals, and 85 percent of all signals.

Next, the five deficit and financing variables—the overall balance, the primary balance, the actuarial deficit, total financing, and the change in net claims on government—are added to the benchmark specification. All these variables enter the DCSD specification as significant at the 5 percent level, and with the expected sign (i.e., the higher the fiscal deficit, the higher the probability of observing a crisis within the next 24 months), although none leads to a strong improvement of the model's in-sample predictive power (Table A4.8).

Among the deficit and financing variables, the change in net claims on government performs somewhat better than the others in terms of predictive ability. Hence, the model is reestimated with the maximum sample available for the change in net claims on government (Table A4.9). For the increased sample, inclusion of this variable enhances the (in-sample) predictive power of the model compared to the DCSD specification, in terms of the proportion of crises correctly called. As in the reduced sample, the change in net claims on government enters the DCSD specification significantly at the 5 percent level, and suggests that a higher fiscal deficit is associated with an increased probability of observing a crisis within the next 24 months.[51]

This procedure is repeated for the variables relating to debt, expenditure, and revenue. The detailed results are not presented, but are available on request. The main points arising are as follows:

- Among the debt variables, only foreign currency debt enters the DCSD model significantly at the 5 percent level and with the expected sign. This tends to confirm the findings of the signals EWS that the composition of debt matters for predicting crises.

- The results for the expenditure variables are mixed. Interest expenditure enters significantly and improves the predictive power of the EWS model when entered in percent of GDP. However, the estimated coefficient changes sign when moving to the maximum sample available, implying that this variable is not robust. Social expenditure enters significantly at the 5 percent level and improves predictive power; and this result is stable when moving to the maximum available sample size.

- Two of the six revenue variables—total revenue and international trade taxes—enter the model significantly but there is little or no improvement in predictive power.

---

[51] The change in net claims on government variable is also available at a monthly frequency, although not for all countries. When reestimated with monthly data, the results are less clear than in Table A4.9. The divergence is likely to arise from sample composition and excessive volatility in the monthly fiscal data compared with the underlying fiscal trend.

Appendix IV

Table A4.8. Regression Results for Deficit and Financing Variables (Joint Sample)

	Benchmark Model		Fiscal Model 1		Fiscal Model 2		Fiscal Model 3		Fiscal Model 4		Fiscal Model 5	
	Coefficient	Wald	Coefficient	Wald	Coefficient	Wald	Coefficient	Wald	Coefficient	Wald	Coefficient	Wald
Observations	2,718		2,718		2,718		2,718		2,718		2,718	
Log likelihood	−977		−969		−966		−966		−971		−973	
Pseudo R^2	0.15		0.16		0.16		0.16		0.15		0.15	
Percent of cases correctly called[1]												
Crisis	61.76		56.25		59.70		60.24		60.56		55.13	
Tranquil periods	86.23		86.02		86.16		86.45		86.25		86.21	
Episodes	85.61		85.32		85.50		85.65		85.58		85.32	
Exchange rate overvaluation	0.017	12.2	0.017	12.4	0.017	12.2	0.017	11.9	0.017	12.4	0.017	12.3
Current account deficit	0.004	3.0	0.004	3.2	0.003	2.5	0.004	3.2	0.004	2.9	0.003	2.8
Reserves growth	0.004	3.2	0.004	3.0	0.004	3.0	0.004	2.9	0.004	3.0	0.004	3.2
Export growth	0.001	1.0	0.001	0.6	0.001	0.5	0.001	0.7	0.001	0.6	0.001	0.7
Short-term debt to reserves	0.010	6.7	0.010	6.9	0.011	7.1	0.010	6.6	0.010	6.6	0.009	6.4
M2 to reserves	0.005	3.3	0.005	3.2	0.005	3.2	0.005	3.6	0.005	3.6	0.005	3.4
Overall balance			−0.005	−3.7								
Primary balance					−0.005	−4.5						
Change in net claims on government							0.005	4.6				
Total financing									0.004	3.5		
Actuarial deficit											0.003	2.7
Constant	−3.193	−20.9	−2.939	−16.7	−2.904	−16.6	−3.393	−21.9	−3.345	−21.9	−3.309	−20.9

Source: Authors' calculations.
[1] A crisis is called if the predicted probability is greater than 50 percent.

APPENDIX IV

Table A4.9. Regression Results for Reduced Set of Deficit and Financing Variables (Maximum Sample)

	Benchmark Model 1		Fiscal Model 1		Benchmark Model 2		Fiscal Model 2	
Observations	4,025		4,025		4,183		4,183	
Log likelihood	−1,446		−1,442		−1,559		−1,534	
Pseudo R^2	0.15		0.16		0.15		0.16	
Percent of cases correctly called[1]								
Crisis	59.63		59.46		63.91		68.49	
Tranquil periods	86.16		86.18		85.68		86.00	
Episodes	85.44		85.44		84.99		85.39	

	Coefficient	Wald	Coefficient	Wald	Coefficient	Wald	Coefficient	Wald
Exchange rate overvaluation	0.013	12.4	0.013	12.5	0.013	12.4	0.012	11.8
Current account deficit	0.007	6.6	0.007	6.7	0.006	5.7	0.006	5.8
Reserves growth	0.006	5.1	0.005	4.8	0.005	5.1	0.005	4.3
Export growth	0.002	1.8	0.002	1.7	0.002	2.3	0.002	2.0
Short-term debt to reserves	0.013	11.7	0.013	11.7	0.013	12.4	0.013	12.3
M2 to reserves	0.001	0.9	0.001	0.6	0.002	2.0	0.002	2.1
Overall balance			−0.003	−2.7				
Change in net claims on government							0.006	6.9
Constant	−3.231	−25.5	−3.075	−21.1	−3.183	−26.8	−3.409	−27.3

Source: Authors' calculations.
[1] A crisis is called if the predicted probability is greater than 50 percent.

Based on the above results, the best performers from each group of fiscal variables are included jointly in the DCSD model. These variables are the change in net claims on government, foreign currency debt, interest expenditure, social expenditure, total revenue, and international trade taxes. When insignificant fiscal variables, and fiscal variables for which the estimated coefficient are highly sensitive to sample size, are subsequently dropped from the model, only the change in net claims on government and foreign currency debt remain (Table A4.10, Model 5). Compared with the DCSD specification (Table A4.10, Benchmark Model 2), including these two variables improves the model's overall predictive power for tranquil episodes, although it marginally reduces the number of correctly called crisis signals. A similar conclusion emerges when an EWS model that only includes the six best performing fiscal variables is estimated (Fiscal Model 6). This purely fiscal EWS appears to be reasonably well suited to delivering tranquil signals, but it falls short of the DCSD capacity for delivering crisis signals.

Explaining the Severity of Currency Crises

This section investigates the empirical relationships between a variety of fiscal indicators and the depth of currency crises. The latter is measured by the FMP index. There is now a growing part of the empirical crisis literature that attempts to explain variations in the severity of crises using this index.[52] The approach is to build on the existing models, again focusing on fiscal variables, and then to try a novel approach based on panel estimation techniques.

A Regression Approach

As a first step in investigating the linkages between fiscal vulnerability and the severity of currency crises, a variant of the Sachs, Tornell, and Velasco (1996) (STV) model is estimated.[53] The sample of countries, the fiscal variables, and the currency crisis index are all as described in Section III of the main text; the 58 currency crisis episodes become the maximum sample for estimation. This approach differs from STV who include all countries in their sample for a year in which a major crisis occurred, whether a country was directly affected by the crisis or not.

As the benchmark model, an augmented version of the STV model is estimated. The starting point is a variation of the STV specification with five regressors: exchange rate overvaluation in the year before the crisis; growth of credit to the private sector; the M2 to reserves ratio; weak fundamentals; and low reserves (Table A4.11, Benchmark Model 1). The change in credit to the private sector and the dummy for low reserves are individually and jointly insignificant and therefore dropped (Benchmark Model 2). To this specification, the variables used in the IMF's main EWS model are added. However, none of the variables enters significantly (Benchmark Models 3–6).

The preferred benchmark specification (Benchmark Model 2) thus includes exchange rate overvaluation in the year before the crisis, the M2 to reserves ratio, and weak fundamentals. The greater the overvaluation before the crisis, and the higher the ratio of M2 to reserves, the more severe the crisis as measured by the FMP index. Likewise, countries with weak fundamentals during a crisis experience a larger deterioration in the FMP index. These results are consistent with findings of related studies. To this specification was added, in turn, variables reflecting deficits, debt, expenditure, and revenue. However, none of these variables entered significantly at the 5 percent level and the results are not reported.

Next, the "best" performers among the fiscal variables—the change in net claims on government, public external debt, and long-term debt—are added jointly to the benchmark specification (Table A4.12, Fiscal Models 1 and 2). As expected, the fiscal variables do not enter significantly. Among the fiscal variables, the change in net claims on government has the highest t-ratio; two specifications focusing on this variable are then estimated. The first drops M2 to reserves to account for a possible correlation between that variable and the change in net claims on government; now the change in net claims on government enters significantly at the 5 percent level (Table A4.12, Fiscal Model 3). Second, the FMP index is estimated as a function of change in net claims on government only, leaving aside the benchmark regressors. The variable enters significantly at the 5 percent level, but the adjusted R-squared of this regression is 6 percent, compared with 22 percent for the benchmark specification (Table A4.12, Fiscal Model 4).

Thus the results suggest that fiscal variables are not strongly correlated with the severity of crises as measured by the change in the FMP index. None of the fiscal variables enters significantly, even at the 10 percent level. While the severity of crisis is positively correlated with the change in net claims on

---

[52]Other studies have measured the severity of crises in terms of deviations of output from trend, falls in stock market indices, and so on (see Appendix I).

[53]See Appendix I for a description of the STV model.

APPENDIX IV

Table A4.10. Regression Results for Selected Fiscal Variables

	Benchmark Model 1	Fiscal Model 1	Fiscal Model 2	Benchmark Model 2	Fiscal Model 3	Fiscal Model 4	Fiscal Model 5	Fiscal Model 6
Observations	1,525	1,525	1,525	2,289	2,289	2,289	2,289	2,658
Log likelihood	–409	–333	–333	–655	–629	–630	–634	–858
Pseudo R²	0.21	0.35	0.35	0.22	0.25	0.25	0.24	0.17
Percent of cases correctly called[1]								
Crisis	100.00	76.06	76.06	81.03	69.89	68.75	78.05	42.47
Tranquil periods	90.63	92.57	92.57	89.76	90.43	90.56	90.53	87.81
Episodes	90.75	91.80	91.80	89.54	89.59	89.65	90.08	86.57

	Coefficient	Wald	Coefficient	Wald	Coefficient	Wald	Coefficient	Wald	Coefficient	Wald	Coefficient	Wald	Coefficient	Wald	Coefficient	Wald
Exchange rate overvaluation	0.015	5.9	0.017	6.5	0.017	6.7	0.018	10.6	0.019	11.6	0.019	11.7	0.019	11.5		
Current account deficit	0.015	9.0	0.012	6.7	0.012	6.4	0.010	7.6	0.009	6.5	0.009	6.7	0.010	7.4		
Reserves growth	0.005	2.5	0.012	5.2	0.012	5.3	0.003	2.2	0.004	2.6	0.004	2.5	0.004	2.1		
Export growth	0.001	0.8	–0.001	–0.5	–0.001	–0.6	0.004	2.6	0.003	2.2	0.004	2.3	0.004	2.4		
Short-term debt to reserves	0.009	4.1	0.000	0.1	0.000	0.1	0.013	7.4	0.012	6.8	0.012	7.0	0.013	7.1		
M2 to reserves	–0.004	–1.9	–0.008	–2.9	–0.008	–3.0	0.002	1.5	0.004	2.5	0.004	2.4	0.004	2.5		
Change in net claims on government			0.008	4.0	0.008	4.1			0.003	1.8	0.003	1.8	0.003	2.0	0.008	5.8
Foreign currency debt			0.017	9.7	0.017	9.7			0.008	6.5	0.008	6.7	0.008	6.6	0.008	5.8
Interest expenditure			0.001	0.4											–0.013	–9.6
Social expenditure			0.013	4.7	0.013	5.2									0.009	6.6
Total revenue			0.009	4.2	0.009	4.2			0.004	2.9	0.004	3.0			0.014	9.3
International trade taxes			–0.014	–5.5	–0.014	–6.4			0.000	–0.3					0.011	6.8
Constant	–3.429	–13.0	–5.333	–15.2	–5.279	–14.6	–3.917	–18.1	–4.804	–21.2	–4.835	–22.3	–4.578	–20.7	–3.091	–16.7

Source: Authors' calculations.
[1] A crisis is called if the predicted probability is greater than 50 percent.

Appendix IV

Table A4.11. Explaining Crisis Depth (Benchmark Specification)

	Benchmark Model 1		Benchmark Model 2		Benchmark Model 3		Benchmark Model 4		Benchmark Model 5		Benchmark Model 6	
Observations	57		57		57		57		57		49	
Test for joint significance	$F(5, 51)$ 27.9		$F(3, 53)$ 27.9		$F(4, 52)$ 34.1		$F(4, 52)$ 30.9		$F(4, 52)$ 30.9		$F(4, 44)$ 41.6	
R^2	0.26		0.25		0.25		0.25		0.26		0.23	
Adjusted R^2	0.20		0.22		0.21		0.21		0.22		0.17	
	Coefficient	t-ratio	Coefficient	t-ratio	Coefficient	t-ratio	Coefficient	t-ratio	Coefficient	t-ratio	Coefficient	t-ratio
Exchange rate overvaluation (in the previous period)	0.0001	6.86	0.0001	8.62	0.0001	7.59	0.0001	8.38	0.0001	8.44	0.0001	7.88
Growth in credit to private sector	0.0000	1.10										
M2 to reserves	0.0063	3.07	0.0063	3.15	0.0063	3.12	0.0063	3.12	0.0060	2.89	0.0057	2.58
Weak fundamentals	1.4311	2.20	1.4566	2.29	1.4667	2.22	1.4904	2.32	1.4254	2.21	0.8754	1.92
Low reserves	0.1094	0.25										
Current account deficit					0.0018	0.09	0.0020	0.43				
Reserves growth (in the previous period)									−0.0069	−0.71		
Export growth											0.0003	0.86
Short-term debt to reserves	0.7467	1.16	0.7923	1.39	0.7764	1.23	0.7398	1.25	0.8479	1.45	1.3291	3.99
Constant												

Source: Authors' calculations.

APPENDIX IV

Table A4.12. Best Performers Among Fiscal Variables

	Benchmark Model 2		Fiscal Model 1		Fiscal Model 2		Fiscal Model 3		Fiscal Model 4	
Observations	57		38		45		54		54	
Test for joint significance	$F(3, 53)$	27.9	$F(5, 32)$	17.3	$F(5, 39)$	82.2	$F(3, 50)$	36.0	$F(1, 52)$	4.9
R^2		0.25		0.37		0.27		0.17		0.06
Adjusted R^2		0.22		0.30		0.20		0.14		0.06
	Coefficient	t-ratio	Coefficient	t-ratio	Coefficient	t-ratio	Coefficient	t-ratio	Coefficient	t-ratio
Exchange rate overvaluation (in the previous period)	0.0001	8.62	0.0001	6.80	0.0001	7.20		7.85		
M2 to reserves	0.0063	3.15	0.0066	2.39	0.0057	2.46				
Weak fundamentals	1.4566	2.29	1.9147	2.24	1.2196	3.33		3.09		
Change in net claims on government			0.0518	0.75	0.0418	1.39	2.0215	2.20	0.0587	
Total debt			−0.0001	−0.01			0.0573			
Long-term debt					0.0150	1.19				
Constant	0.7923	1.39	0.1124	0.14	0.7457	2.46	0.3811	0.63	2.2931	9.11

Source: Authors' calculations.

government, this relationship becomes insignificant when other explanatory variables are included. This suggests that, consistent with similar empirical studies, fiscal variables have at most an indirect impact on crisis severity.

A Panel Approach

The modified STV approach described above models the FMP index conditional on a country undergoing a crisis. As an alternative, the FMP index is modeled independent of whether there is a crisis or not. This approach is akin to modeling the exchange rate, with all the attendant difficulties. Nonetheless, this approach allows many more observations than the modified STV approach—the sample now becomes a panel consisting of the 29 emerging market economies over the period from 1971 to 2000—and may therefore result in more precise estimates of the effect of fiscal variables on changes in the FMP index.

The panel is estimated with fixed effects and with random effects.[54] Only the fixed effects results are reported, although for completeness the Hausman test statistic for random effects is also reported. In each case this indicates that a random effects model would not lead to different results.

The benchmark model is specified using the standard variables in the STV model and from the EWS literature discussed in Section III. From the STV literature, exchange rate overvaluation in the previous period, growth of credit to the private sector, M2 to reserves, and dummies for weak fundamentals and low reserves are included. From the IMF's main EWS model, the current account deficit, reserves growth lagged one period, export growth, and short-term debt are included. Following Girton and Roper (1976), domestic GDP growth, U.S. GDP growth, domestic CPI inflation, and the London interbank offered rate (LIBOR) are also included.

For the general specification, the joint sample includes 681 observations for 29 countries (Table A4.13, column 1). Six regressors are insignificant at the 10 percent level: growth of credit to the private sector; the current account deficit; reserves growth lagged one period; U.S. GDP growth; domestic CPI inflation; and LIBOR. When these variables are dropped, the dummy for low reserves becomes insignificant at the 5 percent level (column 2). Dropping the dummy gives the benchmark specification (column 3),[55] which models the FMP index as a function of the exchange rate overvaluation in the previous period, the change in M2 to reserves, weak fundamentals, export growth, short-term debt to reserves, and GDP growth. As expected, overvaluation leads to an increased FMP index (i.e., a bigger combination of nominal depreciation and reserves loss) in the next period. A higher M2 to reserves ratio, which is thought to reflect increased vulnerability to a capital inflow reversal, increases the FMP index. Likewise, a high short-term debt to reserves ratio puts upward pressure on the FMP index. Having weak fundamentals in general increases the FMP index. High export growth and high GDP growth ameliorate exchange market pressure.

Including Fiscal Variables in the Benchmark Specification

Now fiscal variables are added to the benchmark specification. First they are added separately, and then the best performers are entered jointly.

Of the deficit and financing variables, only the actuarial deficit enters significantly in the benchmark specification (Table A4.14). Next, GDP growth and export growth are dropped from the benchmark regression because these variables typically move with the fiscal stance. Now, total financing enters significantly in addition to the actuarial deficit (results not reported). Likewise, short-term debt to reserves is dropped from the benchmark regression because short-term debt could also move with the fiscal stance. This results in the overall balance, the actuarial deficit, and total financing entering significantly. The results are similar if deficit and financing variables are added to a model including only the STV variables (not reported). Taken together, this is reasonably robust evidence that loose fiscal policy is associated with increased pressure in the foreign exchange market, controlling for a number of other determinants.

Four debt variables enter significantly (Table A4.15): total debt; public external debt; long-term debt; and foreign debt. When these four variables are entered jointly in the benchmark specification, public external debt as well as foreign debt become insignificant (results not reported). Given the colinearity between the different debt variables this is not surprising. Overall, the results suggest that high public external debt is associated with increased pressure in the foreign exchange market. Several debt indicators capture this relationship.

Of the expenditure variables, two measures of interest expenditure enter significantly (Table A4.16): interest expenditure in percent of total expenditure and in percent of GDP. No revenue variables enter significantly.

---

[54]In a fixed effects model, the time-invariant country-specific unobserved effects are assumed to be correlated with the explanatory variables; in a random effects model, they are assumed to be uncorrelated with the explanatory variables.

[55]Note that the Hausman test rejects the null hypothesis of the validity of the random effects model compared with the fixed effects model for this specification.

APPENDIX IV

Table A4.13. Benchmark Specification for Panel Approach (Fixed Effects)

	Benchmark Model 1		Benchmark Model 2		Benchmark Model 3	
Observations		681		709		709
Countries included		29		29		29
Per country						
Minimum observations		5		6		6
Average observations		23.5		24.4		24.4
Maximum observations		28		29		29
R^2						
Within		0.40		0.40		0.40
Between		0.07		0.12		0.16
Overall		0.38		0.38		0.38
Test for joint significance	$F(13, 639)$	32.68	$F(7, 673)$	63.72	$F(6, 674)$	73.66
Hausman test for random effects	$\chi^2(13)$	19.82	$\chi^2(7)$	30.46	$\chi^2(6)$	26.77
Results similar for random effects		Yes		Yes		Yes

	Coefficient	t-ratio	Coefficient	t-ratio	Coefficient	t-ratio
Exchange rate overvaluation						
(in the previous period)	0.0000	1.87	0.0000	2.36	0.0000	2.32
Growth of credit to the						
private sector	0.0001	0.62				
Change in M2 to reserves	0.0124	12.65	0.0127	13.86	0.0129	14.26
Weak fundamentals	0.4539	3.54	0.4532	3.64	0.4502	3.62
Low reserves	0.2584	1.78	0.2408	1.69		
Current account deficit	0.0047	0.71				
Reserves growth						
(in the previous period)	−0.0001	−0.21				
Export growth	−0.0175	−7.02	−0.0170	−7.12	−0.0169	−7.08
Short-term debt to reserves	0.0005	1.74	0.0006	2.37	0.0008	3.12
Real GDP growth	−0.0153	−2.20	−0.0180	−2.68	−0.0177	−2.63
U.S. real GDP growth						
(in the previous period)	0.0065	0.29				
CPI inflation	0.0001	0.45				
LIBOR	0.0192	1.21				
Constant	−0.3749	−1.83	−0.1843	−1.46	−0.1515	−1.21

Source: Authors' calculations.

As a last step, the "best" performers among the fiscal variables are entered jointly, using only one variable at a time from each group (Table A4.17). The results largely confirm the above findings. Loose fiscal policy, high debt, and high interest expenditure (based on either the economic or functional classification of expenditure) increase pressure in the foreign exchange market, over and above the effect of other factors influencing the exchange market. The relationships are robust over different specifications, choice of measures, and sample composition.

Appendix IV

Table A4.14. Including Deficit and Financing Variables in the Benchmark Specification (Panel Approach, Fixed Effects)

	Fiscal Model 1		Fiscal Model 2		Fiscal Model 3		Fiscal Model 4		Fiscal Model 5	
Observations	566		295		668		579		670	
Countries included	27		24		27		27		27	
Per country										
Minimum observations	6		6		5		4		6	
Average observations	21		12.3		24.7		21.4		24.8	
Maximum observations	29		25		29		29		29	
R^2										
Within	0.36		0.32		0.42		0.41		0.41	
Between	0.10		0.04		0.14		0.17		0.16	
Overall	0.34		0.27		0.40		0.39		0.40	
Test for joint significance	$F(7,532)$ 43.66		$F(7,264)$ 17.53		$F(7,634)$ 64.44		$F(7,545)$ 53.05		$F(7,636)$ 62.59	
Hausman test for random effects	$\chi^2(7)$ 14.00		$\chi^2(7)$ 15.98		$\chi^2(7)$ 13.79		$\chi^2(7)$ 10.93		$\chi^2(7)$ 35.41	
Results similar for random effects	Yes		Yes		Yes		Yes		Yes	

	Coefficient	t-ratio	Coefficient	t-ratio	Coefficient	t-ratio	Coefficient	t-ratio	Coefficient	t-ratio
Exchange rate overvaluation (in the previous period)	0.0000	0.55	0.0000	0.00	0.0000	2.39	0.0000	2.29	0.0000	2.31
Change in M2 to reserves	0.0121	11.52	0.0096	6.47	0.0133	14.36	0.0120	12.26	0.0131	13.84
Weak fundamentals	0.5119	3.78	0.6219	3.41	0.4001	3.13	0.4015	3.04	0.4410	3.46
Export growth	−0.0144	−4.85	−0.0140	−2.75	−0.0162	−6.65	−0.0169	−5.81	−0.0169	−6.96
Short-term debt to reserves	0.0010	3.38	0.0011	1.63	0.0008	2.88	0.0008	3.18	0.0008	3.20
Real GDP growth	−0.0127	−1.78	−0.0212	−1.96	−0.0117	−1.67	−0.0263	−2.76	−0.0174	−2.45
Overall balance	−0.0144	−1.30								
Primary balance			−0.0018	−0.09						
Actuarial deficit					0.0173	2.68				
Total financing							0.0193	1.27		
Change in net claims on government									−0.0024	−0.29
Constant	−0.3126	−2.10	−0.2423	−1.28	−0.1495	−1.18	−0.1126	−0.77	−0.1548	−1.20

Source: Authors' calculations.

APPENDIX IV

Table A4.15. Including Public Debt Variables Individually in the Benchmark Specification (Panel Approach, Fixed Effects)

	Fiscal Model 1		Fiscal Model 2		Fiscal Model 3		Fiscal Model 4		Fiscal Model 5		Fiscal Model 6	
Observations	674		460		649		674		439		322	
Countries included	27		26		27		27		26		18	
Per country												
Minimum observations	6		4		6		6		4		4	
Average observations	25		17.7		24		25		16.9		17.9	
Maximum observations	29		29		29		29		29		29	
R^2												
Within	0.41		0.44		0.43		0.41		0.43		0.47	
Between	0.13		0.15		0.08		0.12		0.40		0.13	
Overall	0.39		0.42		0.39		0.39		0.42		0.44	
Test for joint significance	$F_{(7,640)}$	64.66	$F_{(7,427)}$	47.79	$F_{(7,615)}$	65.48	$F_{(7,640)}$	62.94	$F_{(7,406)}$	43.65	$F_{(7,297)}$	37.15
Hausman test for random effects	$\chi^2(7)$	31.77	$\chi^2(7)$	16.66	$\chi^2(7)$	16.37	$\chi^2(7)$	19.82	$\chi^2(7)$	35.31	$\chi^2(7)$	22.65
Results similar for random effects	Yes		Yes		Yes		Yes		Yes		Yes	

	Coefficient	t-ratio	Coefficient	t-ratio	Coefficient	t-ratio	Coefficient	t-ratio	Coefficient	t-ratio	Coefficient	t-ratio
Exchange rate overvaluation (in the previous period)	0.0000	2.08	0.0000	2.02	0.0000	2.13	0.0000	2.36	0.0000	1.98	0.0005	2.53
Change in M2 to reserves	0.0134	14.55	0.0125	11.83	0.0132	14.36	0.0132	14.18	0.0122	11.16	0.0120	10.26
Weak fundamentals	0.4132	3.25	0.4156	3.04	0.4419	3.42	0.4393	3.45	0.4384	3.15	0.4993	3.25
Export growth	−0.0156	−6.40	−0.0163	−5.13	−0.0147	−5.84	−0.0162	−6.57	−0.0165	−5.07	−0.0175	−4.47
Short-term debt to reserves	0.0007	2.75	0.0009	3.12	0.0007	2.86	0.0007	2.34	0.0009	3.27	0.0009	2.96
Real GDP growth	−0.0171	−2.55	−0.0216	−2.22	−0.0257	−3.15	−0.0164	−2.42	−0.0205	−2.05	−0.0091	−0.86
Public external debt	0.0082	2.99										
Total debt			0.0085	2.89								
Long-term debt					0.0201	4.66						
Short-term debt							0.0143	1.35				
Foreign debt									0.0087	2.16		
Foreign currency debt											0.0070	1.70
Constant	−0.3824	−2.58	−0.5103	−2.84	−0.4366	−3.01	−0.2462	−1.69	−0.3368	−2.12	−0.6471	−2.70

Source: Authors' calculations.

Table A4.16. Including Government Expenditure Variables in the Benchmark Specification (Panel Approach, Fixed Effects)

	Fiscal Model 1		Fiscal Model 2		Fiscal Model 3		Fiscal Model 4	
Observations		571		583		336		500
Countries included		27		29		19		26
Per country								
Minimum observations		4		4		4		4
Average observations		21.1		20.1		17.7		19.2
Maximum observations		29		29		28		28
R^2								
Within		0.41		0.40		0.38		0.41
Between		0.13		0.13		0.17		0.33
Overall		0.39		0.38		0.36		0.40
Test for joint significance	F(7,357)	53.43	F(7,547)	52.10	F(7,310)	27.12	F(7,467)	46.44
Hausman test for random effects	$\chi^2(7)$	12.25	$\chi^2(7)$	37.92	$\chi^2(7)$	4.71	$\chi^2(7)$	8.74
Results similar for random effects		Yes		Yes		Yes		Yes
	Coefficient	t-ratio	Coefficient	t-ratio	Coefficient	t-ratio	Coefficient	t-ratio
Exchange rate overvaluation	0.0000	2.25	0.0000	2.30	0.0000	2.09	0.0000	2.07
Change in M2 to reserves	0.0124	12.79	0.0123	12.75	0.0112	8.53	0.0118	11.34
Weak fundamentals	0.3446	2.62	0.3237	2.45	0.4077	2.08	0.3949	2.83
Export growth	−0.0163	−5.59	−0.0156	−5.31	−0.0133	−3.07	−0.0160	−5.27
Short-term debt to reserves	0.0009	3.46	0.0009	3.34	0.0008	2.21	0.0010	3.63
Real GDP growth	−0.0243	−2.57	−0.0275	−2.92	−0.0707	−3.99	−0.0237	−2.41
Interest expenditure (in percent of total expenditure)	0.0137	2.14						
Interest expenditure (in percent of GDP)			0.0596	2.76				
Defense expenditure							−0.0291	−1.92
Social expenditure					0.0218	1.55		
Constant	−0.1921	−1.28	−0.1861	−1.27	−0.2083	−0.63	0.2798	1.26

Source: Authors' calculations.

APPENDIX IV

Table A4.17. Best Performers Among Fiscal Variables (Panel Approach, Fixed Effects)

	Fiscal Model 1		Fiscal Model 2		Fiscal Model 3		Fiscal Model 4	
Observations		566		559		544		551
Countries included		27		27		27		27
Per country								
Minimum observations		4		4		4		4
Average observations		21		20.7		20.1		20.4
Maximum observations		29		29		29		29
R^2								
Within		0.42		0.44		0.44		0.43
Between		0.12		0.15		0.15		0.11
Overall		0.40		0.41		0.41		0.41
Test for joint significance	F(9,530)	43.43	F(9,523)	44.74	F(9,508)	44.00	F(9,515)	42.67
Hausman test for random effects	$\chi^2(9)$	13.81	$\chi^2(9)$	14.83	$\chi^2(9)$	87.92	$\chi^2(9)$	13.85
Results similar for random effects		Yes		Yes		Yes		Yes

	Coefficient	t-ratio	Coefficient	t-ratio	Coefficient	t-ratio	Coefficient	t-ratio
Exchange rate overvaluation (in the previous period)	0.0000	2.35	0.0000	2.35	0.0000	2.26	0.0000	2.35
Change in M2 to reserves	0.0130	13.20	0.0131	13.39	0.0132	13.38	0.0130	13.11
Weak fundamentals	0.3085	2.36	0.3091	2.34	0.3174	2.36	0.3156	2.37
Export growth	−0.0146	−4.92	−0.0138	−4.56	−0.0132	−4.29	−0.0141	−4.68
Short-term debt to reserves	0.0007	2.75	0.0007	2.81	0.0007	2.71	0.0008	2.78
Real GDP growth	−0.0204	−2.14	−0.0212	−2.21	−0.0209	−2.15	−0.0193	−1.99
Actuarial deficit	0.0176	2.67	0.0133	1.98	0.0167	2.39	0.0215	3.12
Public external debt	0.0033	1.06					0.0007	0.21
Long-term debt			0.0149	3.05	0.0142	2.88		
Interest expenditure (in percent of GDP)[1]	0.0549	2.39	0.0461	2.07				
Interest payments (in percent of GDP)[2]					0.0474	2.07	0.0632	2.64
Constant	−0.3078	−1.92	−0.4206	−2.66	−0.4389	−2.74	−0.2725	−1.67

Source: Authors' calculations.
[1]Taken from the IMF's Government Finance Statistics (GFS) functional classification.
[2]Taken from GFS economic classification.

Appendix V   Case Studies

This appendix contains case studies of 11 emerging market crises of the 1990s: Mexico (1994–95); Argentina (1995); Bulgaria (1996–97); the Czech Republic (1997); Thailand (1997); Korea (1997); Pakistan (1998–99); Russia (1998); Ukraine (1998–2000); Brazil (1998–99); and Ecuador (1999).

Mexico, 1994–95

Background

Following the "lost decade" of the 1980s, Mexico's performance was generally impressive during the early 1990s. This was underpinned by a reform program launched in 1988, the main elements of which were a predetermined nominal exchange rate anchor, extensive privatization and deregulation, an opening to international competition, and a broad social and economic agreement on wages, key prices, and the exchange rate (the "Pacto"). The fiscal position improved considerably, and overall balance was achieved in 1992; this compared with a deficit of around 12 percent of GDP in 1987. Inflation fell from 160 percent in 1987 to single digits in 1993. Real growth picked up, averaging 2.8 percent between 1988 and 1994, although it varied considerably from year to year, and was on average below that in some neighboring countries such as Chile and Colombia. There were substantial capital inflows (6 percent of GDP in 1993, roughly one-fifth of all flows to developing countries, and mainly short term in nature), which resulted in a buildup of reserves, real exchange rate appreciation, and a growing current account deficit (up from 3 percent of GDP in 1989 to 7 percent of GDP in 1993).

How Did the Crisis Manifest Itself?

Capital outflows and pressures on the exchange rate emerged in early 1994, following political shocks (the Chiapas uprising and assassination of the PRI presidential candidate) and an increase in U.S. interest rates. The exchange rate depreciated to the top of the band, despite intervention that saw interest rates double from 9 percent to 18 percent. Since the authorities were reluctant to let interest rates rise further in an election year, rates were capped on domestic government paper (Cetes) and increased amounts of dollar-denominated debts (Tesobonos) were issued. In addition, reserve losses were sterilized and domestic credit expanded rapidly. Investor confidence largely returned until further political turmoil in October prompted a decline in the stock market and a resumption of outflows. Monetary policy was not tightened, and by mid-November reserves were far lower than public short-term debt. Interest rates were eventually allowed to increase in mid-December, but outflows continued and, with reserves falling lower than US$6 billion, the currency was floated (in December). The currency plummeted as investors doubted Mexico's ability to service its short-term dollar liabilities. An initial international rescue package of US$18.5 billion proved insufficient to restore confidence, and the situation deteriorated to the brink of default until the announcement of a US$50 billion package in January 1995. However, capital outflows and depreciation continued through March and the adjustment program had to be tightened further. This stemmed capital outflows but caused a sharp contraction in output that, combined with high real interest rates, led to severe strains on the banking system. The crisis resulted in the abandonment of the pegged exchange rate regime and a sharp devaluation, a run on government debt—although no default, and a banking crisis in 1995. GDP contracted by 7 percent in 1995.

What Were the Main Causes of the Crisis?

There is no consensus on the causes of the Mexican crisis, but the following hypotheses have been suggested in the literature:

- The use of the exchange rate as a nominal anchor, in the face of inflation inertia, led to overvaluation of the real exchange rate and unsustainable current account deficits. According to

APPENDIX V

this view (associated with Dornbusch, Goldfajn, and Valdés, 1995), a sharp exchange rate correction was inevitable at some point, and was triggered by the domestic and external shocks during 1994.

- Others, such as Ötker and Pazarbaşioğlu (1995), have put more emphasis on policy inconsistencies and mistakes during 1994: decisions to sterilize large interventions, to keep domestic interest rates low, and to avoid any fiscal tightening; large-scale conversion of domestic currency government debt into Tesobonos, intended to keep the monetary base stable and avoid an increase in interest rates (to avoid further difficulties in a fragile banking system) but which added to tensions in the exchange market; and a lack of transparency about the reserves position leading to a sudden loss of investor confidence.

- Some analyses, for example, Calomiris (1998), have emphasized the role of moral hazard related to expectations that the IMF would bail out loans by Mexican banks, thereby inducing capital inflows and risky lending by the banks.

- Related to this, and reinforced by developments in subsequent emerging market crises, other analyses of the Mexican crisis (e.g., Ghosh and others, 2002) have emphasized the role of financial sector fragilities and weak supervision, which prevented the efficient intermediation of capital inflows and led to firm-level vulnerabilities. Other balance sheet problems, primarily added vulnerability of the public sector balance sheet as a result of the switch into dollar-denominated debt, were also a contributing factor.

- Finally, the fact that the scale and timing of the crisis was largely unexpected has led many to interpret the Mexican crisis as self-fulfilling panic rather than "inevitable." The main sources of the problem are typically seen as the buildup of a large stock of foreign currency public debt of short maturity, and herding behavior in financial markets (e.g., Calvo and Mendoza, 1996; Cole and Kehoe, 1996; and Sachs, Tornell, and Velasco, 1996).

These various hypotheses, which are to some extent competing and to some extent overlapping, have been scrutinized in a number of papers by Gil-Diaz and Carstens (e.g., Gil-Diaz and Carstens, 1996a and 1996b). They found that explanations of the Mexican crisis that emphasize inappropriate policies and resulting misalignment of real phenomena do not hold up under careful analysis. While macroeconomic management could certainly have been improved, they conclude that the fundamental causes of the crisis were the politically triggered speculative attack on the pegged exchange rate regime, the large current account deficit (reflecting rapid credit expansion and not exchange rate overvaluation), and a sharp increase in U.S. interest rates.

What Was the Nature of Fiscal Vulnerabilities?

There is general agreement that fiscal policy was not the main cause of the crisis, at least in the sense of a persistent deficit undermining the pegged exchange rate as in the classic Krugman (1979) model. Most advocates of the "overvaluation" explanation agree that the dynamics were driven by the private sector and not by public sector deficits. That said, as noted above, some have argued that the failure to tighten fiscal policy in 1994, in response to the initial exchange market pressures, was a contributory factor to the crisis. In the same vein, Bléjer and del Castillo (1998) note the sharp increase in lending by state-owned development banks (not captured in conventional measures of the deficit at the time), which exacerbated the expansion of domestic credit in 1994. Taking a longer-term perspective, Kalter and Ribas (1999) argue that a significant increase in the level of government expenditure (financed by higher taxes and therefore not reflected in an increasing deficit) over 1987–94 raised production costs in the private sector. With a fixed exchange rate, the relative price of nontradables rose, as higher costs could be passed on in this sector but not in the tradable sector, contributing to the real appreciation.

Public sector debt, and its management, played a major role in the crisis. This was not so much related to the level of total debt, which had declined by some 40 percentage points of GDP between 1985 and 1994, but more to the reduction in average maturity during 1992–94, and hence continuous rollover pressures, the sharp increase in dollar-denominated debt in 1994, and the increase in short-term debt relative to reserves.

Fiscal Vulnerability Indicators

Table A5.1 reveals little or no indication of fiscal vulnerability: the deficit measure published by the authorities had been declining strongly since 1987 and was close to balance between 1991 and 1993; correspondingly, the ratio of public debt to GDP was falling over this period. The quarterly fiscal figures in Table A5.2 show that the fiscal position was deteriorating during 1994, but this deterioration was not dramatic. However, the official deficit measure understated the "true" deficit in several dimensions—it included privatization receipts as revenue, and excluded some investment expenditure and

Table A5.1. Mexico: Selected Fiscal Vulnerability Indicators (Annual)

	1991	1992	1993	1994	1995	1996	1997
(In percent of GDP)							
Traditional budget measures[1]							
Total revenue	25.8	26.1	25.8	22.7	22.3	22.9	23.0
Of which							
Petroleum revenue	3.1	3.0	2.9	2.2	3.5	4.2	3.9
Total expenditure	26.2	24.6	25.0	23.1	23.0	23.1	23.7
Of which							
Interest	4.6	4.1	4.2	2.3	4.6	4.4	4.1
Extrabudgetary balance	—	—	—	0.1	0.2	0.1	—
Adjustments	—	—	—	0.1	—	0.1	−0.1
Primary balance	4.1	5.5	3.5	2.1	4.1	4.4	3.3
Overall balance	−0.5	1.5	0.7	−0.2	−0.5	—	−0.8
Adjusted measure (authorities)[2]							
Primary balance	4.0	5.3	3.1	1.9	3.6	3.5	2.2
Overall balance	−1.4	0.3	−2.3	−3.5	−2.8	−3.7	−3.9
Augmented measure (IMF)[3]							
Overall balance	−1.4	0.3	−2.3	−3.5	−6.6	−11.0	−6.9
Public sector debt	43.1	33.6	30.9	35.8	54.0	54.4	51.2
Domestic	17.7	12.7	11.4	13.8	9.4	8.4	9.3
External	25.4	20.8	19.5	20.3	35.7	29.6	22.0
Bank restructuring and debtor support	—	—	—	1.7	8.9	16.4	19.9
(In percent of gross reserves)							
Total short-term debt	194.9	235.5	236.8	1,005.8	306.2	262.8	...
Of which							
Public sector	69.8	121.1	128.6	508.6	117.0	89.8	57.8
External debt	40.4	48.6	42.8	202.6	97.6	72.4	45.9
Nonresident holdings of treasury bills	29.3	72.5	85.7	306.0	19.4	17.3	11.5
(In percent of debt outstanding)							
Public debt repayable within five years	33.2	37.2	41.0	45.7	59.3	56.3	53.6
One year	8.6	11.7	13.1	15.2	14.5	13.5	8.3
Two–five years	24.6	25.5	27.9	30.5	44.9	42.8	45.3

Source: IMF.
[1] Authorities' definition.
[2] Excludes privatization receipts and unrealized valuation gains; includes inflation adjustment to indexed bonds, imputed interest cost of bank restructuring, and financial requirements of development banks.
[3] Adjusted to include net nonrecurrent capital costs of bank restructuring and debtor support.

quasi-fiscal activities—and an adjusted balance measure now published by the authorities shows a steady widening of the deficit during 1992–94. With the benefit of hindsight, it is apparent that more informative signals of impending problems were given by various debt indicators: note in particular the increase in the various ratios of short-term debt to reserves during 1994, and the steady shortening of the average maturity of public debt between 1991 and 1994.

The Mexican crisis caught the markets, and most analysts, by surprise. Risk measures based on interest differentials—the devaluation premium measured by the difference between interest rates on Cetes and Tesobonos, and the country risk premium measured by the difference between Tesobono and U.S. treasury bill rates—only increased sharply in the fourth quarter of 1994 (and, in fact, only in early December 1994; see Edwards (1997) and Table A5.2).

What Was the Fiscal Impact of the Crisis and How Did Fiscal Policy Respond?

The original intention was to target an improvement in the overall balance of 1 percent of GDP in 1995, based on reductions in noninterest spending. The main reason for this tightening was the acute short-term financing problem; medium-term debt

APPENDIX V

Table A5.2. Mexico: Selected Fiscal Vulnerability Indicators (Quarterly)
(In percent of GDP)

	1994				1995			
	Q1	Q2	Q3	Q4	Q1	Q2	Q3	Q4
Traditional budget measures[1]								
Total revenue	22.2	21.8	23.9	22.8	21.5	22.1	22.0	23.1
Of which								
Petroleum revenue	1.9	1.9	2.5	2.4	2.5	4.9	3.7	2.9
Total expenditure	22.3	20.7	24.0	25.0	20.7	21.6	19.9	28.3
Of which								
Interest	2.8	2.2	2.5	1.9	4.1	4.1	3.3	6.5
Extrabudgetary balance	0.6	0.1	0.1	−0.4	0.3	0.5	0.2	−0.1
Adjustments	0.6	−1.5	−0.3	1.6	1.2	0.1	−1.1	−0.3
Primary balance	3.9	1.9	2.2	0.9	6.4	5.2	4.5	0.9
Overall balance	1.1	−0.3	−0.3	−1.0	2.3	1.1	1.2	−5.6
Short-term interest rates								
(in percent, end of period)								
Cetes[2]	9.7	16.2	13.8	18.5	69.5	47.3	33.5	48.6
Tesobonos	4.4	7.0	6.0	6.3	16.2	n.a.	n.a.	n.a.
EMBI spread (basis points)	469	546	445	890	1,637	1,000	1,067	1,052
Foreign currency long-term debt rating								
Moody's	Ba2	Ba2	Ba2	Ba2	Ba2	Ba2	Ba2	Ba2
Standard & Poor's	BB+	BB+	BB+	BB+	BB	BB	BB	BB

Sources: IMF; and market information.
[1] Authorities' definition.
[2] Average of 28-day treasury bill rate.

sustainability was not a major concern. The targeted tightening was larger than necessary to stabilize the debt, but judged necessary to accommodate the carrying cost of financial sector restructuring (see Ghosh and others, 2002). However, market confidence was not restored and capital outflows continued during the first quarter of 1995. The primary balance target was tightened by a further 1 percent of GDP, based mainly on increases in the value-added tax (VAT) and further cuts in noninterest expenditure; this offset higher interest costs, leaving the target for the overall balance unchanged. At the same time, monetary policy was tightened and the official financing package strengthened. These measures were sufficient to stem capital outflows. The overall fiscal deficit was ½ percent of GDP in 1995, which represented a substantial tightening given the much sharper-than-anticipated fall in output. On the revenue side, shortfalls in VAT and import duties were offset by higher-than-expected oil revenues; on the spending side, higher interest payments were offset by delays in investment projects and cuts in social sector spending.

As regards public debt, the authorities managed to remain current on their obligations. The large stock of Tesobonos was amortized during 1995, and the government was able to return to international bond markets from mid-1995. The stock of external public debt was reduced sharply during 1995–97, though overall public debt increased as a result of the costs of restructuring the banking sector (around 9 percent of GDP).

At the structural level, significant reforms to tax administration were implemented during 1996–98. To improve the targeting of social expenditures and transfers, a program of direct cash benefits to the poor was introduced in 1997 to replace various price subsidies. However, a much-needed overhaul of tax policy made little progress in years following the crisis.

Argentina, 1995

Background

In 1991 Argentina launched a comprehensive stabilization plan, centered on the March 1991 "Convertibility Plan," which established a currency board and strict limits on central bank financing of the nonfinancial public sector and of financial institutions, including provincial banks. Other elements of the plan included trade reforms, the abolition of price controls, deregulation of wholesale and retail trade, privatization, and reforms to the financial sector.

A major effort to reduce discretionary spending, combined with a sharp reduction in interest payments, led to a dramatic improvement in the public finances through 1993. Annual inflation was reduced from nearly 5,000 percent at the end of 1989 to 3.7 percent by end-1994. The reforms led to a very fast pace of re-monetization, with bank deposits fueled by capital inflows allowing a rapid growth in bank credit. The government also eliminated arrears and restored access to domestic and international credit markets. The return of credibility, confidence, and foreign investment caused a sharp increase in GDP growth, which averaged close to 8 percent a year in real terms between 1991 and 1994, driven by consumption and investment in particular. A steady appreciation of the real exchange rate and a growing current account deficit, to almost 4 percent of GDP in 1994, accompanied the credit boom. Fiscal policy was loosened in 1994, reflecting a shift of employees' social security contributions to the private pension system, increased discretionary expenditure by the federal government, and a deterioration in provincial finances. As a result, the IMF program went off track in the second half of 1994. The public sector deficit reached 2.3 percent of GDP and public debt 32 percent of GDP by end-1994.

How Did the Crisis Manifest Itself?

A combination of factors toward the end of 1994—the growing current account and budget deficits, failure to adhere to an IMF-supported program, the prospect of elections in May 1995, and the Mexican crisis of December 1994—prompted investors to doubt the government's commitment to the exchange rate peg and the repayment of debt. Funds were withdrawn from banks and by foreign investors; this escalated sharply following the collapse of a small bond trader (heavily exposed to Mexican bonds) in January 1995, with large-scale withdrawals first from wholesale banks and then by retail depositors from weak provincial, cooperative, and small retail banks. Interest rates rose sharply (the interbank rate peaking at 70 percent, and peso and U.S. dollar loan rates at 40 percent and 19 percent, respectively, during March); the central bank's gross reserves fell by around one-third during the first quarter; and stock and bond markets fell by roughly one half between December 1994 and March 1995.

The authorities initially responded to the crisis by increasing assistance to the financial system as far as was consistent with the currency board arrangement. Reserve requirements on U.S. dollar and peso deposits were reduced; bank deposits at the central bank were dollarized in an attempt to give confidence to the markets; and a fund was set up to purchase nonperforming loans of distressed financial institutions. Despite these measures, deposit withdrawals and reserve losses continued, until the central bank's ratio of reserves to monetary liabilities approached the statutory ratio of 80 percent, in effect eliminating the scope for further central bank support for the financial system. In March 1995, the authorities announced details of an IMF-supported program with two main components: first, a fiscal tightening designed to demonstrate the government's commitment to servicing its debt obligations; second, the setting up of two new trust funds, capitalized by domestic and foreign loans, to provide resources for restructuring the financial sector. There was a positive market reaction, with interest rates falling sharply, and in April Argentina was able to place two US$1 billion bond issues with domestic and foreign investors, respectively.

Despite a return of deposits and capital inflows during the remainder of 1995, credit to the private sector remained tight as banks sought to rebuild their liquidity positions while increasing lending to the public sector. This contributed to a significant decline in economic activity, with GDP falling by 3 percent in 1995 as a whole, and unemployment jumping from 12.2 percent in October 1994 to 18.6 percent in May 1995.

Overall, therefore, the crisis was characterized by a sharp reversal of capital flows, leading to a dramatic fall in reserves, although the peg to the dollar was maintained; large withdrawals of deposits, almost pushing the banking system into crisis, which in the event was avoided because the banks were able to withstand a period of high interest rates and because the authorities acted promptly; and a sharp fall in GDP. Debt default and restructuring were avoided.

What Were the Main Causes of the Crisis?

Although the Argentine crisis has generated less controversy regarding its causes than the Mexican crisis, different studies have nonetheless emphasized different factors:

- Radelet and Sachs (1998) emphasize illiquidity—in the sense that short-term liabilities to foreigners exceeded short-term assets—as the key vulnerability. They argue that the same vulnerability was the source of the Mexican crisis of late 1994–95, although most of the debt to foreign banks was owed by the bank and nonbank private sector.

APPENDIX V

- Choueiri and Kaminsky (1999) put more emphasis on international contagion to explain the crisis. They find evidence that the shift to a contractionary monetary stance in the United States during 1994 was a major factor precipitating the Mexican crisis, which in turn was transmitted to Argentina through common bank creditors and cross-market hedging.

- Underlying both these explanations is Argentina's heavy reliance on external sources of finance, and hence vulnerability to shifts of sentiment in international capital markets.

- García-Herrero (1997) emphasizes weaknesses in the banking system. Although improved supervision and regulation during the early 1990s made the financial sector more resilient, problems remained among the provincial banks. They continued to be used to finance the deficits of provincial governments (which, unlike the federal deficit, had not decreased during the early 1990s) and were poorly managed, leading to a large volume of underperforming loans. This undermined confidence, which was already low following a history of banking crises. Balance sheet mismatches also emerged, with increasing issuance of dollar-denominated credit and a declining maturity of peso and dollar deposits. The run on deposits caught several provincial and small private banks short of liquidity, and the ensuing contagion spread to other (apparently solvent) banks.

- While the currency board arrangement was in some respects a source of credibility and stability, certain aspects of the regime added to vulnerability: it reduced the scope for the central bank to cushion the impact of capital outflows on the banking system; it precluded the option of using inflation to shrink bank balance sheets through devaluation; and it tightened the financing constraint on the government, leading to heavy reliance on external funding and the possibility of rollover problems.

- Finally, traditional macroeconomic disequilibria were increasingly evident in the run-up to the crisis. The real exchange rate appreciated by 13 percent in 1992 and 12 percent in 1993; the current account deficit widened from 2.8 percent of GDP in 1992 to 4.3 percent of GDP in 1992; and the fiscal position deteriorated in 1994 (discussed further below).

What Was the Nature of Fiscal Vulnerabilities?

Most analyses of the crisis in Argentina in 1995 do not put fiscal issues center stage, although they acknowledge that it was a contributory factor. With the improvement in the deficit during the early 1990s and reduction in the debt-to-GDP ratio through 1993, there were no long-standing concerns about fiscal sustainability. However, the increase in the deficit in 1994, reflecting higher spending at the federal and provincial levels, and subsequent break with the IMF, raised doubts about the commitment to the exchange rate peg, especially given the proximity of presidential elections due in 1995 and Argentina's recent history of hyperinflation. Moreover, it seems clear (at least with hindsight) that the economy was growing at an unsustainable rate in 1992–93, and hence that the fiscal stance was more expansionary than implied by the headline numbers. In addition, the very positive market reaction to the IMF-supported program that took effect in March 1995, with fiscal tightening as a major component, points to the importance of fiscal problems in causing the crisis.

As mentioned above, the currency board constraints on monetary financing, combined with underdeveloped domestic capital markets and a heavy reliance on external borrowing, made the financing of even a relatively small deficit a potential source of vulnerability. Difficulty in rolling over public debt in March 1995 was a major reason that fiscal policy needed to be tightened. That said, the authorities managed to avoid the severe debt management problems that were at the core of the Mexican crisis.

There were two main structural fiscal weaknesses underlying the crisis of 1995. The first related to intergovernmental fiscal relations. Through revenue-sharing agreements, the provinces benefited from the strong improvement in federal revenue collection in the early 1990s, but did not reduce their deficits or improve their own revenue effort. Wages made up around 50 percent of provincial expenditure, a legacy of the 1980s when provincial governments operated as an employer of last resort. The second was the rigidity of expenditure: nondiscretionary pensions and transfers to provinces constituted two-thirds of federal spending.

Fiscal Vulnerability Indicators

The deterioration in the fiscal position in 1994 is evident from the increase in expenditure and also in the fiscal impulse estimates shown in Table A5.3, although the latter were produced after the crisis. But there is little indication of sustainability problems in the public debt figures prior to the crisis. Some higher frequency market-based indicators are shown in Table A5.4. Both short-term interest rates and spreads on foreign currency borrowings increased sharply during the fourth quarter of 1994. Sovereign debt ratings were unchanged throughout 1994 and 1995.

Table A5.3. Argentina: Selected Fiscal Vulnerability Indicators (Annual)

	1991	1992	1993	1994	1995	1996	1997
	(In percent of GDP)						
Consolidated public sector operations							
Revenue	18.8	17.1	17.4	17.3	23.2	22.1	23.1
Total tax revenue	...	11.7	11.4	11.4	15.6	15.8	16.8
Social security contributions	...	4.3	4.6	4.8	5.3	4.4	4.2
Other revenues	...	1.1	1.4	1.1	2.3	1.9	2.1
Expenditure	22.0	17.3	16.5	17.7	25.5	23.2	22.8
Of which							
Interest	2.6	1.5	1.1	1.2	1.9	2.1	2.3
Overall balance	−3.2	−0.2	0.9	−0.4	−2.3	−1.1	0.3
Primary balance	−5.8	−1.7	−0.2	−1.6	−4.2	−3.2	−2.0
Fiscal impulse[1]	...	...	0.5	1.5	−0.9	−0.3	−0.5
Public sector debt	35.7	30.3	30.1	32.1	37.0	38.5	37.4
Federal government	32.4	27.5	27.0	28.4	31.8	33.1	32.0
Provinces	3.3	2.8	3.1	3.7	5.2	5.4	5.4
	(In billions of U.S. dollars)						
Public sector debt	58.4	59.1	67.8	79.5	89.7	99.7	101.1
Local currency	1.2	0.7	5.9	7.3	6.7	10.7	10.7
Foreign currency	57.2	58.4	61.9	72.2	83.0	89.0	90.4
External debt	57.2	57.4	60.3	69.6	68.2	72.5	74.8
Domestic debt	—	1.0	1.6	2.6	14.8	16.5	15.6

Sources: IMF; and Argentine authorities.
[1]The annual change in the fiscal stance; the latter is the difference between the actual fiscal balance and an estimate of the cyclically adjusted balance.

Table A5.4. Argentina: Selected Fiscal Vulnerability Indicators (Quarterly)

	1994				1995			
	Q1	Q2	Q3	Q4	Q1	Q2	Q3	Q4
Short-term interest rate (in percent, end of period)[1]	5.59	6.07	5.47	19.71	13.69	7.28	7.28	8.49
Spreads on foreign currency debt (basis points)[2]	768	791	712	1,141	1,509	1,248	1,254	962
Foreign currency debt rating								
Moody's	B1	B1	B1	B1	B1	B1	B1	B1
Standard & Poor's	BB−	BB−	BB−	BB−	BB−	BB−	BB−	BB−

Source: Market information.
[1]Seven-day interbank peso rate (mid-rate).
[2]From JP Morgan EMBI.

What Was the Fiscal Impact of the Crisis and How Did Fiscal Policy Respond?

Fiscal measures were at the heart of the IMF-supported reforms announced in March 1995. They were expected to yield 2 percent of GDP in 1995 and included a temporary increase in VAT and broad-based cuts in expenditure (worth an estimated 0.7 percent of GDP). The reaction to announcement of these measures was favorable, and sufficient to mobilize funds from international financial institutions and the private sector to enable the government to meet its debt-service obligations, capitalize two funds set up to restructure the banking system, and rebuild international reserves. Provincial finances improved in 1995 and 1996, due to increased privatization receipts, shifts in pension liabilities to the federal government, and increased transfers. However, the overall fiscal deficit in fact widened in 1995, due to the sharp fall in revenues following the contraction in economic activity; adjusted for this, the fiscal stance was tightened in 1995 (and broadly neutral in 1996). The debt-to-GDP ratio increased in the years following the crisis, reflecting the deficit in 1995 and the costs of financial sector restructuring, although widespread sustainability concerns did not arise until the late 1990s. Finally, no significant structural fiscal reforms were implemented in the two to three years following the 1995 crisis.

Bulgaria, 1996–97

Background

Bulgaria's economic performance in the 1990s was weaker than in most other transition countries in the region. Between 1990 and 1997, real output declined by a cumulative 37 percent, and inflation remained in high double and even triple digits. The origins of this poor performance can be found in the difficult initial conditions inherited from the communist era. In the second half of the 1980s, the country substantially increased its debt burden through large external borrowing, both official and private. In the early 1990s, there were major disruptions associated with the start of transition, and external shocks in the form of the collapse of markets in member countries of the Council for Mutual Economic Assistance and the crises in the Middle East and former Yugoslavia. This combination of factors proved too much for a succession of weak and fractured governments, which failed to achieve a durable stabilization and proved unwilling to tackle deep-rooted structural problems. In particular, the failure to establish market discipline fostered a rent-seeking culture of soft budget constraints that affected public finances. Some time was bought by external debt rescheduling in 1994, although this was offset by bank recapitalization operations. Meanwhile, asset-stripping of state-owned enterprises and banks continued throughout the 1990s, adding to public debt levels and undermining an already weak banking system.

How Did the Crisis Manifest Itself?

Bulgaria had tried to use a fixed exchange rate as a nominal anchor, but the continuing flow of funds to insolvent banks led to a collapse in official reserves. A last-ditch attempt at stabilization was made in mid-1996. A money-based stabilization was chosen, as official reserves were deemed insufficient and the banking sector too weak to support the exchange rate as a nominal anchor. However, the demand for real money continued to decline rapidly, and a lack of credibility precluded the authorities from gathering sufficient external financing. Delays in enterprise restructuring combined with a loss of confidence in the banking system[56] led to the collapse of the stabilization program after only a few months. The ensuing sharp increase in interest rates turned out to be fiscally unsustainable, and could not halt the collapse of money demand and capital flight. An increasing awareness of the scale of bank insolvency—prompted in part by the government's decision to introduce a limited deposit insurance scheme—and skepticism concerning the government's ability to meet its debt-service obligations led to fears that foreign exchange deposits would be blocked. Speculation mounted against the lev, as depositors withdrew funds. Even solvent banks were not immune to the panic. The exchange rate, which had been relatively stable at 70 leva per US$1 at the end of 1995, plummeted to almost 500 leva per US$1 a year later.

The government fell in December 1996; subsequent political instability led to a full-blown crisis—a collapse of output, a rapidly depreciating currency (reaching 2,000 leva per U.S. dollar), and annual inflation approaching 2,000 percent (fueled by liquidity injections to support the banking sector, central bank financing of the budget deficit, and a precipitous fall in money demand). Real GDP declined by 11 percent in 1996, and a further 7 percent in 1997. However, there was no default on government debt.

The caretaker government that was formed in February 1997 decided to implement a stabilization strategy underpinned by a currency board arrangement. With IMF support, the currency board was put in place on July 1, 1997. This succeeded in restoring confidence, and GDP growth turned positive within a year while inflation remained low.

What Were the Main Causes of the Crisis?

Essentially, poor policies—rather than adverse shocks or a self-fulfilling panic—were the cause of the crisis. In addition to long-standing political un-

---

[56]Nine out of the 10 state banks (which accounted for more than 80 percent of banking sector assets) had negative capital, and more than half of all state banks' portfolios were nonperforming. About half of the private banks, among them the largest, were also technically insolvent.

willingness or inability to tackle deep-rooted structural and governance problems, the crisis arose from skepticism about the ability of the government to meet its obligations, especially debt service, combined with increasing insolvency in the banking system.

- A secular decline in revenue and rising debt-service costs, exacerbated by the government repeatedly assuming nonperforming loans of state-owned banks, led to an unsustainable fiscal position. This is discussed more fully below.

- The roots of the problems in the banking sector lay in the nonperforming loans inherited from central planning and extended in the early 1990s—quasi-fiscal support that bypassed the budget. In the absence of structural reforms, state-owned enterprises continued to be unable to service debts and state-owned banks continued to roll over outstanding credits, while capitalizing interest payments. Private banks were established in the early 1990s under a lax regulatory regime; a close connection between management and debtors emerged, and nonperforming loans rose dramatically. More generally, weak governance facilitated asset-stripping and insider lending by private banks; this was compounded by ineffective recapitalization and general economic instability.

- Given the banking crisis, the authorities were unable to respond appropriately to the pressures facing the lev. They continued to extend loans to ailing banks, while higher interest rates only served to weaken banks further, requiring additional liquidity injections.

What Was the Nature of Fiscal Vulnerabilities?

First, in common with many transition economies, Bulgaria experienced a secular decline in tax revenues in the early 1990s. The decline was temporarily reversed in 1994 due to the introduction of VAT and a jump in company profitability. But revenue fell by 4 percentage points of GDP in 1995 despite favorable macroeconomic developments. The decline was due to the inability of the tax administration to deal with high inflation rates (collection lags leading to a real loss in revenues), deteriorating compliance, and a decline in nontax revenues because of a fall in central bank profits as it supported ailing banks.

Second, partly as a result of the deteriorating macrofiscal situation, directed lending to state-owned enterprises increased during the 1990s. Combined with lax supervision and a tradition of nonrepayment on the part of borrowers, this led to the growth of nonperforming loans in bank portfolios.

Third, Bulgaria faced volatile and ultimately unsustainable public debt dynamics. The position in the early years of transition was strained due to high levels of communist era debt, a sharp contraction in real GDP, real exchange rate depreciation, and extensive bank recapitalization. During 1996, inflation eroded the domestic component of public debt, but depreciation of the lev raised the burden of external debt, which was then compounded by falling revenues and declining real output. Doubts about debt sustainability prevented Bulgaria from accessing international capital markets at this time, and official lending was intermittent, which meant that external debt could be serviced only by severe expenditure compression.

Finally, attempts to increase the primary surplus by squeezing discretionary expenditure proved unsustainable. In the third quarter of 1996, a primary surplus of 9 percent of GDP coexisted with an overall deficit of 16 percent of GDP. Monthly public sector wages and pensions were cut to US$25 and US$11, respectively; many embassies in Sofia opened soup kitchens. Expenditure arrears also proliferated, which in turn led to increasing revenue arrears (reaching 5 percent of GDP in the first quarter of 1997).

Fiscal Vulnerability Indicators

The main elements of the fiscal vulnerabilities described above were strikingly evident in standard fiscal indicators (Table A5.5): falling revenues, mushrooming interest expenditures, contracting discretionary spending, a rapidly growing overall deficit, and increasing external debt. It is also clear that this was a very different type of crisis to that experienced by Mexico in 1994–95, with short-term debt remaining a very small share of overall debt. Growing problems were also evident in domestic short-term interest rates, although not in Brady bond spreads, perhaps reflecting the commitment to remain current on external obligations.

What Was the Fiscal Impact of the Crisis and How Did Fiscal Policy Respond?

One immediate impact of the banking crisis was on government debt markets. Participation in these markets declined precipitously at the height of the crisis, as even those banks with adequate liquidity feared further deposit withdrawals and preferred to retain cash balances. This threatened to paralyze government debt markets and required massive liquidity injections by the central bank (see Enoch, Gulde, and Hardy, 2002).

APPENDIX V

Table A5.5. Bulgaria: Selected Fiscal Vulnerability Indicators
(In percent of GDP, unless otherwise indicated)

	1994	1995	1996					1997					1998
			Q1	Q2	Q3	Q4	Annual	Q1	Q2	Q3	Q4	Annual	
General government													
Revenue	39.9	36.1	27.7	36.4	31.5	33.5	32.6	19.3	29.7	30.7	39.7	31.6	36.8
Expenditure	45.7	42.4	38.3	47.9	40.9	49.5	45.2	31.2	30.5	31.8	40.5	34.1	35.8
Of which													
Interest	13.5	14.6	14.0	14.3	20.4	25.1	20.3	19.5	9.9	8.9	1.7	8.4	4.4
Overall balance	−5.8	−6.3	−10.6	−11.5	−9.5	−16.1	−12.7	−11.9	−0.9	−1.1	−0.8	−2.5	1.0
Primary balance	7.7	8.3	3.4	2.8	10.9	9.1	7.7	7.6	9.1	7.8	0.9	5.9	5.4
Total debt	140.2	100.9	95.1	110.5	114.8	119.1	105.8	139.2	122.9	110.6	104.1	104.1	79.7
Domestic debt	42.7	37.3	35.3	30.5	29.0	24.7	22.0	22.2	26.1	23.1	24.3	23.3	20.3
Lev-denominated debt	24.1	29.9	28.3	20.8	18.2	12.9	11.5	7.7	6.5	5.5	5.3	5.3	4.8
Direct credit			8.7	6.5	5.1	3.3		1.2	0.6	0.4	0.8		
Deficit financing			19.6	14.3	13.1	9.7		6.5	5.9	5.1	4.5		
SDR-denominated debt	0.0	0.0	0.0	0.0	0.0	0.0	0.0	0.0	0.0	6.8	9.0	9.0	8.0
U.S. dollar-denominated debt	18.6	7.4	7.0	9.7	10.8	11.8	10.5	14.5	11.7	10.8	10.1	10.1	7.6
External debt	97.5	63.7	59.8	80.0	85.8	94.3	83.8	117.0	96.9	87.6	79.8	79.8	59.4
Total external debt	117.0	77.0	...	...	...	...	97.0	...	...	...	...	96.0	82.0
Of which													
Short-term debt	4.0	1.0	...	...	...	...	1.0	...	...	...	...	4.0	2.0
Short-term interest rate													
(in percent, end of period)[1]	101.2	39.8	59.9	181.3	264.1	435.0	n.a.	628.8	42.7	6.3	7.0	n.a.	5.2
EMBI spread (basis points)	1,690	1,347	1,480	1,391	1,452	1,212	n.a.	1,071	642	463	622	n.a.	850
Foreign currency long-term debt rating[2]	...	...	...	...	B3	B3	n.a.	B3	B3	B3	B2	n.a.	B2

Sources: IMF; and market information.
[1]Bulgarian National Bank basic rate.
[2]Moody's; Standard & Poor's only rated Bulgaria from November 1998.

As regards fiscal policy more generally, the government responded to the emerging crisis by reducing noninterest expenditure. But, as described above, this became increasingly difficult during 1996. Administered prices for energy, utilities, and transportation were also increased. Following the decision to adopt a currency board arrangement in February 1997, inflation and real interest rates fell rapidly. The 1997 budget emphasized short-term tax administration measures to bolster revenue. On the expenditure side, the key measure was a reduction in public sector employment by 58,000. In an effort to improve transparency, the budget also included an expenditure contingency of 0.7 percent of GDP to cover potential subsidy and bank bailout costs. Toward the end of 1997, revenues rebounded sharply and interest costs declined dramatically, reflecting the erosion of lev-denominated debt and lower nominal interest rates. This permitted a recovery of noninterest expenditure to more adequate levels. The outturn for 1997 was an overall deficit of 2.5 percent of GDP, which was better than budgeted.

A number of structural fiscal reforms were introduced in 1997 and subsequent years, designed in particular to address weaknesses in tax administration and public expenditure management, to broaden the tax base while lowering marginal rates, and to improve fiscal transparency. The success of these measures was reflected in the first post-communist era overall budget surplus being recorded in 1998, and deficits under 1 percent of GDP since.

Czech Republic, 1997

Background

Following the adoption of an exchange rate peg in 1991, inflation was rapidly reduced, to below 10 percent by 1994; growth turned positive in 1994 and accelerated during 1995. However, macroeconomic imbalances built up during the mid-1990s, with large capital inflows that complicated monetary management and spurred credit growth. Combined with excessive wage increases in the state enterprise sector, this fueled inflation and overheated the economy. The resulting loss of competitiveness and boom in domestic demand led to a widening current account deficit, which reached 8 percent of GDP in 1996. The fiscal deficit increased slightly, to above 2 percent of GDP. In response to these pressures, the government initially widened the exchange rate band in early 1996 and increased interest rates. This then led to further real appreciation and a marked deceleration in growth.

How Did the Crisis Manifest Itself?

In March 1997 concerns about the current account, combined with the government's public calls for a looser monetary policy, led to a worsening of investor sentiment and a turnaround in capital inflows; contagion from Asia exacerbated these pressures. To counter this, in April 1997, the government announced expenditure cuts of 1¾ percent of GDP and, later in May, a second round of cuts of ¾ percent of GDP. Despite these efforts, there was a speculative attack in mid-May. This was initially countered by a sharp increase in interest rates and unsustainable foreign exchange intervention by the central bank. The government was, however, soon forced to abandon the exchange rate peg in May, which was followed by a 12 percent depreciation. The resulting period of monetary turbulence was short-lived, and its impact on the economy was contained. However, pressures emerged again in the last quarter of 1997, as a result of political uncertainties and further contagion from the Asian crisis. High interest rates (coinciding with extensive flooding) caused the economy to slow significantly in 1997 which, combined with the depreciation, caused the external balance to improve by the second half of the year.

The speculative attack was not accompanied by a banking sector crisis. Although, like most former communist countries in the early years of transition, the solvency of banks was questionable and there was insufficient emphasis on supervision, banks typically had limited exposure to foreign exchange movements and liquidity risks. Nevertheless, the economic slowdown and high real interest rates did adversely affect the quality of the banks' loan portfolios.

What Were the Main Causes of the Crisis?

Begg (1998) reviews several competing explanations for the crisis. One possibility is that the real exchange rate appreciation experienced during 1991–96 caused the economy to become uncompetitive and the external position to become unsustainable. He cites evidence—unit wage costs substantially above productivity growth and slowing export growth—which suggests that while the real exchange rate had not reached an unsustainable level, the trend was clearly in that direction. On the other hand, the real exchange rate returned to its precrisis level within a year of the crisis, suggesting that it was not fundamentally overvalued before the crisis.

A related possibility is that solvency was deteriorating. Since the public finances were close to bal-

APPENDIX V

ance—at least using the data available at the time—Begg argues that the relevant measure is external solvency. The enormous capital inflows during the mid-1990s were premised on the expectation of successful and continued structural adjustment; they were therefore vulnerable to changes in expectations about the commitment to reform. Moreover, because a large share of imports of capital goods were for infrastructure projects with long gestation periods, any positive impact on productivity or competitiveness was slow to materialize. But, in the meantime, competitiveness and solvency were deteriorating and the policy mix was unbalanced.

The third element was government policy. Despite the overheating of the economy in 1996, political constraints made the government unwilling to countenance a fiscal tightening as a response to pressure on the currency. This forced a monetary policy response that increased further the capital inflow problem and resulted in an unsustainable fiscal-monetary policy mix. In addition to this fundamental policy inconsistency, there was political uncertainty at home, weak governance of state enterprises—with a lack of corporate restructuring leading to high wage increases—and poor lending practices by state-controlled banks softening the budget constraints of the corporate sector.

Begg concludes that the combination of these three factors, together with contagion from Asia, ultimately caused foreign investors to lose their nerve.

What Was the Nature of Fiscal Vulnerabilities?

The primary fiscal problem reflected political opposition to a sufficiently large fiscal adjustment to avert the collapse of the exchange rate peg. Since the budget did not have a large deficit, a move toward a fiscal surplus would have eased overheating and pressures on monetary policy, reduced the costs of sterilized intervention, and lowered vulnerability to capital outflows. It is also important to note that the reported fiscal figures understated fiscal activity in two important respects. First, there was substantial expenditure through off-budget institutions (such as Konsolidacni Banka and the National Property Fund). Brixi, Ghanem, and Islam (1999) estimate these to have added 3 percent to the deficit in 1993, although declining to around 1 percent of GDP by 1997. Second, implicit liabilities were incurred via the banking system. Privatization receipts were frequently pledged as collateral for guarantees to banks for loans to ailing enterprises that the government was keen to support. These guarantees reached over 15 percent of GDP in 1997; and they had a subsidy element that added 1 percent of GDP to expenditure in 1996, 3 percent of GDP in 1997, and 1.5 percent of GDP in 1998.

Fiscal Vulnerability Indicators

Three points can be made about the indicators shown in Table A5.6. First, data on the central government, which was typically available on a more timely basis than more comprehensive measures of the deficit, implied that the fiscal position was stronger than it would have been had the finances of local governments and extrabudgetary funds, as well as the off-budget spending and contingent liabilities mentioned above, been considered. Official figures also treated depletion of the Privatization Fund as revenue rather than financing. Second, figures on tax arrears indicate growing difficulties in tax administration (VAT accounts for around half of the total). Third, the rising proportion of central government expenditure on mandatory social insurance transfers to households—from 37 percent of the total in 1995 to 42 percent in 1997—points to increasing rigidity on the expenditure side.

What Was the Fiscal Impact of the Crisis and How Did Fiscal Policy Respond?

Following the crisis there was a strong adjustment in the fiscal position, primarily through lower discretionary spending, that contained the deficit to 2 percent of GDP, despite significant increased spending on the floods. The tight fiscal stance was maintained through most of 1998—in the 1998 budget, corporate tax rates were reduced, while indirect taxes were raised, government wages were frozen, and discretionary spending was reduced—which contributed to a reduction in the current account deficit and low inflation. However, the tightening of both fiscal and monetary policy caused the 1997 slowdown to become a severe recession in 1998. As a result, by late 1998 fiscal and monetary policies were eased and the 1999 budget was reoriented to stimulate growth. The deficit was increased to accommodate higher capital spending, real wage increases to government employees, and higher transfers to the enterprise sector (to mitigate the impact of the economic downturn). The deficit grew further in 2000 and 2001 which, combined with medium-term pressures related to accession to the European Union and financial sector restructuring, raised some concerns about the sustainability of fiscal policy.

Finally, the crisis was accompanied by, and may indeed have prompted, some important structural reforms aimed at improving fiscal transparency:

Table A5.6. Czech Republic: Selected Fiscal Vulnerability Indicators
(In percent of GDP, unless otherwise indicated)

	1995	1996	1997	1998
General government				
Revenue	40.4	39.7	39.5	39.1
Expenditure	42.5	41.8	41.4	41.4
Of which				
Interest	1.1	1.0	1.2	1.2
Overall balance (cash)	−2.1	−2.1	−1.9	−2.3
Primary balance	−1.0	−1.1	−0.7	−1.1
Central government				
Revenue[1]	32.2	30.3	29.7	29.1
Expenditure	31.7	30.4	30.7	30.7
Of which				
Social insurance transfers	11.8	12.0	13.0	12.3
Interest	1.0	0.9	1.1	1.1
Overall balance (cash)	0.5	−0.1	−0.9	−1.6
Primary balance	1.5	0.8	0.2	−0.5
Total debt	11.2	9.9	10.3	10.7
Total loan guarantees	...	13.1	17.0	17.0
Tax arrears	1.7	2.3	2.6	...
Short-term interest rate				
(in percent, end of period)[1]	11.2	12.6	16.7	10.6
Foreign currency debt rating				
Moody's	Baa1	Baa1	Baa1	Baa1
Standard & Poor's	A	A	A	A−

Sources: IMF; and maket information.
[1]Seven-day interbank rate.

- A resolution was passed in February 1998 requiring that hidden debts and liabilities be included in budget documentation.

- Rules on government guarantees were tightened, with each guarantee requiring a separate law.

- Budgetary decisions became set in a medium-term framework.

Thailand, 1997

Background

Thailand grew rapidly in the decade leading up to the crisis; between 1987–95, its growth rate averaged 10 percent a year. In tandem with this high growth, net capital inflows averaged an annual 10 percent of GDP during these years. These inflows did not give rise to concern in light of the stable macroeconomic situation, high growth, and the fact that the inflows were financing investment (which grew at an average 20 percent a year) rather than consumption. However, aggressive deregulation in the early 1990s combined with buoyant capital inflows to create asset bubbles, especially in the real estate sector and stock market. In 1996, Thailand experienced slowing export growth, as a result of an overvalued exchange rate (exacerbated by the rise in the U.S. dollar to which the baht was pegged), weakening demand in export markets, and a sharp decline in the prices of key exports. This led to a widening current account deficit, to almost 8 percent of GDP.

How Did the Crisis Manifest Itself?

The combination of an overvalued exchange rate, large current account deficit, and adverse terms of trade shocks led to mounting pressures on the baht during 1997. Reserve money growth increased sharply as the central bank provided liquidity support for ailing financial institutions. The policy response was centered on interventions in the foreign exchange market, the introduction of capital con-

Table A5.7. Thailand: Selected Fiscal Vulnerability Indicators (Annual)

	1994/95[1]	1995/96	1996/97	1997/98	1998/99	1999/2000
	(In percent of fiscal year GDP)					
Consolidated nonfinancial public sector						
Revenue and grants	23.5	23.6	22.0	20.0	19.4	20.0
Expenditure	20.7	20.8	25.3	28.5	31.7	24.0
Of which						
Interest[2]	0.3	0.2	0.3	0.2	1.0	1.2
Capital	9.5	9.5	13.3	15.5	16.7	9.0
Overall balance	2.7	2.8	−3.2	−8.4	−12.3	−4.1
Public sector debt[3]	11.4	14.5	36.3	45.3	55.5	57.9
Domestic	4.3	5.4	5.7	10.3	20.0	23.9
External	7.1	7.8	11.6	13.9	17.8	17.9
Bank restructuring/debtor support	—	1.3	19.0	21.1	17.7	16.1
	(In billions of U.S. dollars, calendar year)					
Total external debt	100.8	108.7	109.3	105.1	95.1	79.7
Short term	52.4	47.7	38.3	28.4	19.5	14.7
Medium and long term	48.4	61.0	71.0	76.6	75.5	65.0
Of which						
Public sector	16.3	16.7	24.1	31.6	36.2	33.9

Source: IMF.
[1] The fiscal year runs October 1–September 30.
[2] For central government only.
[3] Figures for 1994/95 refer to central government only.

trols, and minor fiscal tightening. But following a series of speculative attacks, and difficulties in rolling over short-term debt, the baht was floated in July 1997. However, the accompanying policy package failed to inspire credibility and the baht depreciated 20 percent against the U.S. dollar in July alone.

In August 1997, the IMF approved a three-year Stand-By Arrangement amounting to US$4 billion, with additional financing worth US$13 billion. Key elements of the package included financial restructuring (with closure of insolvent financial institutions), significant fiscal adjustment (amounting to 3 percent of GDP), and control of domestic credit. But the baht continued on its downward path and the government continued to find it difficult to roll over its short-term debt. Political uncertainty, coupled with delays in introducing necessary structural reforms, undermined market confidence in the package. Furthermore, the downturn proved to be steeper than anticipated: excess capacity built up in the 10 years preceding the crisis led to a sharp fall in gross investment and to a rapid increase in unemployment rates. A new government took office in November, strengthened the program, and announced additional fiscal measures. The baht finally began to strengthen in February 1998 as market confidence improved and regional growth rebounded.

What Were the Main Causes of the Crisis?

The vulnerabilities that exposed Thailand to a shift in market sentiment were primarily in the private sector. Large capital inflows were used to accumulate low-quality loans in banks and other financial intermediaries. Financial weakness, arising from inadequate regulation and supervision, combined with weak governance, caused this misallocation of credit and inflated asset prices. Large unhedged private short-term foreign currency debt (encouraged by a variety of special facilities and the implicit guarantee of the exchange rate peg) increased the risk of self-fulfilling liquidity attacks, and created exchange rate exposure. The macroeconomic weakening in 1996 exacerbated the deteriorating asset portfolio, making underlying financial sector problems increasingly evident. Furthermore, these problems made it harder for the authorities to use interest rates to defend the exchange rate, leading to credibility problems.

Appendix V

Table A5.8. Thailand: Selected Fiscal Vulnerability Indicators (Quarterly)
(In percent of GDP, unless otherwise indicated)

	1995/96				1996/97				1997/98			
	Q1	Q2	Q3	Q4	Q1	Q2	Q3	Q4	Q1	Q2	Q3	Q4
Central government												
Revenue	15.3	17.7	22.3	21.6	14.1	18.4	20.9	18.5	14.0	15.9	18.3	14.2
Expenditure	13.6	16.9	16.8	20.1	18.0	22.8	19.0	20.5	16.5	15.7	17.4	22.3
Of which												
Interest	0.3	0.2	0.3	0.2	0.2	0.6	0.1	0.4	0.2	0.1	0.2	0.2
Budgetary balance	1.7	0.8	5.5	1.5	–4.0	–4.4	1.9	–2.0	–2.5	0.2	0.9	–8.1
Nonbudgetary balance	0.0	1.1	–0.4	–0.3	0.4	0.4	0.0	0.4	0.4	–0.2	–0.3	–0.5
Total budgetary balance	1.7	1.9	5.1	1.2	–3.6	–4.0	1.8	–1.7	–2.2	0.0	0.6	–8.6
Primary balance	2.0	2.1	5.4	1.3	–3.4	–3.4	2.0	–1.3	–2.0	0.2	0.8	–8.3
Total debt	...	...	...	...	14.7	14.7	16.2	20.1	26.5	23.2	40.9	45.1
Domestic	5.9	5.1	4.5	4.5	3.7	3.6	3.5	3.0	2.6	2.3	15.9	20.4
Of which												
Short term	3.8	3.7	2.7	2.6	2.5	2.5	2.5	2.2	2.0	2.0	1.8	1.6
External	...	...	...	...	11.0	11.2	12.7	17.1	23.9	20.9	25.0	24.7
Short-term interest rate (in percent)[1]	11.2	6.0	8.5	11.7	9.7	8.3	15.1	23.9	21.7	20.6	18.6	7.2
EMBI spread (basis points)	...	...	...	...	...	...	...	...	398	240	394	555
Foreign currency long-term debt rating												
Moody's	A2	A2	A2	A2	A2	A2	A3	A3	Ba1	Ba1	Ba1	Ba1
Standard & Poor's	A	A	A	A	A	A	A	A–	BBB	BBB–	BBB–	BBB–

Sources: IMF; Thai authorities; and market information.
[1]Interbank lending rates.

What Was the Nature of Fiscal Vulnerabilities?

Prior to the crisis, public finances were apparently sound. Low debt ratios were accompanied by a series of fiscal surpluses or modest deficits. Standard statistics, however, did not reflect large contingent liabilities, both implicit and explicit, associated with government guarantees granted to weak and poorly supervised financial institutions. Indeed, Burnside, Eichenbaum, and Rebelo (1999) argue that it is was the prospect of large fiscal deficits following bailouts of the banking system that was the main cause of the crisis in Thailand (and Korea). They cite the fact that agents knew that banks were in trouble before the crisis and that the size of the bailout would be large. The implication is that attention should be focused on information relevant to forecasting prospective deficits.

From a tax policy perspective, generous tax treatment of corporate debt compared to equity contributed to the high leveraging of large corporations. Moreover, and with the benefit of hindsight, it is now recognized that growth rates in Thailand were well above potential, masking the underlying fiscal position.

Fiscal Vulnerability Indicators

The coverage of fiscal accounts was broader in Thailand than other Asian crisis countries, including local governments and public enterprises. But long reporting lags compromised the quality of fiscal information available prior to the crisis. Table A5.7 confirms the apparent strength of the macrofiscal position in the years prior to the crisis, but the deficit did widen substantially during 1996/97; this is also clear from the quarterly data on central government—particularly the total budgetary balance and external debt—in Table A5.8. Note however that the various market indicators in Table A5.7 give virtually no advance warning of the crisis. Data on the growth of implicit government liabilities during the 1990s is hard to find; Burnside, Eichenbaum, and Rebelo (1999) make some estimates for 1997, based on data in Corsetti, Pesenti, and Roubini (1999) on loan default rates.

What Was the Fiscal Impact of the Crisis and How Did Fiscal Policy Respond?

The objective of the original IMF-supported program was for a 2½ percent of GDP improvement in the fiscal balance in 1997/98 compared with 1996/97; Ghosh and others (2002) estimate that this was some 2 percentage points greater than required to stabilize the debt-to-GDP ratio, even allowing for the carrying cost of debt issued to recapitalize the banking sector. However, the extent of the recession was underestimated. It had a substantial effect on the budget, primarily through corporate tax revenues (where rising domestic costs of foreign currency debt led to a fall in taxable income); in the absence of large unemployment and social programs there was relatively little impact on nominal spending levels. After the first review of the IMF-supported program in November 1997, the fiscal targets were repeatedly revised to offset the greater-than-anticipated weakness in the private sector. With output falling by 9 percent in 1997/98, the public sector deficit widened to 8 percent of GDP while the debt ratio soared from 14 percent in 1995/96 to 45 percent by September 1998. With the recovery taking longer than earlier expected, the need to support economic activity by providing a fiscal stimulus was reiterated in preparing the 1998/99 budget.

Fiscal policy could not respond promptly to the crisis. The limited coverage of social safety nets and unemployment insurance, narrow tax bases, and lags in tax collection all militated against the operation of fiscal stabilizers. This meant that discretionary measures had to be employed to offset the sharp decline in output: increases in social spending, public works schemes, other capital projects, and tax deferrals. However, as implementation delays risked reducing the planned fiscal stimulus by as much as 1 percent of GDP, a new stimulus package was launched in April 1999, consisting of tax cuts (0.6 percent of GDP) and additional spending (0.4 percent of GDP), mainly in the form of block grants for local governments. Nonetheless, the fiscal deficit fell short of its target in 1998–99 and 1999–2000 owing to the tradition of fiscal conservatism and difficulties in implementing increased public spending.

The fall in output in the aftermath of the crisis meant that overall there was a very large increase in the deficit—the public sector balance shifted from a 3 percent of GDP surplus in 1995/96 to a 3 percent of GDP deficit in 1996/97. Public debt levels also increased dramatically: around two-third of the debt was directly attributable to the cost of financial sector restructuring, and the remainder to discretionary expansionary policies. Finally, at the structural level, one consequence of the crisis was an increase in spending on transfer programs for the poor and on public works.

Korea, 1997

Background

The rapid growth and low inflation seen in Korea throughout the 1990s masked deep-rooted structural

Table A5.9. Korea: Selected Fiscal Vulnerability Indicators (Annual)

	1994	1995	1996	1997	1998	1999
	(In percent of GDP)					
Consolidated central government						
Revenue	19.1	19.3	20.4	20.6	21.8	23.4
Expenditure	19.0	19.0	20.4	22.3	25.7	26.5
Of which						
Interest	0.6	0.6	0.5	0.5	1.1	2.0
Capital	2.7	3.5	4.1	4.1	4.6	5.1
Overall balance (cash)	0.1	0.3	0.0	−1.7	−4.0	−3.2
Primary balance	0.7	0.9	0.5	−1.2	−2.9	−1.1
Public sector debt	10.6	12.5	11.9	16.0	32.8	35.6
Domestic	8.8	11.1	10.7	9.8	8.3	15.2
External	1.8	1.4	1.2	4.7	11.5	7.3
Bank restructuring and debtor support	—	—	—	1.5	13.0	13.1
	(In billions of U.S. dollars)					
Total external debt	88.7	127.1	164.4	159.2	148.7	137.1
Short term	58.4	71.6	93.0	63.6	30.7	39.2
Medium and long term	30.3	55.5	71.4	95.6	118.0	97.9
Of which						
Public sector	7.2	6.7	6.1	22.3	36.5	29.5

Sources: IMF; and market information.

problems, including an overleveraged corporate sector and chaebols that focused on gaining market share rather than profitability. At the same time, weak prudential control over banks and forbearance by supervisors left the banking system with large exposures to such corporations. A slowdown in export growth in 1996 worsened the deterioration in the current account deficit. As a result, and despite lower levels of capital inflows than in many other emerging market economies during the 1990s, Korea found itself with a huge amount of short-term foreign debt and very exposed to changes in market sentiment. In early 1997, 6 of the top 30 chaebols declared bankruptcy, increasing the banking sector's stock of nonperforming loans. Following the eruption of crisis in Thailand, its spread to the Hong Kong SAR stock market in October, and downgrades by the main rating agencies, Korean financial markets came under mounting pressure. As investors became increasingly unwilling to roll over Korean exposure, the central bank rapidly lost reserves, which were used to repay the short-term debts of Korean commercial banks.

How Did the Crisis Manifest Itself?

On November 20, 1997 facing a complete loss of reserves, Korea requested IMF assistance. On December 4 the IMF approved a US$21 billion Stand-By Arrangement, with additional financing totaling US$37 billion. Interest rates were increased and the exchange rate band—limiting daily changes to ±10 percent—was eliminated. Following an initially positive reaction, market sentiment quickly turned negative as the true loss of reserves became known. The won depreciated by 70 percent during December 5–24 (to W 2,000 per US$1) at the same time as the country experienced a further decline in reserves. In defense of the currency, the overnight call rate was raised from 12 percent to 32 percent, causing market interest rates to also increase sharply.

In January 1998, Korea reached an agreement with foreign banks on a voluntary rescheduling of US$22 billion of short-term private sector debt in return for an explicit sovereign guarantee. The conclusion of the agreement stabilized foreign exchange markets and facilitated a sovereign upgrade and a return by Korea to international capital markets (a US$4 billion sovereign global bond was placed in April). By June, the won had appreciated to W 1,300 per US$1 and call rates were brought down to precrisis levels. By the fourth quarter 1998 there were the initial signs of a return of economic growth. Nonetheless, the effect of the crisis on the economy was severe: real GDP fell by nearly 7 percent in 1998, with private consumption and

APPENDIX V

Table A5.10. Korea: Selected Fiscal Vulnerability Indicators (Quarterly)
(In percent of GDP, unless otherwise indicated)

	1997				1998			
	Q1	Q2	Q3	Q4	Q1	Q2	Q3	Q4
Consolidated central government								
Revenue	23.2	18.6	18.2	22.4	21.2	20.0	23.1	22.7
Expenditure	18.0	19.2	17.1	32.7	21.2	22.2	28.2	31.9
Of which								
Interest	0.5	0.4	0.5	0.7	0.7	0.4	0.8	1.1
Overall balance (cash)	5.2	–0.6	1.1	–10.4	—	–2.2	–5.2	–9.2
Primary balance	5.7	–0.3	1.6	–9.7	0.7	–1.8	–4.4	–8.1
Short-term interest rate (in percent)[1]	11.9	12.2	12.3	16.3	23.7	18.8	10.2	7.2
EMBI spread (basis points)	...	...	...	589	359	493	710	412
Foreign currency long-term debt rating								
Moody's	A1	A1	A1	Ba1	Ba1	Ba1	Ba1	Ba1
Standard & Poor's	AA–	AA–	AA–	B+	BB+	BB+	BB+	BB+
Fitch	BB+	BB+	BB+	BB+	BBB–	BBB–	BBB–	BBB–

Sources: IMF; and market information.
[1]Thirty-day call rate.

fixed investment falling by 12 percent and 21 percent, respectively.

What Were the Main Causes of the Crisis?

The proximate cause of the crisis was a sharp capital account reversal, following years of ready access to cheap, short-term foreign borrowing, triggered by a combination of contagion from other Asian countries undergoing capital market pressures and growing concerns about corporate indebtedness. The shift in sentiment left the corporate sector unable to finance its rollover requirement and left Korea's financial institutions virtually bankrupt. The underlying vulnerabilities were rooted in the private sector: weak governance, indebtedness, and balance sheet mismatches in the corporate sector (due, in part, to continuing controls on longer-term borrowing and the implicit guarantee of a fixed exchange rate); and a fragile financial sector, poorly regulated and supervised, and ill-equipped to intermediate large capital inflows. Moreover, structural weaknesses in the corporate and financial sectors were closely interrelated because of the corporate sector's heavy reliance on bank finance. These fragilities undermined the effectiveness of a traditional defense of the currency, since rising interest rates only worsened the state of highly leveraged corporations.

What Was the Nature of Fiscal Vulnerabilities?

There were no macrofiscal origins to the crisis, at least not in the traditional sense. The government had pursued prudent fiscal policy for much of the 1990s and sovereign debt had fallen to single digits as a share of GDP, one of the lowest levels among OECD countries. However, this picture belied the considerable contingent liabilities the government had on its balance sheet, or would soon assume.

At the structural level, Korea had a history of directed lending to big industrial conglomerates and government bailouts of distressed companies. This encouraged excessive risk taking and overinvestment, and left the financial system with large nonperforming loans.

As in Thailand, there were also "policy vulnerabilities" in the sense that it proved difficult to implement fiscal expansion rapidly in response to evolving circumstances. This was primarily due to a history of fiscal conservatism—manifested in a tradition of securing revenue before making expenditure—which hampered attempts to put in place an activist fiscal policy in response to the economic downturn, both in terms of the government's unwillingness to initiate such policies and of the capacity of the fiscal authorities (typically at the local level) to implement an expansionary policy.

Fiscal Vulnerability Indicators

The indicators in Tables A5.9 and A5.10 above confirm the apparent strength of the macrofiscal position in the run-up to the crisis. Only in the final quarter of 1997 did the overall balance deteriorate.[57] There was equally no advance warning of the crisis in the various market indicators reported in Table A5.10.

What Was the Fiscal Impact of the Crisis and How Did Fiscal Policy Respond?

The primary impact of the Korean crisis on the macrofiscal situation was a significant increase in the stock of sovereign-guaranteed debt, albeit from a very low starting point. This increase came from two sources. First, the costs of recapitalizing the banking sector added around 10 percent of GDP to the stock of public debt. Second, government programs to guarantee corporate debt—initially for small- and medium-size enterprises and later expanded more widely, justified as a response to the difficulties of raising finance after the crisis—added further to the stock of contingent liabilities. At the structural level, the crisis resulted in a major and long-term expansion of the existing social safety net system, with social protection expenditure increasing from 0.6 percent of GDP in 1997 to 1.6 percent in 1999, and a significant increase in (mostly small-scale) public works spending in response to the increase in unemployment.

In terms of the stance of fiscal policy, the original IMF-supported program called for a tightening of the overall balance by 1½ percentage points of GDP (and more in cyclically adjusted terms, given the expected fall in output). However, confidence was not restored, and private capital outflows continued for several months after the initial program was announced. It seems that markets judged that Korea's vulnerabilities lay in the private sector, and hence that fiscal tightening (beyond conveying the impression that restructuring costs would be addressed responsibly) was not helpful; see Ghosh and others (2002). The unexpected continued fall in output prompted a reconsideration of the original fiscal targets. The government introduced a large stimulus package that moved the fiscal position from balance to a deficit of 4 percent of GDP in 1998, which resulted in a positive fiscal impulse, despite some implementation lags. The fiscal measures were almost entirely discretionary, because automatic stabilizers were small. The temporary stimulus was reversed in 2000, and the fiscal position was restored to a surplus of 1 percent of GDP.

Pakistan, 1998–99

Background

Despite a series of adjustment and reform programs supported by IMF arrangements, Pakistan's economic performance was consistently poor during the 1990s. Successive governments failed to carry through sustained reforms to improve the efficiency of the tax system, diversify the export base, and attract private sector investment. Persistent budget deficits caused public debt to increase from around 65 percent of GDP in 1980 to around 90 percent of GDP by 1990, where it remained throughout the following decade. Gradually rising interest rates caused debt servicing to become progressively more burdensome through the 1990s. An external crisis was finally triggered by sanctions imposed by bilateral official creditors following Pakistan's nuclear tests in May 1998.

How Did the Crisis Manifest Itself?

The cessation of official capital inflows posed the risk of massive withdrawals of foreign currency deposits and the authorities responded by freezing these deposits. This followed the buildup of arrears on debt servicing and other foreign exchange obligations, and adversely affected the confidence of local and foreign investors. The rating agencies downgraded Pakistan's debt, portfolio investments and overseas worker remittances fell sharply, and the Karachi Stock Exchange index declined over 50 percent between May and July 1998. To avoid a total loss of reserves, the government imposed restrictions on foreign payments in addition to debt service. In July it also imposed a temporary dual exchange rate system to support exports (which had been hit by the Asian crisis) while easing the pressure on the official exchange rate. The composite exchange rate fell 7.4 percent against the dollar between July and November but then stabilized. Agreement was reached with the Paris Club to reschedule official debt service in January 1999, but this required comparable restructuring of some Eurobonds (with a face value of US$608 million, or around 1 percent of GDP). Negotiations on a voluntary restructuring began in May 1999 and led to an official exchange offer in November 1999, shortly after a new government assumed office in October. In view of the continuing fragility of the external position, the authorities floated the rupee.

---

[57]As mentioned above, data on the growth of implicit government liabilities during the 1990s is hard to find. See Burnside, Eichenbaum, and Rebelo (1999) for some estimates.

Despite all the external financial disruption, there was no banking crisis, in part because the exposure of the banking sector to restructured debt was small (only around 10 percent of the US$608 million restructured). Wider economic disruption was also much less severe than in most other financial crises of the 1990s, with growth and inflation hardly affected. This reflected the limited impact of the crisis on the banking sector and the exchange rate, and the small balance sheet exposure to currency risk as a result of limited capital account openness.

What Were the Main Causes of the Crisis?

The adverse effects on export markets of the Asian crisis, compounded by the sanctions imposed in May 1998, were the proximate factors that crystalized a number of underlying vulnerabilities:

- A narrow production base—high dependence on cotton-based manufactures—rendered the economy vulnerable to exogenous shocks such as adverse weather and fluctuating prices. A noncompetitive exchange rate and a strongly regulated foreign exchange regime discouraged export diversification.

- Persistent macroeconomic imbalances, manifested in large public sector and external deficits, led to high interest rates and crowded out private investment.

- The buildup of external debt, particularly of the private sector, and the rise in interest rates on private debt during the 1990s meant that solvency and liquidity concerns developed rapidly following the events of May 1998. External debt service rose from 44 percent of current foreign exchange receipts in 1995–96 to 75 percent in 1998–99. Pakistan's external debt problem was primarily a liquidity problem, arising from an unfavorable amortization profile, rather than a solvency problem.

- Governance problems and poor investor protection kept private sector foreign capital inflows very modest.

What Was the Nature of Fiscal Vulnerabilities?

While the private sector was responsible for most of the increase in external debt—and short-term debt in particular—during the 1990s, high levels of public debt added to external vulnerability. There were also significant structural fiscal problems. These included a low tax ratio, reflecting a narrow tax base together with weak administration and enforcement of taxes and tariffs, and a high proportion of unproductive and inflexible public spending, especially on defense and debt service (although the former had fallen during the 1990s).

Fiscal Vulnerability Indicators

Fiscal vulnerabilities are clearly evident from Table A5.11 (although it should be noted that serious discrepancies in fiscal reporting emerged in 1999, which clouded the fiscal picture prior to 1999). The deteriorating external financing situation is illustrated clearly by the external debt servicing as a proportion of current foreign exchange receipts. Adverse public debt dynamics were driven by increases in external debt, which in turn reflected exchange rate depreciation. The effective real interest rate on external debt was increasing during the mid-1990s, albeit from a very low level, reflecting the predominance of concessional official lending. Domestic public debt stabilized as a ratio to GDP during the late 1990s. With revenues fairly stable relative to GDP, fiscal consolidation was achieved by cutting noninterest expenditure (especially capital and development spending). The overall rigidity of public spending is confirmed by the figures for debt service and military expenditure.

The deteriorating external situation was not reflected in domestic short-term interest rates, but the two major rating agencies downgraded Pakistan's sovereign debt in May 1998, following the imposition of sanctions.

What Was the Fiscal Impact of the Crisis and How Did Fiscal Policy Respond?

The crisis had limited impact on fiscal policy. The overall deficit increased marginally in 1999–2000 to 6.5 percent of GDP, compared with 6.1 percent of GDP in 1998–99, but this change was accounted for by an increase in debt-service costs as a result of higher interest rates. With the primary balance unchanged between these two years, there was no net fiscal stimulus or withdrawal in the fiscal year following the imposition of sanctions. There was some tightening the following year, with the primary surplus improving by ½ percent of GDP. Domestic debt changed little, as a ratio to GDP, although there was an almost 10 percentage point increase in the overall public debt ratio, to 100.9 percent of GDP, mainly as a result of valuation effects due to a fall in the exchange rate.

As regards structural fiscal policy, the military government that took office in October 1999 made an effort to improve tax policy by eliminating some

Table A5.11. Pakistan: Selected Fiscal Vulnerability Indicators

	1995/96[1]	1996/97	1997/98	1998/99	1999/2000	2000/01
	(In percent of GDP)					
Consolidated general government						
Total revenue (excluding grants)	17.5	16.1	15.8	16.2	16.3	16.2
Tax revenue	15.0	13.4	13.0	13.2	12.9	12.9
Of which						
Central board of revenue	12.5	11.6	10.8	10.6	11.0	11.5
Surcharges	2.1	1.3	1.8	2.1	1.2	0.9
Nontax revenue	2.5	2.7	2.8	2.9	3.4	3.3
Total expenditure	25.5	23.1	23.5	21.9	22.5	21.0
Current expenditure	20.1	19.2	19.5	19.3	20.3	18.8
Of which						
Interest	6.2	6.5	7.3	7.3	7.8	6.9
Defense	5.1	5.0	4.5	4.2	4.8	3.1
Development and net lending	5.2	3.7	3.9	3.0	2.6	2.1
Budget balance	–7.8	–6.8	–7.7	–6.0	–6.6	–5.3
Primary balance	–1.7	–0.3	–0.3	1.3	1.2	1.6
Public sector net debt	86.2	88.5	92.7	94.3	92.5	104.5
Domestic	39.8	40.8	43.0	43.0	43.3	43.3
External	46.4	47.7	49.7	51.3	49.2	61.2
Total external debt	51.4	54.1	53.7	58.1	55.9	59.4
Of which						
Effective short-term debt[2]	5.5	5.8	6.5	7.7	8.8	7.6
	(In percent of current foreign exchange receipts)					
External debt service						
Total	27.7	28.8	29.1	34.3	38.4	22.5
Public and publicly guaranteed	23.5	23.8	24.7	31.9	35.6	20.3
Private	4.2	5.0	4.5	2.4	2.7	2.2
	(In percent, adjusted for inflation)					
Implied interest rates on public debt	–3.4	–4.1	0.6	2.2	4.6	2.4
Domestic	1.4	1.0	7.0	7.5	9.2	6.2
External	–7.9	–8.9	–5.4	–2.9	–0.4	–1.4
Short-term interest rates (in percent, end of period)[3]	12.8	15.6	15.7	13.1	8.8	10.4
Foreign currency long-term debt rating						
Moody's	B1	B2	B3	Caa1	Caa1	Caa1
Standard & Poor's	B+	B+	B–	SD	B–	B–

Sources: IMF; and market information.
[1]The fiscal year runs July–June.
[2]Short-term debt at original maturity plus amortization of medium-term debt in the next year.
[3]Six-month treasury bill rate.

general sales tax and income tax exemptions, and modernizing the income tax. But tax administration continues to be weak, and revenue targets were missed repeatedly in 2000–01. Expenditure management procedures have been strengthened following the emergence of fiscal reporting problems in 1999.

Russia, 1998

Background

Since embarking on market-oriented reforms in 1992, Russia had been unable to bring its fiscal situation under control, with a trend decline in cash revenue and an inability to reduce unproductive spending and contain spending commitments. This resulted in a buildup of expenditure arrears and recurrent recourse to noncash ("offset") mechanisms to net out tax and spending arrears which, in turn, served to further undermine tax compliance. However, despite these fiscal problems, 1997 had witnessed a return of positive growth in Russia for the first time since the beginning of the transition. In addition, by mid-1997 domestic interest rates had fallen to below 20 percent, there were large private capital inflows into the government debt market, reserves were increasing, inflation had been brought down to single digits, and Russia had the world's best performing stock market.

In October 1997, fallout from the Asian crisis hit Russia, causing a reversal of some of the capital inflows, rapidly rising domestic interest rates, and a significant loss of reserves as the central bank strived to protect the currency band. The reduced availability of financing and an inability to adjust the fiscal stance resulted in a further buildup in expenditure arrears and heavy recourse to the use of tax offsets.

How Did the Crisis Manifest Itself?

During the first half of 1998, the Russian economy was hit by domestic political uncertainties, including a new prime minister, continued emerging market malaise, and a negative terms of trade shock as international energy prices declined. Short-term interest rates rose to over 100 percent and revenues continued to fall well short of targets, in part because of weaknesses in the energy sector; pension and local wage arrears also grew. From early 1998, the government had trouble meeting its domestic debt rollover and large-scale capital outflows resumed as investors became increasingly unwilling to roll over maturing treasury bills. In addition, Russian equities fell precipitously throughout the period, to less than 20 percent of the August 1997 highs by the time the crisis hit in August 1998.

In July 1998, the IMF together with other international financial institutions and bilateral creditors, put together a large financing package that calmed markets somewhat, producing a decline in interest rates. The government also conducted a voluntary swap of some of the shorter-term domestic debt into longer-term Eurobonds (although many domestic debt holders chose not to participate so that the ultimately small scale of the swap had little impact on the government's large monthly rollover requirement). But the relief provided by the international financing package was short-lived and, by August, pressures from nonresidents to exit the market were mounting and the ministry of finance had difficulty placing new paper.

The central bank began to extend credit to cover the debt obligations coming due[58] and to increase liquidity support for the banking system that fueled the capital outflows and led to a rapid loss of reserves. On August 17, the government announced the devaluation of the ruble, a unilateral restructuring of its domestic debt obligations, and a 90-day moratorium on payments of private sector external debt enforced through extensive capital and exchange controls. Shortly after, the Kiriyenko government was dissolved.

Overall, the crisis was characterized by a rapid depreciation of the currency (from a precrisis exchange rate of ruble 6 per US$1 to an exchange rate of ruble 20 per US$1 by end-September); a sovereign debt default (initially, only on domestic currency instruments but the government subsequently ran arrears on Soviet era external debt); a collapse of the banking sector;[59] a spike in monthly inflation to nearly 40 percent; and a sharp decline in output (GDP fell by 4 percent in 1998).

What Were the Main Causes of the Crisis?

Although external shocks such as the Asian crisis and the associated fall in energy prices contributed to Russia's difficulties, the main cause of the crisis was a protracted failure of domestic policy to address structural economic distortions and governance problems (including weak property rights and the dominant influence of certain interest groups). At a macroeconomic level, the primary cause of the crisis was the inability to get the government deficit under control. With relatively high short-term debt and a large net financing requirement, the government was unable to finance its gross needs at a sustainable interest rate in the face of the Asian crisis and a general retreat from emerging markets. Interest rates rose rapidly following the Asian crisis and stayed high as the government was unable to deliver a convincing policy response to the market turmoil.

What Was the Nature of Fiscal Vulnerabilities?

The fiscal vulnerabilities were twofold. First, there was a clear tax administration problem despite a large investment of technical assistance resources to improve the state tax service. Problems

---

[58]Despite a prohibition on direct lending, the central bank provided overdrafts to the government while redeeming treasury bills from the market in its capacity as fiscal agent for the government.

[59]Not only were the banks heavily invested in domestic debt instruments, but they had also sold dollars in forward contracts to hedge the ruble exposure of foreign investors holding the same debt, and so were very vulnerable to a devaluation.

Table A5.12. Russia: Selected Fiscal Vulnerability Indicators (Annual)
(In percent of GDP)

	1996	1997	1998	1999	2000
Federal budget					
Revenue	12.5	12.5	10.9	12.8	15.4
Expenditure	20.9	19.8	16.7	17.1	14.6
Of which					
Interest	5.9	4.8	4.4	6.0	3.4
Overall balance	−8.4	−7.3	−5.8	−4.3	0.8
Primary balance	−2.5	−2.5	−1.4	1.8	5.2
Enlarged government					
Revenue	33.5	37.1	32.9	34.0	37.1
Expenditure	42.4	45.1	40.7	37.2	34.4
Primary balance	−3.0	−3.3	−3.3	2.9	7.1
Overall balance	−8.9	−8.0	−7.9	−3.2	2.7
Domestic debt	18.9	19.8	17.8	12.3	7.5
Of which					
Short-term treasury bills	...	11.0	0.6	0.1	—
Medium and long-term bonds	...	6.6	16.8	10.8	7.2
External debt	32.6	39.2	59.2	96.8	66.9
Sovereign	32.6	31.4	49.2	80.5	54.1
Nonsovereign	—	7.8	10.0	16.3	12.8

Source: IMF.

of corruption, poorly trained personnel, inadequate resources, and the lack of political will to take on the large tax debtors all conspired to undermine compliance, with large taxpayers simply negotiating their tax obligations rather than complying with statutory obligations. In addition, the continual recourse to offsets and the noncollection of interest or penalties provided a strong incentive for taxpayers to accrue arrears. Second, despite efforts to put in place a centralized treasury, a large part of the budgetary sphere—the "power" ministries—remained outside the control of the Ministry of Finance. Such agencies could freely accrue spending arrears and appeared not to be subject to budget constraints. In addition, there were no ex post controls to prevent suppliers from overcharging on invoices, providing poor quality goods, or even not delivering supplies at all. Weak controls were compounded by a lack of information about the execution of expenditure, which prevented a rational process of expenditure reduction and prioritization, and by a high share of nondiscretionary spending (over 50 percent of spending went to interest costs and statutory transfers to the regions). Further, regional governments were politically fairly strong, enabling them to increase their share of revenue and expenditure with little control or accounting to the federal government.

Fiscal Vulnerability Indicators

Several of the indicators in Table A5.12 provided warnings of an impending crisis in Russia. The overall picture of the fiscal position—continually falling revenue, growing noninterest expenditure arrears, high levels of nondiscretionary spending, short-maturity debt, and a large overall deficit—was one of a deterioration in the fiscal authorities' control. This was clearly an unsustainable trend. By late 1997, it became apparent that the initial optimism about bringing the deficit under control had faded. The clearest sign of the impending crisis was the difficulty the Ministry of Finance had in placing domestic debt during its weekly auctions. Indeed, as shown in Table A5.13, the average maturity of domestic liabilities, right up until the crisis, actually lengthened (rather than the usual pattern of shortening maturities) as the government refused to roll over short-maturity debt at the prevailing high interest rates. As with other crisis cases, credit ratings seemed to be clearly reactive rather than predictive.

APPENDIX V

Table A5.13. Russia: Selected Fiscal Vulnerability Indicators (Quarterly)
(In percent of GDP, unless otherwise indicated)

	1997				1998				1999			
	Q1	Q2	Q3	Q4	Q1	Q2	Q3	Q4	Q1	Q2	Q3	Q4
Federal budget												
Revenue[1]	9.6	12.4	8.8	17.9	10.7	10.3	8.0	14.5	10.6	13.1	12.6	16
Expenditure	18.5	21.3	12.8	25.3	16.5	17.2	15.3	18.5	19.0	19.2	15.4	18.4
Of which												
Interest	6.2	5.3	3.8	3.8	5.2	5.4	4.4	3.5	6.9	8.1	5.5	5.4
Overall balance (cash)	−8.8	−8.9	−4.1	−7.3	−5.8	−6.8	−7.3	−4.0	−8.4	−6.1	−2.9	−2.5
Primary balance	−2.7	−3.6	−0.2	−3.5	−0.6	−1.5	−2.8	−0.5	−1.5	2.0	2.7	2.9
Enlarged government overall balance	−9.1	−9.2	−4.8	−8.9	−10.2	−10.7	−10.3	−2.5	−7.7	−4.6	−1.1	−1.7
Enlarged government primary balance	−2.9	−3.9	−0.9	−5.1	−5.0	−5.3	−5.9	1.0	−0.8	3.5	4.5	3.7
Tax arrears (percent of year-end GDP)	3.1	3.2	3.8	4.1	4.1	4.8	5.4	5.9	...	...	...	...
Expenditure arrears	...	...	...	1.8	...	...	...	2.2	...	...	...	...
Domestic debt market												
Stock of gross domestic debt[2,3]	9.1	10.6	11.2	12.5	12.5	15.9	12.7	...	...	...	...	...
Average treasury bill interest rate (percent)[2]	35.3	20.6	18.7	38.3	27.5	65.6	109.7	...	...	...	...	...
Average maturity (months)[2]	5.8	7.3	8.7	9.1	11.9	12.2	13.9	...	...	...	...	...
Gross rollover requirement	17.0	17.9	16.1	13.4	18.2	16.3	12.8	...	...	...	...	...
Net domestic debt financing	7.3	6.4	3.7	3.3	4.1	0.6	−7.2	...	...	...	...	...
External debt												
Eurobond ratings (Fitch)	BB+	BB+	BB+	BB+	BB+	BB	CCC	CCC	CCC	CCC	CCC	CCC
Eurobond 2007 premia (basis points)	...	355	295	554	507	944	4,440	3,823	3,476	1,846	2,311	1,419

Sources: IMF; and market information.
[1]Cash revenue.
[2]1998Q3 data are for July 1998.
[3]Tradable GKO-OFZ debt as a percent of end-year GDP.

What Was the Fiscal Impact of the Crisis and How Did Fiscal Policy Respond?

In the immediate aftermath of the measures introduced in August 1998, cash revenue plummeted to 7 percent of GDP in the third quarter of 1998. This was in part due to the collapse of the payments system, but it also reflected the general chaos in the economy following the crisis. Significant expenditure arrears were accumulated, which were reduced somewhat in the following quarter through large-scale offset operations and a large amount of financing supplied by the Central Bank, which served to further the downward spiral in the ruble.

The economic situation stabilized during the first half of 1999, as the Central Bank of Russia sought to bring inflation under control, and decisive measures were implemented to improve the fiscal position. In particular, expenditure control was tightened, with the treasury system expanded to cover all earmarked funds, a series of export taxes (on a range of primary exports) were reintroduced to capture some of the windfall gains to exporters arising from the devaluation, and revenue was recentralized. In addition, the federal government ended the use of offsets, which led to a rapid decline in barter arrangements, and long-standing efforts to enforce tax compliance contributed to higher cash revenue. The position improved further in the latter part of 1999 as international energy prices increased sharply.

The fiscal position has continued to improve, with the enlarged government primary surplus increasing to 8 percent of GDP in 2000, reflecting a sharp compression of noninterest expenditure and higher revenue due to output growth and a rise in oil prices. The combination of the real appreciation of the ruble, debt restructuring operations by the Paris Club, London Club, and other creditor groups, and the strong fiscal surpluses that have sharply reduced gross financing needs, cut debt to below 50 percent of GDP at the end of 2001. Since then the fiscal position has been broadly sustainable, although it remains vulnerable to a protracted fall in energy prices.

Ukraine, 1998–2000

Background

The initial years following independence in 1991 were characterized by very high inflation (peaking at 10,200 percent in 1993), currency depreciation, large budget deficits, and rapidly declining GDP. A new government in 1994 introduced a stabilization program that, by and large, succeeded in arresting inflation, stabilizing the exchange rate, and slowing the decline in output. By 1997 private capital was flowing in, encouraged by a stable and open foreign exchange market. Initially, treasury bills were the preferred investment vehicle, but as confidence diminished in this instrument the government resorted increasingly to international capital markets and short-term foreign sources of funding. This allowed the government to delay necessary fiscal reforms, and the government's financial situation deteriorated in late 1997 and early 1998 as debt service became a significant burden on the budget.

How Did the Crisis Manifest Itself?

Capital inflows slowed in the wake of the Asian crisis and dried up completely following the Russian debt default in August 1998. The authorities had used most of their reserves to prop up the exchange rate during 1997 and the first half of 1998, which left little alternative but to move the exchange rate band downward when the currency came under heavy pressure in September 1998. The authorities also introduced a number of measures to restrict capital outflows. Despite these developments, and severe cash-flow problems for budget financing, the authorities, imposing large losses on debt holders, restructured part of the domestic and foreign debt in September and October 1998. In March 1999, restrictions on current transactions were lifted (though some capital controls were retained), and the exchange rate was floated (but remained extensively managed). The hryvnia lost about half of its value against the dollar between the fall of 1999 and early 2000. Continuing negotiations with creditors resulted in further piecemeal restructurings, against the background of continued concerns about the government's ability to service its debt. The bunching of repayment obligations and the threat of a full-blown liquidity crisis in early 2000 forced the government to mount a comprehensive restructuring bid for US$2.7 billion of commercial debt falling due in 2000–01. This was successful, with agreement from 98 percent of creditors to accept replacement Eurobonds maturing in 2007. In early 2000, the government stopped servicing its Paris Club obligations and sought a restructuring of these debts.

Hence, as in the case of Pakistan, sovereign default was avoided, although the possibility of default loomed large and led to negotiated restructurings of government debt. Unlike the case of Pakistan, the exchange rate was affected, with the hryvnia eventually suffering a major depreciation. A meltdown of the banking system was avoided: exchange rate exposure had been limited by tight controls, and the banks' holdings of government paper was a relatively small share of their assets. At no point were

APPENDIX V

Table A5.14. Ukraine: Selected Fiscal Vulnerability Indicators
(In percent of GDP, unless otherwise indicated)

	1996	1997	1998	1999	2000	2001
Consolidated general government						
Total revenue	35.0	36.7	34.5	31.9	33.4	33.5
Tax revenue	32.9	33.4	32.8	30.1	28.0	27.9
Nontax revenue	2.1	3.2	1.7	1.7	5.4	5.6
Memorandum item: earmarked revenue	...	10.8	11.5	11.4	12.1	14.7
Total expenditure	38.2	42.2	37.3	34.2	34.7	35.1
Of which						
Social security and welfare	...	14.8	14.9	13.7	13.2	14.0
Interest	1.6	1.8	2.3	2.4	3.1	2.0
Defense	1.5	1.6	1.4	1.2	1.3	1.4
Budget balance	−3.2	−5.6	−2.8	−2.4	−1.3	−1.6
Primary balance	−1.6	−3.7	−0.4	0.0	1.8	0.4
Budgetary payments arrears (stock)[1]	3.7	2.8	4.2	6.1	2.0	1.3
Of which						
Wages	1.5	1.4	1.6	0.8	0.3	0.0
Pensions	1.5	0.9	2.0	1.0	0.1	0.0
Energy	...	...	...	2.8	0.7	0.5
Total tax arrears (stock)	3.6	5.3	13.0	10.0	6.7	3.3
State tax administration	1.7	2.5	9.5	9.0	5.9	3.1
Pension fund	1.9	2.8	3.5	1.0	0.8	0.2
Official debt	24.4	29.9	38.5	50.9	45.3	37.3
Domestic	4.5	10.9	11.1	11.5	12.2	10.4
Held by						
Banks	1.7	1.5	2.3	2.7	6.2	5.2
Nonbank institutions	2.8	9.4	8.8	8.8	6.0	5.2
External	19.9	19.0	27.5	39.4	33.1	26.9
Short-term interest rates (in percent, end of period)[2]	40.0	35.0	19.0	56.0	9.0	17.0
Spread on benchmark bonds (basis points)	...	...	...	...	1,430	780

Sources: IMF; and market information.
[1]Incomplete data.
[2]Money market rate; weighted average rate on daily loans between financial institutions in national currency.

deposits frozen. But the banking system was weakened by the crisis with a deterioration in already low capitalization, and as a result of the imposition of high mandatory reserve requirements as a means to stabilize the currency.

The financial crisis of 1998–2000 did not have a significant impact on output trends. Growth rates had been improving since the mid-1990s, and eventually turned positive in 2000, helped by the large real depreciation and recovering domestic and Russian demand. The modest growth impact of the crisis was due to a combination of limited exposure of domestic agents to restructured debt, low levels of bank intermediation, and a relatively closed capital account, which created little exposure to currency risk.

What Were the Main Causes of the Crisis?

Disruptions in international capital markets following the Asian crisis, and particularly following the Russian default of August 1998, were the proximate causes of Ukraine's crisis. The reversal of the favorable external environment of the mid-1990s put reserves under heavy pressure, given the decision to defend the exchange rate. But fiscal problems—persistent budget deficits, low cash revenue (relative to total revenue), and a reliance on short-term external financing—were central to the underlying vulnerability to liquidity concerns on the part of investors. Fiscal problems are discussed in more detail below.

More generally, there had been a lack of progress on institutional reform and governance (in contrast to the relative success of the stabilization program of the mid-1990s). Fundamental institutional weakness and poor governance were manifest in poor contract enforcement, capture of public institutions by private interests, particularly in the energy sector, and various public sector problems. The lack of progress in addressing these problems reflected the complexity of moving away from a centrally planned economy, but also a lack of resolve on the part of successive administrations, growing paralysis in the legislature, and rising encroachment of the oligarchs.

What Was the Nature of Fiscal Vulnerabilities?

Persistent budget deficits indicated problems on both the revenue and the expenditure sides.

- Cash revenue performance was hit by the general economic decline, an increasing reliance on barter transactions throughout the economy, and netting-out operations conducted by the government. Widespread tax exemptions narrowed the tax base. This intensified pressure on those enterprises not benefiting from preferential treatment, driving more companies into the shadow economy and encouraging the transfer of profits into foreign accounts or private intermediary firms.

- Slow progress in expenditure reduction reflected a lack of clear priorities, the inability of government and parliament to reach consensus on difficult issues, and obsolete public administration.

Poor debt management—in particular, a growing reliance on short-term foreign borrowing when domestic interest in the treasury bill market declined—contributed significantly to liquidity problems in 2000. Access to external finance also allowed pressing fiscal reforms to be further delayed.

Fiscal Vulnerability Indicators

The underlying fiscal problems were apparent in the standard fiscal aggregates, at least when considered together with data on tax and spending arrears. Some indication of the inflexibility of the fiscal regime is apparent, for example, in a high proportion of total revenue that was earmarked, although this was to a large extent the consequence of absorbing extrabudgetary funds into the budget, which was an appropriate move. The acute liquidity problems in the public debt market in 1999 and 2000 are not apparent from the standard fiscal indicators in Table A5.14, and would only have been apparent from detailed information on the profile of gross financing requirements. Overall, although there were concerns about solvency, the prime concern was liquidity.

What Was the Fiscal Impact of the Crisis and How Did Fiscal Policy Respond?

The drying up of private sector financing in mid-1998 forced a sharp reduction in the cash deficit. But this was not accompanied by underlying adjustment, and therefore resulted in the accelerated buildup of spending arrears. Significant fiscal reform did begin in 2000, however, under the new government led by Mr. Yushenko. There were considerable discretionary expenditure cuts, recourse to noncash offsets virtually ceased, government guarantees were banned, and project loans were put on budget. A modern budget code was enacted, putting fiscal management and intergovernmental fiscal relations on a firmer footing. New indirect tax collection procedures were also introduced. These reforms, combined with a surge in growth following the devaluation and the regional recovery, resulted in primary surplus of around 1½ percent of GDP in 2000, compared with a primary deficit of around 3½ percent of GDP in 1997. The depreciation of the exchange rate increased the external public debt burden in 1999, but it has since fallen as a result of the fiscal adjustment efforts and the debt restructuring operations.

Brazil, 1998–99

Background

The 1994 *Real Plan*, an exchange rate–based stabilization program, succeeded in reducing Brazil's very high inflation to around 3 percent by 1998, while maintaining an average growth rate of 4 percent during 1994–98. There was also progress in structural reform, in the areas of privatization, deregulation, external liberalization, and financial reform. However, the real exchange rate appreciated and the current account widened from approximate balance in 1994 to a deficit of 4 percent of GDP in 1997. This, together with deterioration on the fiscal front worsened by high real interest rates, left Brazil vulnerable to the contagion that followed the Asian crisis in late 1997. Pressure on the reserves and the exchange rate was only ameliorated by a sharp increase in interest rates, to around 45 percent, and the adoption of a fiscal package yielding around 2½ percent of GDP. Early in 1998 capital inflows resumed, allowing interest rates to return to precrisis levels of around 20 percent; nonetheless, growth slowed sharply during 1998.

APPENDIX V

How Did the Crisis Manifest Itself?

The fiscal stance was relaxed in 1998, and doubts grew about the authorities' commitment to fiscal adjustment in an election year. Contagion following the Russian crisis put pressure on the exchange rate peg and caused a large fall in reserves. The authorities adopted a series of measures to improve expenditure control and tighten the fiscal stance, and raised short-term interest rates to around 40 percent. This was followed by the adoption of an IMF-supported program built on medium-term fiscal adjustment aimed at stabilizing the debt ratio, and maintenance of the crawling peg supported by tight monetary policy. Pressure eased on the currency immediately following the announcement of the program. The central bank promptly cut interest rates (from 40 percent in November 1998 to 29 percent in December), but this coincided with the defeat in congress of an important part of the fiscal package and the announcement that a state would not honor its debt to the federal government. Doubts about the authorities' ability to implement the program grew, putting the currency under serious pressure in late December and early January 1999 as foreign bank creditors refused to roll over their maturing credit lines.

After increases in interest rates and a one-day experiment with a wider band, the real was floated in mid-January. Interest rates were raised further, but the exchange rate and the stock of reserves fell sharply until March, when confidence was restored following the introduction of a revised monetary framework, an increase in interest rates to 45 percent, a revised IMF-supported program, and an agreement with foreign banks to maintain their credit lines with Brazilian banks. Despite the currency crisis, there was no banking crisis; bank loan portfolios were generally strong, and they were not exposed to devaluation risk. There was no default on public debt. Voluntary capital inflows resumed from as early as April, allowing the currency to stabilize while interest rates were reduced from a peak of 45 percent to 21 percent in July. Growth recovered faster than expected, reaching 1 percent in 1999 compared with original program projections of a 4 percent decline, which in large part reflected the strength of the banking sector.

What Were the Main Causes of the Crisis?

The proximate causes of the crisis were domestic policy mistakes in 1998 and early 1999—such as fiscal slippages and delays in implementing fiscal reforms, premature interest rate cuts, and insufficient interest rate increases at various points—and external shocks in the form of contagion from the Asian and Russian crises. Underlying these were several key vulnerabilities:

- A growing current account deficit—rising steadily from 2½ percent of GDP in 1995 to 4½ percent of GDP in 1998—financed mainly by short-term portfolio inflows;

- An external imbalance driven in large part by a growing fiscal deficit from 1995, reflecting increases in outlays on private pensions and other social assistance benefits, as well as due to growing provincial deficits. In 1998, a comprehensive subnational debt restructuring program contributed to the fiscal stimulus.

- A structure of public debt that made the government's finances very sensitive to changes in short-term interest rates and the exchange rate: by the end of 1998 the average maturity of public debt was around seven months, with two-thirds of the stock indexed to short-term interest rates and one-fifth linked to the dollar.

What Was the Nature of Fiscal Vulnerabilities?

Fiscal factors were at the core of Brazil's crisis. The *Real Plan* failed to address the key structural fiscal weaknesses, namely an expensive and actuarially unbalanced public pension system, excessive government payrolls, especially at the state level, a rigid expenditure structure with a high share of mandated expenditures, and a complex and inefficient system of indirect taxation. Although public debt levels in relation to GDP were not high by international standards, market fears about medium-term sustainability—given the apparent lack of political will to implement meaningful fiscal adjustment, high real interest rates, and the sensitivity of debt to changes in short-term interest rates and the exchange rate—were critical precipitating factors for several episodes of extreme exchange rate pressure. On the other hand, it is interesting to note that the structure of government debt provided a hedge to the private sector as the government absorbed much of the cost of the devaluation, allowing the private sector to recover quickly from the interest rate and exchange rate shocks of 1998–99.

Fiscal Vulnerability Indicators

As shown in Table A5.15, fiscal problems were evident in the public sector deficit, which was rising in the run-up to the crisis and was almost 8 percent of GDP in 1998. Debt levels did not appear high by international standards as a share of GDP, but were clearly very high in relation to gross reserves, and

Table A5.15. Brazil: Selected Fiscal Vulnerability Indicators

	1996	1997	1998	1999	2000	2001
	(In percent of GDP)					
Federal government						
Nonfinancial revenue	17.8	18.4	20.2	21.7	21.5	22.7
Total primary expenditure	17.4	18.7	19.6	19.3	19.6	20.9
Of which						
Wages and salaries	5.0	4.8	5.0	5.1	5.1	5.4
Transfers and pension benefits	9.0	8.2	8.9	9.2	9.4	10.0
Primary balance	0.4	−0.3	0.6	2.3	1.9	1.8
Borrowing requirement[1]	2.6	2.6	5.4	2.7	2.3	2.1
States and municipalities						
Nonfinancial revenue	10.8	10.6	10.9	11.0	11.1	12.1
Total primary expenditure	11.3	11.3	11.1	10.8	10.5	11.3
Of which						
Wages and salaries	6.1	5.9	6.1	6.0	5.7	5.7
Primary balance	−0.5	−0.7	−0.2	0.2	0.5	0.9
Borrowing requirement	2.7	3.0	2.0	3.1	2.1	2.0
Public enterprises						
Primary balance	0.1	0.1	−0.4	0.6	1.1	0.9
Borrowing requirement	0.6	0.4	0.5	−0.1	−0.8	−0.6
Public sector						
Primary balance	−0.1	−1.0	—	3.2	3.5	3.6
Borrowing requirement[1]	5.9	6.1	7.9	5.8	3.6	3.6
Public sector net debt	33.3	35.4	42.2	53.0	51.1	55.1
Domestic	29.2	31.0	36.0	41.9	41.0	44.2
Federal government[2]	14.9	17.3	21.1	23.9	24.3	25.7
States and municipalities	10.3	12.8	13.6	16.6	15.8	18.0
Public enterprises	4.0	0.9	1.3	1.4	0.9	0.4
External (net of reserves)	4.1	4.4	6.3	11.2	10.1	10.9
	(In percent of gross reserves)					
Total external debt	299.4	386.6	549.5	675.9	715.4	585.1
Medium and long term	236.6	315.7	489.4	599.2	624.6	508.2
Public sector	147.2	154.6	209.2	272.5	272.0	258.6
Private sector	89.4	161.1	280.3	326.7	352.6	249.6
Short term	62.9	71.0	60.1	76.7	90.8	76.8
Public sector	8.7	11.1	7.7	9.3	7.8	1.1
Private sector	54.2	59.9	52.4	67.4	83.0	75.8
Short-term interest rates (in percent, end of period)[3]	23.9	42.0	31.2	19.0	16.2	19.1
Spreads on long term for current debt (basis points)	523	521	1,231	636	749	883
Foreign currency long-term debt rating						
Moody's	B1	B1	B2	B2	B1	B1
Standard & Poor's	B+	BB−	BB−	B+	B−	BB−

Sources: IMF; and market information.
[1]Harmonized definition after 1999 (excludes the impact of exchange rate movements that is accrued but not paid).
[2]Includes central bank.
[3]SELIC interest rate.

given the rise in interest rates in 1997. Problems on the expenditure side were evident in the high proportion of expenditure on wages and salaries, and in the growing cost of pension benefits and other social assistance transfers. Credit ratings failed to predict the crisis.

APPENDIX V

What Was the Fiscal Impact of the Crisis and How Did Fiscal Policy Respond?

The impact of the crisis on interest rates and the exchange rate put upward pressure on the public sector deficit in 1999, and there was a strong underlying adjustment with the public sector recording a primary surplus of 3.2 percent of GDP, compared with a primary deficit of 1 percent of GDP in 1997. The consolidation was mostly at the central government level (deriving evenly from both sides of the budget), although the state governments and public enterprises also contributed. Revenue increases reflected some tax measures, but also improved enforcement and collection of arrears; expenditure restraint focused on government wages and capital spending, with some moderation in the real growth of social security spending following the reforms to the pension system of 1998. Strong fiscal performance continued in 2000, with more of the adjustment coming from states (and municipalities).

Despite the rapid turnaround in growth and the absence of a banking crisis, public debt increased somewhat in 1999, reflecting the impact of the depreciated exchange rate on foreign currency–indexed debt and the continued recognition of previously unrecorded liabilities (the latter adding around 11 percentage points of GDP since 1996). However, the structure of public debt improved, with a lower share of debt linked to short-term interest rates and foreign currencies, and an increase in the average maturity.

It would seem that the public finances showed a fair degree of flexibility following the crisis, despite the rigidity of expenditure noted above. The tightening of fiscal policy that followed the crisis was underpinned by the Fiscal Responsibility Law, passed in May 2000, which mandates the setting of limits on personnel expenditure and on debt at each level of government, eliminates the scope for bailouts of state governments, and increases transparency and accountability; and by subnational debt restructuring agreements with the treasury that require minimum primary surpluses. But other aspects of structural fiscal reforms, such as the reform of indirect taxation and public sector employment regulations, continued to be impeded by congress.

Ecuador, 1999

Background

Following strong growth in the 1970s, driven largely by oil exports, economic performance has been weak over the last two decades. GDP per capita in 1998 was at the same level as in 1981, while poverty and inequality had increased. In general terms, this poor performance has resulted from structural rigidities, weak macroeconomic policies, and fractious domestic politics; these have rendered the economy vulnerable to external shocks, which have been frequent and severe. Three major external shocks hit Ecuador in 1998, triggering the crisis of 1999. First, the El Niño weather phenomenon, which is estimated to have caused US$2.6 billion (13 percent of GDP) of economic damage; second, the collapse in world oil prices, which caused a decline in public sector revenue of around 3½ percent of GDP in 1998; and third the turbulence in international financial markets following the Russian crisis in August 1998, which led to a marked reduction in external credit for an already strained banking system.

How Did the Crisis Manifest Itself?

The external shocks caused growth to stagnate in 1998 and fall by 7½ percent in real terms in 1999, while unemployment increased from 9 percent in 1997 to 16 percent in 1999. Annual inflation accelerated from 25–30 percent in 1995–97 to over 60 percent by the end of 1999 and to over 100 percent in July 2000. Short-term interest rates increased through 1998 and 1999, peaking at 160 percent. As the investment climate deteriorated and external finance dried up, reserves fell sharply and the real effective exchange rate depreciated by almost 50 percent in 1998 and 1999. The sucre was floated in February 1999. Ongoing liquidity and solvency problems in the banking sector culminated in a deposit freeze in March 1999, which persisted until 2000. Finally, facing a tight cash flow in September 1999, the government missed coupon payments on discount Brady bonds and shortly after announced the suspension of servicing on all Brady bonds, Eurobonds, all domestic public debt (both in domestic and foreign currency), and external credit lines in closed banks. Full dollarization was announced in January 2000. After being in default for almost a year, an external debt exchange offer was made in July–August 2000.

What Were the Main Causes of the Crisis?

While the proximate cause of the crisis was the external shocks of 1998, the economy was vulnerable due to a combination of factors.

- Structural rigidities were evident in several areas: a banking sector characterized by connected lending practices and high foreign currency exposure; a rigid labor market; high barriers to trade; a system of regulated and subsidized prices for goods produced by public utilities; and an underdeveloped oil sector hampered by restrictions on foreign investment and limited public investment. The key structural fiscal problems are discussed below.

- Civilian governments have held power since 1979, but a lack of party discipline, deep-seated regionalism, and political opportunism have hindered the formation of stable governments with coherent policy agendas. Powerful interest groups and public sector unions have resisted the structural reform attempts of successive governments.

- During 1997 and 1998 macroeconomic policies were too loose. Monetary policy was expansionary, to contain the public sector interest bill and shore up the banking system, and the fiscal stance was considerably relaxed in 1998 and 1999, as discussed below.

- The banking system, already fragile as a result of connected lending practices and currency mismatches, was hit hard by the shocks of 1998 (disruption to payments caused by El Niño, and a reversal of capital flows associated with domestic problems and turbulence in emerging markets generally). There was a failure to address the early manifestations of the banking crisis in 1998, with lax supervision and no strategy for government intervention.

What Was the Nature of Fiscal Vulnerabilities?

At the macrofiscal level, the nonfinancial public sector deficit widened from an average of 1.8 percent of GDP in 1993–97 to around 6 percent of GDP in 1998 and 1999, reflecting a decline in oil revenue, a big public sector wage rise, and rapidly growing interest costs due to the depreciation of the currency and the cost of bank restructuring. This put upward pressure on interest rates, crowding out private sector investment and aggravating the effects of the external credit squeeze.

There were three main sources of fiscal vulnerability at the structural level. First, a heavy reliance on oil revenue (accounting for 28 percent of total revenue in 1998) made revenue unpredictable. Second, a very low tax yield from the non-oil sector, even by regional standards; this primarily reflected extensive exemptions from personal income taxes and weak tax administration. Third, a lack of central government autonomy over expenditure, due to a very high proportion of revenue—around 64 percent in 2000—being earmarked (partly for expenditure items such as pensions and education, and partly for transfers to subnational institutions), and the very high interest bill (almost 10 percent of GDP in 1999–2000). In addition, at a more general level, political and social difficulties delayed the implementation of fiscal adjustment and led to some counterproductive measures.

Fiscal policy also contributed to the banking crisis, in several respects. First, the introduction of a 1 percent financial transactions tax in January 1999 prompted a surge in demand for dollars as funds were withdrawn from domestic banks. Second, the US$1.4 billion of government bonds issued to the agency set up to guarantee deposits (announced in December 1998) contributed to the monetary expansion and increased the vulnerability of the public finances to a depreciation. Third, the widening budget deficit created doubts about the government's ability to sustain the deposit guarantee, precipitating a run on deposits in early 1999. Finally, banks held large quantities of government paper that was rescheduled and then had to be written down.

Fiscal Vulnerability Indicators

The deteriorating fiscal situation was evident in the combined balance reported in Table A5.16, which in turn was mostly driven by a near doubling of interest costs in 1999. Vulnerability to devaluation was also apparent in the sharp increase in external debt (more than 80 percent of which is public) in 1998 and 1999. Declining foreign investor confidence and funding was evident in the marked widening of spreads during 1999. Pressures were also evident, but less markedly, in domestic interest rates; the central bank did not significantly raise official rates until November 1999, only six weeks before dollarization. Overall, and with the benefit of hindsight, the impending crisis was apparent in a number of standard fiscal indicators, most of which were available with a relatively short time lag.

What Was the Fiscal Impact of the Crisis, and How Did Fiscal Policy Respond?

The early (and largely unexpected) success of dollarization helped restore confidence in the banking system quickly. Economic activity rebounded strongly in 2000 (real GDP growth was 2.5 percent, following a decline of 7.2 percent in 1999), while inflation decelerated sharply, although it remained high. The fiscal position improved dramatically in 2000, with the combined public sector (including the quasi-fiscal activities of the central bank) recording a surplus of 1.6 percent of GDP compared with a deficit of 7 percent of GDP in 1999. This improvement derived from the revenue side, thanks to more buoyant non-oil revenue, im-

APPENDIX V

Table A5.16. Ecuador: Selected Fiscal Vulnerability Indicators
(In percent of GDP, unless otherwise indicated)

	1997	1998	1999	2000	2001
Nonfinancial public sector					
Total revenue	21.6	19.1	22.5	27.6	24.7
Of which					
Petroleum revenue	5.4	3.9	6.2	9.2	6.4
Total expenditure	23.7	24.1	27.2	26.5	25.1
Of which					
Interest	4.3	4.2	8.1	6.6	4.7
Primary balance	2.2	–0.9	3.4	7.7	4.3
Nonfinancial public sector balance	–2.1	–5.1	–4.6	1.0	–0.5
Central bank quasi-fiscal balance	0.1	0.3	–0.4	0.3	0.1
Combined balance	–2.0	–4.8	–5.0	1.3	–0.4
Public sector debt	62.6	66.1	101.6	91.4	70.2
Of which					
External	55.3	56.2	82.8	72.0	54.5
Short-term interest rate (in percent, end of period)[1]	29.1	54.0	47.7	13.2	15.8
Spread of EMBI+ (basis points)	648	1,631	3,353	1,415	1,233
Foreign currency long-term debt rating					
Moody's	...	B2–	Caa2	Caa3	Caa3
Standard & Poor's	...	...	...	B–	CCC+

Sources: IMF; Ecuadoran authorities; and market information.
[1]Central bank auction rate up to the end of 1999; discount rate from 2000.

proved tax administration, and higher oil prices; noninterest expenditure increased slightly in 2000. Overall expenditure was kept broadly unchanged as a share of GDP, with the immediate costs of the banking crisis offset by lower interest payments. At a structural level, several reforms have been introduced since the crisis. The financial transactions tax has been eliminated and import tariffs have been reduced, offset by a reduction in subsidies on domestic fuels. And an oil stabilization fund was approved in 2002 as part of a new Fiscal Responsibility Law.

The total cost of the banking crisis is estimated at around 15.7 percent of 2001 GDP, with an interest carrying cost in 2001 of 2.1 percent of GDP. But offsetting this, the bond exchange with private creditors finalized in August 2000 reduced the external debt stock by some 40 percent; combined with the restructuring of domestic debt, this has resolved the medium-term sustainability problem, provided at least some of the additional oil revenue resulting from the expansion of a new oil pipeline is saved and a primary surplus of around 6 percent of GDP is maintained.

References

Agénor, Pierre-Richard, and Peter Montiel, 1999, *Development Macroeconomics* (Princeton, New Jersey: Princeton University Press, 2nd ed.).

Alesina, Alberto, and Roberto Perotti, 1995, "The Political Economy of Budget Deficits," *Staff Papers*, International Monetary Fund, Vol. 42 (March), pp. 1–31.

Allen, Mark, Christoph Rosenberg, Christian Keller, Brad Setser, and Nouriel Roubini, 2002, "A Balance Sheet Approach to Financial Crisis," IMF Working Paper No. 02/210 (Washington: International Monetary Fund).

Aziz, Jahangir, Francesco Caramazza, and Ranil Salgado, 2000, "Currency Crises: In Search of Common Elements," IMF Working Paper No. 00/67 (Washington: International Monetary Fund).

Barth, James, Gerard Caprio, and Ross Levine, 2000, "Banking Systems Around the Globe: Do Regulation and Ownership Affect Performance and Stability?" Policy Research Paper No. 2325 (Washington: World Bank).

Begg, David, 1998, "Pegging Out: Lessons from the Czech Exchange Rate Crisis," *Journal of Comparative Economics* Vol. 26, No. 12, pp. 669–90.

Beim, David O., and Charles W. Calomiris, 2001, *Emerging Financial Markets* (Boston: McGraw-Hill/Irwin).

Bell, James, 2000, "Leading Indicator Models of Banking Crises: A Critical Review," *Financial Stability Report*, December (London: Financial Services Authority).

Berg, Andrew, and Catherine Pattillo, 1999, "Are Currency Crises Predictable? A Test," *IMF Staff Papers*, Vol. 46 (June), pp. 107–38.

Berg, Andrew, Eduardo Borensztein, and Catherine Pattillo, 2003, "Assessing Early Warning Systems: How Have They Worked in Practice?" (unpublished; Washington: International Monetary Fund).

Bléjer, Mario I., and Graciana del Castillo, 1998, "Déja Vu All Over Again?: The Mexican Crisis and the Stabilization of Uruguay in the 1970s," *World Development*, Vol. 26, No. 3, pp. 449–64.

Bordo, Michael, Barry Eichengreen, Daniela Klingebiel, and Maria Soledad Martinez Peria, 2001, "Financial Crises: Lessons From the Last 120 Years," *Economic Policy: A European Forum*, No. 32 (April), pp. 51–82.

Brixi, Hana Polackova, Hafez Ghanem, and Roumeen Islam, 1999, "Fiscal Adjustment and Contingent Liabilities: Case Studies of the Czech Republic and Macedonia," Policy Research Paper No. 2177 (Washington: World Bank).

Brixi, Hana Polackova, and Allen Schick, eds., 2002, *Government at Risk: Contingent Liabilities and Fiscal Risk* (Washington: World Bank).

Brüggemann, Axel, and Thomas Linne, 1999, "How Good Are Leading Indicators for Currency and Banking Crises in Central and Eastern Europe? An Empirical Test" Discussion Paper No. 95 (Halle, Germany: Institut für Wirtschaftsforschung Halle).

———, 2002, "Are the Central and Eastern European Transition Countries Still Vulnerable to a Financial Crisis?" BOFIT Discussion Paper No. 5 (Finland: Bank of Finland Institute for Economies in Transition).

Burnside, Craig, Martin Eichenbaum, and Sergio Rebelo, 1999, "Prospective Deficits and the Asian Currency Crisis," Policy Research Paper No. 2174 (Washington: World Bank).

———, 2001, "On the Fiscal Implications of Twin Crises," NBER Working Paper No. 8277 (Cambridge, Massachusetts: National Bureau of Economic Research).

Bussière, Matthieu, and Christian Mulder, 1999, "External Vulnerability in Emerging Market Economies: How High Liquidity Can Offset Weak Fundamentals and the Effects of Contagion," IMF Working Paper No. 99/88 (Washington: International Monetary Fund).

Calomiris, Charles W., 1998, "The IMF's Imprudent Role as Lender of Last Resort," *Cato Journal*, Volume 17, No. 3 (Winter), pp. 275–94.

Calvo, Guillermo, 1988, "Servicing the Public Debt: The Role of Expectations," *American Economic Review*, Vol. 78 (September), pp. 647–61.

———, 1995, "Varieties of Capital-Market Crises," Working Paper No. 15 (Baltimore, Maryland: University of Maryland Center for International Economics).

Calvo, Guillermo, and Pablo Guidotti, 1990, "Indexation and Maturity of Government Bonds: An Exploratory Model," in *Public Debt Management: Theory and History*, ed. by Rudiger Dornbusch and Mario Draghi (New York: Cambridge University Press).

Calvo, Guillermo, and Enrique G. Mendoza, 1996, "Mexico's Balance of Payments Crisis: A Chronicle of a Death Foretold," *Journal of International Economics*, Vol. 41, pp. 235–64.

Calvo, Guillermo A., and Carmen Reinhart, 2000, "Fixing for Your Life," in *Brookings Trade Forum 2000*, ed. by Susan Collins and Dani Rodrik (Washington: Brookings Institution).

REFERENCES

Caprio, Gerard, and Daniela Klingebiel, 1996, "Bank Insolvencies: Cross Country Experience," Policy Research Paper No. 1620 (Washington: World Bank).

———, 1999, "Episodes of Systemic and Borderline Financial Crisis" (unpublished; Washington: World Bank).

Caramazza, Francesco, Luca Ricci, and Ranil Salgado, 2000, "Trade and Financial Contagion in Currency Crises," IMF Working Paper No. 00/55 (Washington: International Monetary Fund).

Chang, Roberto, and Andrés Velasco, 1999, "Liquidity Crises in Emerging Markets: Theory and Policy," *NBER Macroeconomics Manual*, ed. by Ben Bernanke and Julio Rotemberg (Cambridge, Massachusetts: MIT Press).

Choueiri, Nada, and Graciela Kaminsky, 1999, "Has the Nature of Crises Changed? A Quarter Century of Currency Crises in Argentina," IMF Working Paper No. 99/152 (Washington: International Monetary Fund).

Cohen, Daniel, 1997, "Growth and External Debt: A New Perspective on the African and Latin American Tragedies," CEPR Discussion Paper No. 1753 (London: Centre for Economic Policy Research).

Cole, Harold, and Timothy Kehoe, 1996, "A Self-Fulfilling Model of Mexico's 1994–95 Debt Crisis," *Journal of International Economics*, Vol. 41 (November), pp. 309–30.

———, 2000, "Self-Fulfilling Debt Crises," *Review of Economic Studies*, Vol. 67 (January), pp. 91–116.

Corsetti, Giancarlo, Paulo Pesenti, and Nouriel Roubini, 1999, "Paper Tigers? A Model of the Asian Crisis," *European Economic Review*, Vol. 43 (June), pp. 1211–36.

Corsetti, Giancarlo, and Bartosz Mackowiak, 2001, "Nominal Debt and the Dynamics of Currency Crises," CEPR Discussion Paper No. 2929 (London: Centre for Economic Policy Research).

Demirgüç-Kunt, Asli, and Enrica Detragiache, 1998, "The Determinants of Banking Crises in Developing and Developed Countries," *IMF Staff Papers*, Vol. 45 (March), pp. 81–109.

Detragiache, Enrica, 1996, "Rational Liquidity Crises in the Sovereign Debt Market: In Search of a Theory," *IMF Staff Papers*, Vol. 43 (September), pp. 545–70.

———, and Antonio Spilimbergo, 2001, "Crises and Liquidity: Evidence and Interpretation," IMF Working Paper No. 01/2 (Washington: International Monetary Fund).

Diamond, Douglas, and Philip Dybvig, 1983, "Bank Runs, Deposit Insurance, and Liquidity," *Journal of Political Economy*, Vol. 91 (June), pp. 401–19.

Dooley, Michael, 1998, "A Model of Crises in Emerging Markets," International Finance Discussion Paper No. 630 (Washington: Board of Governors of the Federal Reserve System).

Dornbusch, Rudiger, 2001, "A Primer on Emerging Market Crises," NBER Working Paper No. 8326 (Cambridge, Massachusetts: National Bureau of Economic Research).

———, Ilan Goldfajn, and Rodrigo O. Valdés, 1995, "Currency Crises and Collapses," *Brookings Papers on Economic Activity: 2*, Brookings Institution, pp. 219–93.

Edwards, Sebastian, 1997, "The Mexican Peso Crisis: How Much Did We Know? When Did We Know It?" NBER Working Paper No. 6334 (Cambridge, Massachusetts: National Bureau of Economic Research).

———, and Julio Santaella, 1992, "Devaluation Controversies in the Developing Countries: Lessons from the Bretton Woods Era," NBER Working Paper No. 4047 (Cambridge, Massachusetts: National Bureau of Economic Research).

Eichengreen, Barry, and Carlos Arteta, 2000, "Banking Crises in Emerging Markets: Presumptions and Evidence," CIDER Working Paper No. C00-115 (Berkeley, California: Center for International and Development Economics Research, University of California).

Eichengreen, Barry, and Ricardo Hausmann, 1999, "Exchange Rates and Economic Recovery in the 1930's," *Journal of Economic History*, Vol. 45, No. 4, pp. 925–46.

Eichengreen, Barry, and Andrew K. Rose, 1998, "Staying Afloat When the Wind Shifts: External Factors and Emerging Market Banking Crises," NBER Working Paper No. 6370 (Cambridge, Massachusetts: National Bureau of Economic Research).

Eichengreen, Barry, Andrew K. Rose, and Charles Wyplosz, 1995, "Exchange Market Mayhem: The Antecedents and Aftermath of Speculative Attacks," *Economic Policy: A European Forum*, No. 21 (October), pp. 249–312.

———, 1996, "Contagious Currency Crises," NBER Working Paper No. 5681 (Cambridge, Massachusetts: National Bureau of Economic Research).

Enoch, Charles, Anne-Marie Gulde, and Daniel Hardy, 2002, "Banking Crises and Bank Resolution: Experiences in Some Transition Countries," IMF Working Paper No. 02/56 (Washington: International Monetary Fund).

Fama, E. F., L. Fisher, M. Jensen, and R. Roll, 1969, "The Adjustment of Stock Prices to New Information," *International Economic Review*, Vol. 10 (February), pp. 1–21.

Feldstein, Martin, 2002, "Economic and Financial Crises in Emerging Market Economies: Overview of Prevention and Management," NBER Working Paper No. 8837 (Cambridge, Massachusetts: National Bureau of Economic Research).

Frankel, Jeffrey, and Andrew Rose, 1996, "Currency Crashes in Emerging Markets: An Empirical Treatment," *Journal of International Economics*, Vol. 41 (November), pp. 351–66.

Furman, Jason, and Joseph Stiglitz, 1998, "Economic Crises: Evidence and Insights from East Asia," *Brookings Papers on Economic Activity: 2*, Brookings Institution, pp. 1–135.

García-Herrero, Alicia, 1997, "Banking Crisis in Latin America in the 1990s: Lessons from Argentina, Paraguay, and Venezuela," IMF Working Paper No. 97/140 (Washington: International Monetary Fund).

Gavin, Michael, and Ricardo Hausmann, 1999, "Preventing Crisis and Contagion: Fiscal and Financial Dimensions," Inter-American Development Bank, Office of the Chief Economist, Working Paper Series (International), No. 401 (Washington).

References

Ghosh, Atish, Timothy Lane, Marianne Schulze-Ghattas, Aleš Bulíř, Javier Hamann, and Alex Mourmouras, 2002, *IMF-Supported Programs in Capital Account Crises: Design and Experience*, IMF Occasional Paper No. 210 (Washington: International Monetary Fund).

Ghosh, Swati, and Atish Ghosh, 2002, "Structural Vulnerabilities and Currency Crises," IMF Working Paper No. 02/9 (Washington: International Monetary Fund).

Gil-Diaz, Francisco, and Augustin Carstens, 1996a, "One Year of Solitude: Some Pilgrim Tales About Mexico's 1994–1995 Crisis," *American Economic Review, Papers and Proceedings*, Vol. 86, No. 2 (May), pp. 164–69.

———, 1996b, "Some Hypotheses Related to the Mexican 1994–1995 Crisis," Banco de México, Research Paper No. 9601 (México, D.F.).

Girton, Lance, and Don Roper, 1976, "Monetary Model of Exchange Market Pressure Applied to the Post-War Canadian Experience," International Finance Discussion Paper No. 92 (Washington: Board of Governors of the Federal Reserve System).

Glick, Reuven, Ramon Moreno, and Mark Spiegel, 2001, *Financial Crises in Emerging Markets* (Cambridge, England: Cambridge University Press).

Glick, Reuven, and Andrew Rose, 1998, "Contagion and Trade: Why Are Currency Crises Regional?" NBER Working Paper No. 6806 (Cambridge, Massachusetts: National Bureau of Economic Research).

Goldfajn, Ilan, and Rodrigo Valdés, 1998, "Are Currency Crises Predictable?" *European Economic Review*, Vol. 42 (May), pp. 873–85.

Goldstein, Morris, Graciela Kaminsky, and Carmen Reinhart, 2000, *Assessing Financial Vulnerability: An Early Warning System for Emerging Markets* (Washington: Institute for International Economics).

Green, David Jay, and J. Edgardo Campos, 2001, "Fiscal Lessons from the East Asian Financial Crisis," *Journal of Asian Economics*, Vol. 12, No. 3 (Fall), pp. 309–29.

Gupta, Poonam, Deepak Mishra, and Ratna Sahay, 2003, "Output Response to Currency Crises," forthcoming IMF Working Paper (Washington: International Monetary Fund).

Hausmann, Ricardo, 2002, "Unrewarded Good Fiscal Behavior: The Role of Debt Structure," paper presented at IMF/World Bank Conference on "Rules-Based Fiscal Policy in Emerging Market Economies" (Oaxaca, Mexico).

Hemming, Richard, and Murray Petrie, 2002, "A Framework for Assessing Fiscal Vulnerability," in *Government at Risk: Contingent Liabilities and Fiscal Risk*, ed. by Hana Polackova Brixi and Allen Schick (Washington: World Bank).

Hutchison, Michael, and Kathleen McDill, 1999, "Are All Banking Crises Alike? The Japanese Experience in International Comparison," *Journal of the Japanese and International Economies*, Vol. 13, No. 3, pp. 155–80.

International Monetary Fund, 1998, *World Economic Outlook, May 1998: A Survey by the Staff of the International Monetary Fund*, World Economic and Financial Surveys (Washington).

———, 2002a, *Global Financial Stability Report: Market Developments and Issues*, World Economic and Financial Surveys (Washington, March).

———, 2002b, *World Economic Outlook, April 2002: A Survey by the Staff of the International Monetary Fund*, World Economic and Financial Surveys (Washington).

———, 2002c, "Data Provision to the Fund for Surveillance Purposes." Available on the Internet at http://www.imf.org/external/np/sta/data/prov/2002/042602.htm

Jeanne, Olivier, 2000, "Debt Maturity and the Global Financial Architecture," CEPR Discussion Paper No. 2520 (London: Centre for Economic Policy Research).

Kalter, Eliot, and Armando Ribas, 1999, "The 1994 Mexican Economic Crisis: The Role of Government Expenditure and Relative Prices," IMF Working Paper No. 99/160 (Washington: International Monetary Fund).

Kamin, Steven, and Oliver Babson, 1999, "The Contributions of Domestic and External Factors to Latin American Devaluation Crisis: An Early Warning Systems Approach," International Finance Discussion Paper No. 645 (Washington: Board of Governors of the Federal Reserve System).

Kaminsky, Graciela, 1998, "Currency and Banking Crises: The Early Warnings of Distress," International Finance Discussion Paper No. 629 (Washington: Board of Governors of the Federal Reserve System).

———, Saul Lizondo, and Carmen Reinhart, 1998, "Leading Indicators of Currency Crises," *Staff Papers*, International Monetary Fund, Vol. 45, No. 1 (March), pp. 1–48.

Kaminsky, Graciela, and Carmen Reinhart, 1999, "The Twin Crises: The Causes of Banking and Balance of Payment Problems," *American Economic Review*, Vol. 89 (June), pp. 473–500.

Kharas, Homi, and Deepak Mishra, 2001, "Fiscal Policy, Hidden Deficits and Currency Crises," in *World Bank Economists' Forum*, ed. by S. Devarajan, F. H. Rogers, and L. Squire (Washington: World Bank).

Kopits, George, 2000, "How Can Fiscal Policy Help Avert Currency Crises?" IMF Working Paper No. 00/185 (Washington: International Monetary Fund).

Krugman, Paul, 1979, "A Model of Balance of Payments Crises," *Journal of Money, Credit and Banking*, Vol. 11, pp. 311–25.

———, 1985, "International Debt Strategies in an Uncertain World," in *International Debt and the Developing Countries*, ed. by Gordon Smith and John Cuddington (Washington: World Bank).

———, 1999, "Balance Sheets, the Transfer Problem, and Financial Crises," in *International Finance and Financial Crises: Essays in Honor of Robert P. Flood, Jr.*, ed. by Peter Isard, Assaf Razin, and Andrew Rose (Boston: Kluwer Academic Press; Washington: International Monetary Fund).

Kumar, Manhoman, Uma Moorthy, and William Perraudin, 2002, "Predicting Emerging Market Currency

REFERENCES

Crashes," IMF Working Paper No. 02/7 (Washington: International Monetary Fund).

La Porta, Rafael, Florencio Lopez-de-Silanes, and Andrei Shleifer, 2000, "Government Ownership of Banks," NBER Working Paper No. 7620 (Cambridge, Massachusetts: National Bureau of Economic Research).

Lindgren, Carl-Johan, Gillian Garcia, and Matthew Saal, 1996, *Bank Soundness and Macroeconomic Policy* (Washington: International Monetary Fund).

McKinnon, Ronald, 1991, *The Order of Economic Liberalization: Financial Control in the Transition to a Market Economy* (Baltimore, Maryland: Johns Hopkins University Press).

Milesi-Ferretti, Gian Maria, and Assaf Razin, 1996, "Current-Account Sustainability," Princeton Studies in International Finance No. 81 (Princeton, New Jersey: Department of Economics, Princeton University).

———, 2000, "Current Account Reversals and Currency Crises: Empirical Regularities," in *Currency Crises,* ed. by Paul Krugman (Chicago: University of Chicago Press).

Moreno, Ramon, 1995, "Macroeconomic Behavior During Periods of Speculative Pressure or Realignment: Evidence from Pacific Basin Economies," *Federal Reserve Bank of San Francisco Economic Review*, No. 3, pp. 3–16.

Nitithanprapas, Ekniti, and Thomas Willett, 2000 "A Currency Crises Model That Works: A Payments Disequilibrium Approach," Claremont Working Paper No. 2000-25 (Claremont, California: Claremont University).

Obstfeld, Maurice, 1994, "The Logic of Currency Crises," *Cahiers Economiques et Monétaires* Vol. 43, pp. 189–213.

Osband, Kent, and Caroline Van Rijckeghem, 2000, "Safety from Currency Crashes," *IMF Staff Papers,* Vol. 47 (May), pp. 238–58.

Ötker, İnci, and Ceyla Pazarbaşioğlu, 1995, "Speculative Attacks and Currency Crises: The Mexican Experience," IMF Working Paper No. 95/112 (Washington: International Monetary Fund).

Purcell, John, and Jeffrey Kaufman, 1993, *The Risks of Sovereign Lending: Lessons from History* (New York: Saloman Brothers).

Radelet, Steven, and Jeffrey Sachs, 1998, "The East Asian Financial Crisis: Diagnosis, Remedies, Prospects," *Brookings Papers on Economic Activity: 1,* Brookings Institution, pp. 1–90.

Reinhart, Carmen, 2002, "Default, Currency Crises and Sovereign Credit Ratings," NBER Working Paper No. 8738 (Cambridge, Massachusetts: National Bureau of Economic Research).

Rodrik, Dani, and Andrés Velasco, 1999, "Short-Term Capital Flows," NBER Working Paper No. 7364 (Cambridge, Massachusetts: National Bureau of Economic Research).

Sachs, Jeffrey, Aaron Tornell, and Andrés Velasco, 1996, "Financial Crises in Emerging Markets: The Lessons from 1995," *Brookings Papers on Economic Activity: 1,* Brookings Institution, pp. 147–215.

Stone, Mark, and Melvyn Weeks, 2001, "Systemic Financial Crises, Balance Sheets, and Model Uncertainty," IMF Working Paper No. 01/162 (Washington: International Monetary Fund).

Tornell, Aaron, 1999, "Common Fundamentals in the Tequila and Asian Crises," NBER Working Paper No. 7139 (Cambridge, Massachusetts: National Bureau of Economic Research).

Velasco, Andrés, 1987, "Financial Crises and Balance of Payments Crises: A Simple Model of the Southern Cone Experience," *Journal of Development Economics*, Vol. 27 (October), pp. 263–83.

World Bank, 2000, *Global Economic Prospects and the Developing Countries 2000* (Washington).

Recent Occasional Papers of the International Monetary Fund

218. Fiscal Vulnerability and Financial Crises in Emerging Market Economies, by Richard Hemming, Michael Kell, and Axel Schimmelpfennig. 2003.
217. Managing Financial Crises: Recent Experience and Lessons for Latin America, edited by Charles Collyns and G. Russell Kincaid. 2003.
216. Is the PRGF Living Up to Expectations?—An Assessment of Program Design, by Sanjeev Gupta, Mark Plant, Benedict Clements, Thomas Dorsey, Emanuele Baldacci, Gabriela Inchauste, Shamsuddin Tareq, and Nita Thacker. 2002.
215. Improving Large Taxpayers' Compliance: A Review of Country Experience, by Katherine Baer. 2002.
214. Advanced Country Experiences with Capital Account Liberalization, by Age Bakker and Bryan Chapple. 2002.
213. The Baltic Countries: Medium-Term Fiscal Issues Related to EU and NATO Accession, by Johannes Mueller, Christian Beddies, Robert Burgess, Vitali Kramarenko, and Joannes Mongardini. 2002.
212. Financial Soundness Indicators: Analytical Aspects and Country Practices, by V. Sundararajan, Charles Enoch, Armida San José, Paul Hilbers, Russell Krueger, Marina Moretti, and Graham Slack. 2002.
211. Capital Account Liberalization and Financial Sector Stability, by a staff team led by Shogo Ishii and Karl Habermeier. 2002.
210. IMF-Supported Programs in Capital Account Crises, by Atish Ghosh, Timothy Lane, Marianne Schulze-Ghattas, Aleš Bulíř, Javier Hamann, and Alex Mourmouras. 2002.
209. Methodology for Current Account and Exchange Rate Assessments, by Peter Isard, Hamid Faruqee, G. Russell Kincaid, and Martin Fetherston. 2001.
208. Yemen in the 1990s: From Unification to Economic Reform, by Klaus Enders, Sherwyn Williams, Nada Choueiri, Yuri Sobolev, and Jan Walliser. 2001.
207. Malaysia: From Crisis to Recovery, by Kanitta Meesook, Il Houng Lee, Olin Liu, Yougesh Khatri, Natalia Tamirisa, Michael Moore, and Mark H. Krysl. 2001.
206. The Dominican Republic: Stabilization, Structural Reform, and Economic Growth, by Alessandro Giustiniani, Werner C. Keller, and Randa E. Sab. 2001.
205. Stabilization and Savings Funds for Nonrenewable Resources, by Jeffrey Davis, Rolando Ossowski, James Daniel, and Steven Barnett. 2001.
204. Monetary Union in West Africa (ECOWAS): Is It Desirable and How Could It Be Achieved? by Paul Masson and Catherine Pattillo. 2001.
203. Modern Banking and OTC Derivatives Markets: The Transformation of Global Finance and Its Implications for Systemic Risk, by Garry J. Schinasi, R. Sean Craig, Burkhard Drees, and Charles Kramer. 2000.
202. Adopting Inflation Targeting: Practical Issues for Emerging Market Countries, by Andrea Schaechter, Mark R. Stone, and Mark Zelmer. 2000.
201. Developments and Challenges in the Caribbean Region, by Samuel Itam, Simon Cueva, Erik Lundback, Janet Stotsky, and Stephen Tokarick. 2000.
200. Pension Reform in the Baltics: Issues and Prospects, by Jerald Schiff, Niko Hobdari, Axel Schimmelpfennig, and Roman Zytek. 2000.
199. Ghana: Economic Development in a Democratic Environment, by Sérgio Pereira Leite, Anthony Pellechio, Luisa Zanforlin, Girma Begashaw, Stefania Fabrizio, and Joachim Harnack. 2000.
198. Setting Up Treasuries in the Baltics, Russia, and Other Countries of the Former Soviet Union: An Assessment of IMF Technical Assistance, by Barry H. Potter and Jack Diamond. 2000.
197. Deposit Insurance: Actual and Good Practices, by Gillian G.H. Garcia. 2000.
196. Trade and Trade Policies in Eastern and Southern Africa, by a staff team led by Arvind Subramanian, with Enrique Gelbard, Richard Harmsen, Katrin Elborgh-Woytek, and Piroska Nagy. 2000.
195. The Eastern Caribbean Currency Union—Institutions, Performance, and Policy Issues, by Frits van Beek, José Roberto Rosales, Mayra Zermeño, Ruby Randall, and Jorge Shepherd. 2000.
194. Fiscal and Macroeconomic Impact of Privatization, by Jeffrey Davis, Rolando Ossowski, Thomas Richardson, and Steven Barnett. 2000.

OCCASIONAL PAPERS

193. Exchange Rate Regimes in an Increasingly Integrated World Economy, by Michael Mussa, Paul Masson, Alexander Swoboda, Esteban Jadresic, Paolo Mauro, and Andy Berg. 2000.
192. Macroprudential Indicators of Financial System Soundness, by a staff team led by Owen Evans, Alfredo M. Leone, Mahinder Gill, and Paul Hilbers. 2000.
191. Social Issues in IMF-Supported Programs, by Sanjeev Gupta, Louis Dicks-Mireaux, Ritha Khemani, Calvin McDonald, and Marijn Verhoeven. 2000.
190. Capital Controls: Country Experiences with Their Use and Liberalization, by Akira Ariyoshi, Karl Habermeier, Bernard Laurens, Inci Ötker-Robe, Jorge Iván Canales Kriljenko, and Andrei Kirilenko. 2000.
189. Current Account and External Sustainability in the Baltics, Russia, and Other Countries of the Former Soviet Union, by Donal McGettigan. 2000.
188. Financial Sector Crisis and Restructuring: Lessons from Asia, by Carl-Johan Lindgren, Tomás J.T. Baliño, Charles Enoch, Anne-Marie Gulde, Marc Quintyn, and Leslie Teo. 1999.
187. Philippines: Toward Sustainable and Rapid Growth, Recent Developments and the Agenda Ahead, by Markus Rodlauer, Prakash Loungani, Vivek Arora, Charalambos Christofides, Enrique G. De la Piedra, Piyabha Kongsamut, Kristina Kostial, Victoria Summers, and Athanasios Vamvakidis. 2000.
186. Anticipating Balance of Payments Crises: The Role of Early Warning Systems, by Andrew Berg, Eduardo Borensztein, Gian Maria Milesi-Ferretti, and Catherine Pattillo. 1999.
185. Oman Beyond the Oil Horizon: Policies Toward Sustainable Growth, edited by Ahsan Mansur and Volker Treichel. 1999.
184. Growth Experience in Transition Countries, 1990–98, by Oleh Havrylyshyn, Thomas Wolf, Julian Berengaut, Marta Castello-Branco, Ron van Rooden, and Valerie Mercer-Blackman. 1999.
183. Economic Reforms in Kazakhstan, Kyrgyz Republic, Tajikistan, Turkmenistan, and Uzbekistan, by Emine Gürgen, Harry Snoek, Jon Craig, Jimmy McHugh, Ivailo Izvorski, and Ron van Rooden. 1999.
182. Tax Reform in the Baltics, Russia, and Other Countries of the Former Soviet Union, by a staff team led by Liam Ebrill and Oleh Havrylyshyn. 1999.
181. The Netherlands: Transforming a Market Economy, by C. Maxwell Watson, Bas B. Bakker, Jan Kees Martijn, and Ioannis Halikias. 1999.
180. Revenue Implications of Trade Liberalization, by Liam Ebrill, Janet Stotsky, and Reint Gropp. 1999.
179. Disinflation in Transition: 1993–97, by Carlo Cottarelli and Peter Doyle. 1999.
178. IMF-Supported Programs in Indonesia, Korea, and Thailand: A Preliminary Assessment, by Timothy Lane, Atish Ghosh, Javier Hamann, Steven Phillips, Marianne Schulze-Ghattas, and Tsidi Tsikata. 1999.
177. Perspectives on Regional Unemployment in Europe, by Paolo Mauro, Eswar Prasad, and Antonio Spilimbergo. 1999.
176. Back to the Future: Postwar Reconstruction and Stabilization in Lebanon, edited by Sena Eken and Thomas Helbling. 1999.
175. Macroeconomic Developments in the Baltics, Russia, and Other Countries of the Former Soviet Union, 1992–97, by Luis M. Valdivieso. 1998.
174. Impact of EMU on Selected Non-European Union Countries, by R. Feldman, K. Nashashibi, R. Nord, P. Allum, D. Desruelle, K. Enders, R. Kahn, and H. Temprano-Arroyo. 1998.
173. The Baltic Countries: From Economic Stabilization to EU Accession, by Julian Berengaut, Augusto Lopez-Claros, Françoise Le Gall, Dennis Jones, Richard Stern, Ann-Margret Westin, Effie Psalida, Pietro Garibaldi. 1998.
172. Capital Account Liberalization: Theoretical and Practical Aspects, by a staff team led by Barry Eichengreen and Michael Mussa, with Giovanni Dell'Ariccia, Enrica Detragiache, Gian Maria Milesi-Ferretti, and Andrew Tweedie. 1998.
171. Monetary Policy in Dollarized Economies, by Tomás Baliño, Adam Bennett, and Eduardo Borensztein. 1998.

Note: For information on the titles and availability of Occasional Papers not listed, please consult the IMF's *Publications Catalog* or contact IMF Publication Services.